I0130862

Global Challenges: Peace and War

LUC Texts in Global Challenges

Aiming to 'build knowledge for a better world,' Leiden University College The Hague is founded on the premise that education and research are fundamentally connected. Based in the city of international peace and justice, LUC promotes interdisciplinary and internationally inclusive scholarship into the global challenges of our time.

Global Challenges: Peace and War

Edited by

Yih-Jye Hwang and Lucie Cerna

MARTINUS
NIJHOFF
PUBLISHERS

LEIDEN • BOSTON
2013

Cover illustration: The cover image is inspired by César Baldaccini's "The Freedom Fighter", a formidable bronze sculpture standing tall over the promenade of the Hong Kong Cultural Centre since 1992 in tacit memory of the 1989 events in Tiananmen Square. With its lone wing surviving historical triumphs and tribulations, this monument was later recoined "The Flying Frenchman" and continues to celebrate the tenacity of the human spirit through peace and war.
~ Created by Cissie Fu, Political Arts Initiative (www.politicalarts.org<http://www.politicalarts.org>)

Library of Congress Cataloging-in-Publication Data

Global challenges : peace and war / edited by Yih-Jye Hwang and Lucie Cerna.
    pages cm
    Includes index.
    ISBN 978-90-04-25326-1 (pbk. : alk. paper) — ISBN 978-90-04-24693-5 (e-book) 1. Peace.
2. Peace-building. 3. War. I. Hwang, Yih-Jye, editor of compilation. II. Cerna, Lucie, 1981– editor of compilation.
    JZ5538.G56 2013
    303.6'6—dc23

                                                                                2013016073

This publication has been typeset in the multilingual "Brill" typeface. With over 5,100 characters covering Latin, IPA, Greek, and Cyrillic, this typeface is especially suitable for use in the humanities. For more information, please see www.brill.com/brill-typeface.

ISBN 978-90-04-25326-1 (hardback)
ISBN 978-90-04-24693-5 (e-book)

Copyright 2013 by Koninklijke Brill NV, Leiden, The Netherlands.
Koninklijke Brill NV incorporates the imprints Brill, Global Oriental, Hotei Publishing, IDC Publishers and Martinus Nijhoff Publishers.

All rights reserved. No part of this publication may be reproduced, translated, stored in a retrieval system, or transmitted in any form or by any means, electronic, mechanical, photocopying, recording or otherwise, without prior written permission from the publisher.

Authorization to photocopy items for internal or personal use is granted by Koninklijke Brill NV provided that the appropriate fees are paid directly to The Copyright Clearance Center, 222 Rosewood Drive, Suite 910, Danvers, MA 01923, USA.
Fees are subject to change.

This book is printed on acid-free paper.

CONTENTS

PART TWO

CASE STUDIES

ACKNOWLEDGEMENTS

The idea for this book came some time ago when we were both teaching at Leiden University College (LUC) The Hague. LUC The Hague, founded in 2010, is an international honours college of Leiden University, located in the world's capital of peace and justice, The Hague. It encourages students to engage with global challenges in an interdisciplinary curriculum.

One mandatory course for first year students is on global challenges: peace. The course convenor, Yih-Jye Hwang, had to come up with a brand-new syllabus for the first cohort of students. The course was meant to be interdisciplinary, expose students to a wide range of theoretical and empirical approaches, allow them to do research on peace and war, work together in groups and learn how to write and present on various topics. In the first years in existence, the syllabus drew on a number of different books and articles, and very short introductions to the case studies. Students were then required to find information on the cases and selected readings on their own. There was no book that could provide the necessary theoretical and case study background in one piece, which was a significant drawback. In 2011, we thought that LUC The Hague should have its own book that students and faculty could use every year. The result is this edited volume.

However, this book could not have been written and completed without the efforts of many people. We must express our gratitude to all the contributors for delivering very interesting chapters, and keeping up with our deadlines. We are also grateful to our colleagues at Leiden University, who have assisted us immensely to develop the syllabus at various stages. These colleagues include Arlinda Rustemi, Carsten Stahn, Cissie Fu, Corina Stan, Eric Storm, H.W. (Rico) Sneller, Jaap de Hoop Scheffer, Laurens van Apeldoorn, Maja Vodopivec, Niels van Willigen, Sander Dikker Hupkes, Thomas Bundschuh, and Sara Kendall. Most of them have contributed directly to the course by delivering plenary lectures and/or have taught smaller seminars. We would like to give special thanks to Lieke Schreel for her guidance and help when the course was first taught in 2010. We are indebted to all of them for their help.

We would like to thank the Dean of LUC The Hague, Chris Goto-Jones, for his encouragement and support throughout this project. At Brill, we thank our editor, Nozomi Goto, for her assistance throughout the process, as well as Wilma de Weert for her help with the production of the manuscript. We are grateful to Priya Swamy for copy-editing the whole manuscript and to the LUC Research Centre for its financial support. In addition, we thank Cissie Fu for her book cover design.

Last but not least, our students at LUC The Hague, especially the 2010, 2011 and 2012 student cohorts, deserve special thanks as they served as testing-ground for this new course, and their ideas and evaluations have helped to improve the direction of the course. We hope this book will be useful to future students at LUC The Hague as well as other interdisciplinary programmes.

This book is dedicated to the LUC The Hague students.

Yih-Jye Hwang and Lucie Cerna
The Hague and Oxford, January 2013

ABOUT THE AUTHORS

Laurens van Apeldoorn is Assistant Professor in Philosophy, LUC The Hague.

Lucie Cerna is Lecturer in Politics, Merton College, University of Oxford, and former Assistant Professor in Political Economy, LUC The Hague.

Edmund Frettingham is a freelance writer living in London.

Patsy Haccou is Assistant Professor of Mathematical Biology, LUC The Hague.

Helen Hintjens is Senior Lecturer, International Institute of Social Studies (ISS) in The Hague, Erasmus University Rotterdam.

Yih-Jye Hwang is Assistant Professor of International Relations, LUC The Hague.

William Hynes is economist/policy analyst at the Organisation for Economic Cooperation and Development (OECD) and Research Associate at LUC The Hague.

Sara Kendall is Researcher, Grotius Centre, Leiden University.

Jessica Kroezen is PhD candidate, Institute of Political Science, Leiden University.

Benjamin Pohl is Researcher, Institute of Political Science, Leiden University.

Francesco Ragazzi is Assistant Professor in International Relations, Institute of Political Science, Leiden University.

Håvar Solheim is PhD candidate, Institute for History, Leiden University and Centre for Latin American Research and Documentation (CEDLA), Amsterdam.

Corina Stan is Assistant Professor of Comparative Literature, LUC The Hague.

Eric Storm is Lecturer in History, Institute for History, Leiden University.

Niels van Willigen is Lecturer in International Relations, Institute of Political Science, Leiden University.

Ann Marie Wilson is Assistant Professor of History, LUC The Hague.

INTRODUCTION

Yih-Jye Hwang and Lucie Cerna

Introduction: What is Peace?

What does 'peace' mean? Is peace merely the absence of war, or can it also mean something else? Is peace a condition of emancipation, the maintenance of the status quo, or is it a system of hegemonic stability? Whatever it may mean, how can peace be acquired? And above all, what is the relationship between peace and war?

While peace has been extensively studied and analysed, it is a fact that there is no consensus on what 'peace' actually means, nor does the concept have a clear, comprehensive or satisfying definition. Simply by looking at laureates of the Nobel Peace prize over the past one hundred years (who arguably present a Western idea of peace), one will find many different conceptualisations of peace and various paths to peace. These laureates range from individuals (or organisations) who organised and conducted peace movements, humanitarian works, arms control, peace negotiation, conflict resolution on the one hand, to those who embraced efforts to promote democracy, human rights as well as environmental protection on the other (The Norwegian Nobel Committee 2012). Likewise, academic scholars and students conceptualise the term in various ways across a broad range of disciplines. Some see forms of 'peace' as the pragmatic removal of overt violence, the balancing of power, collective security, rule of law, etc.; others conceptualise the term as harmony, tranquility, a 'divine state', a state of goodness, etc. As such, competing concepts and discourses of peace exist. It is thus vital to problematise peace and ask what it is, or what it should be, at the outset of this book.

The most widely used and all-inclusive contemporary definition of peace was proposed by Johan Galtung, one of the most prominent architects in peace research. In the editorial to the founding edition of *the Journal of Peace Research* in 1964, Galtung originally described the 'absence of war' as negative peace and 'the integration of human society' as positive peace. He further noted that these two types of peace 'should be conceived as two separate dimensions. One can have one without the other' (Galtung 1964: 2). With regards to positive peace, Galtung thereafter developed the concept that denotes the presence of conditions for political equality and social justice (Galtung 1969). In what follows, we will first critically interrogate the term 'peace' when it is conceptualised as negative peace, and then when it is conceptualised as positive peace.

Peace and war are ostensibly contradictory and therefore locked in a dialectical relation. In other words, the negation of a definition of war yields a definition of peace. Nevertheless, this way of defining 'peace' leads to another equally troubled concept: 'war'. What is war? According to Clausewitz, war is 'an act of force to compel our enemy to do our will' (Clausewitz 2007: 13), it 'is not merely an act of policy but a true political instrument, a continuation of political intercourse, carried on with other means' (28). This definition stressed the importance of combat, for which Clausewitz describes war as 'a clash between major interests, which is resolved by *bloodshed*—that is the only way in which it differs from other conflicts' (100, emphasis ours). Similarly, Sun Tzu understands war as the destruction of enemy forces in order to compel one's enemies to submit to one's will. However Sun Tzu believes that the highest objective in war is to compel the enemy to submit to one's will not only through fighting, but also other non-violent elements such as deception and diplomacy. As he notes, 'attaining one hundred victories in one hundred battles is not the pinnacle of excellence. Subjugating the enemy's army without fighting is the true pinnacle of excellence' (Sun 1994: 168). To simplify the discussion, we temporally define war as a 'political movement through violence'.

Nevertheless, the puzzle 'what is war' still needs to be unpacked due to a lack of consensus among scholars about the connotation of two key terms: 'political' and 'violence'. With regards to the former, the conventional use of the term 'politics' refers to the politics that takes place in parliaments, political parties and governments. Yet, this way of understanding politics is highly problematic, as it inherently excludes and delegitimises some important affairs and issues concerning human life that occur outside the institutionalised politics of states. A number of radical philosophers such as Michel Foucault therefore differentiate the term 'politics' from 'political' (Hindess 2005: 390). The former is characterised by its association with the classical, state-oriented conception of politics whereas the latter is a critique of the conception of politics that regards the state as the only actual political institution and legitimate imposition of order. Therefore the term 'political' implicitly signifies a 'power to definition' given the fact that everything is potentially political (Laclau 1990: 31–6).

With regards to violence, the term is commonly left undefined as well. The word often connotes physical attack, yet this way of defining violence implies a wide spectrum of occurrences. More importantly, as suggested by Galtung (1969), a chain of questions can be raised from this kind of definition. For instance, does violence need to be *actual* physical force by one person or group of people directly against another? What about psychological violence such as brainwashing? Similarly, is violence necessarily defined as direct and negative approaches to influence, such as punishment? Is violence something that is 'built into' an individual? More frequent than incidents of physical or psychological violence are incidents of *structural* violence, wherein resources, broadly defined, are unevenly distributed (Galtung 1969). As Levi and Maguire (2002) note, violence is 'a slippery term which covers a huge and frequently changing range of heterogeneous physical and emotional behaviors, situations and victim-offender relationships' (Levi & Maguire 2002: 796).

Leaving aside the problems of defining the terms political and violence, we can pose another important question: what precisely is the *goal* of war? A superficial answer to that question is simply 'victory', with all the satisfaction that it entails. However, the word victory does not provide a satisfactory answer because one can further question what sorts of 'victory' can be achieved through war—domination, resistance, or freedom? Human existence takes diverse forms, and this plurality is the *source* of conflict, whether in terms of territorial expansion and political conquest, scarcity and competition for resources, the sociological tension between unity and discord, or fighting for the preservation of a collective way of life. To rephrase the question of the goal of war, we may ask, what is the effect of peace?

Indeed, the concept of 'peace' is far broader than its antonym, war. Now, questions of justice, equality, and rights begin to emerge at a normative level in relation to peace. These issues coincide with Galtung's idea of 'positive peace', the integration of human society in which justice, rights, needs, and freedom of individuals are guaranteed. Galtung expanded the definition of violence as mentioned above that inevitably enlarges the concept of peace. In order to achieve a state of positive peace, poverty, social injustices, economic inequalities and political injustices must be eliminated. On the one hand, Galtung's idea of 'positive peace' overlaps with the Marxist conceptualisation of peace that hinges on social justice and equality. According to Karl Marx, capitalism is a system of exploitation by the bourgeoisie, and therefore must be replaced by socialism on an international scale in order to provide freedom and equality. Marxists aim to remove certain types of structural violence that often promote economic exploitation and class domination. On the other hand, positive peace is compatible with liberal peace theorists such as Michael Doyle and Francis Fukuyama whose intellectual interest is to extend the domestic peace that rests upon the preservation of a socioeconomic order (i.e. market economy), or the use of a particular type of constitution (i.e. democracy), to an international community. Despite their differences in ideology, both schools share the idea of the emancipation of the individuals derives from the Enlightenment project that seeks to free the humanity from its self-imposed immaturity, and can also be traced back to 'Aristotelian *telos*', which attempts to lead human beings to 'a good and just life' in the polis (Neufeld 1995: 9). Accordingly, Richard Ashley (1981: 227) defined the term 'emancipation' as 'concerned with securing freedom from unacknowledged constraints, relations of domination, and conditions of distorted communication and understanding that deny humans the capacity to make their future through full will and consciousness'. In this vein, positive peace is perceived as a condition of emancipation.

Nevertheless, it is noted that a condition of emancipation may become a form of domination, just like orthodox Marxists' 'class emancipation' turned out to become class domination, at least in the former Soviet Union. A more recent example of such irony is that democratic peace can become a 'democratic crusade' wherein democracy as a political system is imposed via violence (or war) upon non-democracies. Scholars in peace research disagree with each other over the question whether peace *ought to* be *good*, especially when one attempts to consider 'peace' from perspectives of other cultures, religions, or civilisations. They would put the above-mentioned enlightenment-latent, Eurocentric conceptualisation of peace into question.

For instance, theologian Perry Yoder (2005: 3) interestingly puts forward that 'peace is a middle-class luxury, perhaps even a Western middle-class luxury'. What he means here is that espousing a concept of peace and opposing the use of violence can be the rhetoric of those who try to maintain the status quo for the comfort of the their own interests, preserving the existing power structures of an unjust society. As he discovered in his experience working in the Philippines, people there 'saw advocacy for peace as support for their oppression...talking of peace in this context sounded like the language of oppression used by oppressors to keep the oppressed in their place' (Yoder 2005: 3). Likewise, Galtung (1981: 187) noted that the ancient Roman conception of peace, the *pax* (that has dominated the conceptualisation of peace in the Western world) primarily served the interests of the powerful to maintain the status quo through a system of law. He noted that *pax* was 'certainly not in the sense of justice and prosperity for the periphery of the Empire...As a concept it was compatible with the type of system that ultimately proved too exploitative, both of nature and of the internal and external proletariats' (Galtung 1981: 187). As such, peace is understood as the status quo, or even a system of hegemonic domination by a (small) group of people at the expense of the others (masses).

Outline of the Book

This book aims to offer an interdisciplinary and up-to-date introduction to studies of war and peace, from both theoretical and empirical perspectives. Given the ambivalence, richness, and multiplicity of the conceptualisation of peace, this book is designed to make readers contemplate how peace can be conceptualised by investigating its broadly defined opposite—'war'—rather than providing readers *the* answer of what the idea of peace means, while merely accepting popular definitions of the term. Moreover, 'peace studies' requires a research agenda that engages broadly with interdisciplinary perspectives on peace, that bring together history, political science, philosophy, religious studies, law, economics, and culture, allowing for a deep and broad interrogation of 'peace'. With these objectives in mind, the book is divided into two parts.

Part one, 'Theoretical perspectives', intends to look into several aspects of war from different disciplinary perspectives. Topics included here are the history of peace movements, causes of war, biology of war, just war tradition (from both philosophical and legal perspective), representation of war, economics of war and finally the end of war. Each of the chapters features an introduction to the theme and its primary content. Part two, 'Case studies', selects six case studies covering many regions in which students work on their own case study and have the opportunity to put theory into practice. This book aims to examine the nexus between theory and practice in relation to peace and war: each case study can be analysed by a theoretical perspective introduced in part one, and thus serve as a learning tool for students. Selected case studies include: Yugoslav Wars, The Iraq War, The Pacific War, War and Peace in Colombia, Rwanda and Libya.

Chapter one, 'Peace movements in historical perspective', written by historian Ann Marie Wilson introduces readers to the long history of nonviolent responses to conflict and insecurity. Debates about the meaning of peace go back to the ancient and medieval world, but the modern peace movement finds its origins in the late eighteenth and early nineteenth centuries, when a group of small, mostly religiously-based societies began to issue public declarations against war. Since then, a wide variety of political coalitions have coalesced around issues pertaining to peace and conflict resolution. In the nineteenth century, peace advocates worked to establish protocol for international arbitration and called for the regularisation of international law. The outbreak of World War I gave additional weight to the need for an international security organisation, while the disappointments of its aftermath led many to criticise the cultural glorification and romanticisation of warfare. Later in the twentieth century, the experience of World War II and the realities of the Cold War brought about a new focus on arms reduction, disarmament, and nuclear deterrence. Since then, peace organisations increasingly have grappled with the difficult questions raised by humanitarian intervention and alternative missions for military forces. No matter the issue, however, peace advocacy has frequently contributed to changes in the conduct of war. By tracing this history, Wilson shows that military and nonviolent responses to conflict can be seen in a dialectic relationship with one another.

Chapter two, 'Causes of war', by political scientists Niels van Willigen and Benjamin Pohl is designed to consider why (and how) wars occur. There are various ways to answer this question. Political realists may attribute the causes of war to human nature or the structure of the international system (i.e. anarchy). Marxist traditions, such as those proposed by Vladimir Lenin or Immanuel Wallerstein, may blame the logic of capitalism for giving rise to global inequalities which in turn lead to war. Other scholars, like Samuel Huntington, may ascribe the outbreak of war or the forging of peace to cultural factors, referring to civilisation, ethnicity, or nationalism. The variety of explanations shows us that there is no single causal factor that leads to war. Different thinkers have proposed numerous theories that explain the causes of various forms of warfare. Addressing all of them would be impossible in the context of this chapter, therefore the chapter focuses on a few dominant explanations. First, the causes of interstate war are discussed in a level-of-analysis framework. It means that we study war between states at the level of the individual, the state and the international system. Secondly, the causes of intra-state wars, or war within states, are discussed. The focus is on theoretical debates that address the role of factors like ethnicity, ancient hatreds, nationalism, raw materials, poverty and inequality in the outbreak of this type of war.

As human nature can be considered as one of the causes of war, mathematical biologist Patsy Haccou looks at human evolutionary history revealed in biological, anthropological, and archaeological research in chapter three, 'Biology of war'. In evolutionary biology it is now known that not only morphological but also behavioural traits may be subject to selection, and social scientists have started to look at human behaviour from this perspective. This has led to several opposing views of our propensities for war and peace. Observations of our closest living relatives, the chimpanzees, have led some people to argue that same-species aggression leading to murderous raids is an inherent trait of our evolutionary make-up. Among chimps adolescent male behaviour can be violent; this observation has spawned research on the relation between the demography of countries and the incidence of violent conflicts, and a correlation between the two has indeed been confirmed in certain cases. From this point of view, war appears to be a natural state rather than something that needs to be explained by additional factors. Rather, it is the state of peace that has to be explained. However, others have argued that the evolutionary distance between chimps and humans is quite large, and that their social systems are very different. Specifically, the ways of rearing young differ greatly: whereas young chimps and most other apes are predominantly taken care of solely by their mothers, human children traditionally have a large 'extended family' that provides care for them until they can provide for themselves. This could have had a have a large effect on the evolution of human behaviour. From this perspective, our propensity for peace rather than war may be partially explained.

Chapter four by philosopher Laurens van Apeldoorn, and chapter five by the two editors Yih-Jye Hwang and Lucie Cerna give an introduction to the just war argument from both philosophical and legal perspectives respectively. The just war tradition, simply put, is a philosophical, political, ethical, religious, and legal consideration of the idea that resorting to war can only be just under certain conditions. It deals with the justification of how and why wars are fought. The tradition can be traced back to ancient Greek philosophers. However its importance is connected to medieval Christian theologians, such as Augustine and Aquinas. In his renowned book, *Just and unjust war*, Michael Walzer established the foundations of the modern version of just war theory in a secular context. Since the publication of Walzer's book, many contemporary political theorists addressed justice and the use of force in two aspects: *Jus ad bellum* (when it is right to resort to armed force) and *jus in bello* (what is acceptable in using such force). Van Apeldoorn's chapter shows that *jus ad bellum* and *jus in bello* considerations can be understood as deriving from two intellectual traditions—the just war paradigm and the regular war paradigm respectively. He further argues that it is this division that explains the difficulty at the heart of Walzer's theory.

In chapter five Hwang and Cerna explore the dilemmas that arise with the just war tradition, with a critical look at contemporary practice, including the application of the concept of 'responsibility to protect' (R2P). As noted, war and intervention raise complex questions regarding the interplay between sovereignty, justice and accountability. This chapter looks at this relationship from three angles. First, it examines how the idea of 'sovereignty as responsibility' influences moral and legal obligations of states and the international community, and what consequences its violation may entail. Secondly, it examines to what extent judgments on the legality of use of force influence obligations in conflict. And finally, the chapter looks at institutions and mechanisms that have been created to sanction violations of the laws and customs of war.

Chapter six, 'Economics of war', by economist William Hynes, seeks to analyse the economics of war. War is a state of organised, armed conflict between nations. Economics plays an important role in decisions to initiate wars; understanding the role of economics and the tools it provides in analysing different conflicts is therefore illuminating. Concepts such as game theory can be used to model conflictual competition. Cost benefit analysis can be useful in evaluating decisions to go to war. The state of the economy also determines the way in which wars are waged and the eventual outcome: generally those nations that have advantages in economic development tend to win wars through stronger institutionalisation, organisation and the mobilisation of resources. Conversely the global economic environment, international trade and economic prosperity tend to preserve peace between nations. Economic intercourse binds nations together through mutual self-interest, and economic globalisation has made the world safer. Using economic theories and data, this chapter examines several wars in terms of their economic cost and consequences and the economic rationale of these conflicts. In addition it probes the effects of wartime experiences on postwar fortunes. It examines important issues such as if war benefits an economy. It also addresses the questions: do economic sanctions contribute to war or peace? How effective is economic decision making in war?

Chapter seven, 'Representation of war', by comparative literature scholar Corina Stan, contemplates the problematic of the interrelationship between the war and media. Media today, broadly defined, has played a pivotal, if not primary, role in constructing our understanding of world politics. News reports governed the way that a subject is made into a story; the way the world was and continues to be transformed into a text. This process of the textualisation of the world may involve an interplay between questions of identity, language, and power. This chapter employs a Poststructuralist approach, thinking of war and peace by examining the intimate relationship among technology, media, culture and their implications for new politics with relation to wars in the twenty-first century.

Chapter eight, 'The end of war' by Niels van Willigen and Jessica Kroezen, marks the final chapter of part one of this book. Why (and how) do wars end? Francis Fukuyama, a contemporary political theorist, in his 1989 article 'The end of history' famously noted, 'What we may be witnessing is not just the end of the Cold War...but the end of history as such'. To Fukuyama, the end of the Cold War represented the triumph of liberal democracy and liberal capitalism over fascism and communism. Fukuyama argued that this would lead to a more peaceful world. Arguably, the idea that more democracy means less war can be traced back to Immanuel Kant's 1795 essay *Zum ewigen Frieden. Ein philosophischer Entwurf.* In his essay the famous philosopher argues that peace is built on the peaceful union of republican nations. Many contemporary political scientists like Michael Doyle interpret the Kantian notion of 'republican' as 'liberal' or 'democratic', and thus hold the argument that democracies do not fight each other. This came to be known as the democratic peace thesis. This chapter first discusses the democratic peace thesis. The second theme is international peace building. International organisations, such as the United Nations and the European Union, and individual states have become closely involved in large peace operations which aim to build or reconstruct countries that have been torn apart by war. These operations, whether they take place in Bosnia and Herzegovina, Kosovo, East Timor, Iraq, Haiti or Sierra Leone aim to end violent (mostly intra-state) conflict. This chapter gives an introduction to the topic of peace building and explores to what extent peace building is successful in ending wars.

The aforementioned theoretical chapters are followed by selected case studies on the former Yugoslavia, the Iraq War, the Pacific War, Colombia, Rwanda and Libya. The case studies were chosen to represent conflicts in different parts of the world from varying historical periods in the twentieth and twenty-first centuries. The idea was that further cases could be added to this list in the future. As recent events in North Africa, Syria, Israel/Palestine and Mali show, peace and war are part of people's lives, either directly or indirectly.

Chapter nine, 'The Yugoslav Wars' by Francesco Ragazzi, covers not only the facts, but the diverse interpretations (also called narratives) of these facts by the different actors of the war. The chapter revisits the historical context of the conflict, then reviews the reasons and multiple justifications for the war and considers in chronological order the different conflicts in Slovenia, Croatia, Bosnia-Herzegovina, Kosovo and Macedonia.

In chapter ten on 'The Iraq War', Edmund Frettingham narrates the most important events of the war, focusing on two major questions: how did the Iraq War become possible? Why did the Coalition occupation of Iraq descend into sectarian civil war? This chapter examines what lay behind the US decision to remove Saddam Hussein, how the case for war could successfully be made domestically, and why the Bush administration's claims over Iraq received a mixed reception internationally. After describing the brief ground war and the fall of the regime, the chapter moves on to examine the dynamics of the insurgency and the Coalition response against the background of efforts to stabilise and consolidate the Iraqi state. It concludes with a discussion of the costs and long-term implications of the war.

'The Pacific War' is described by Maja Vodopivec in chapter eleven. The chapter's main concerns are to reveal the circumstances in which Japan failed to recognise its colonial and war responsibility in regard to its Asian neighbours. The chapter discusses issues of Hiroshima's peace politics and debates on Japan's pacifist constitution and its Article 9, which is becoming more and more controversial—in an increasingly 'globalised world' the nation-state's sovereignty is losing its meaning in light of the contested human security agenda and 'responsibility to protect' discourse.

Chapter twelve, 'War and peace in Colombia', written by Håvar Solheim and Eric Storm, reviews the historical background, the conflict in its different phases, the international context and the various attempts to negotiate for peace in Colombia.

In chapter thirteen on 'Genocide, war and peace in Rwanda', Helen Hintjes describes Rwanda's civil war from 1990, and the genocide of April to mid-July 1994, in their local, historical and international contexts. Competing explanations of genocide are considered, and the chapter asks why international intervention failed so miserably. Post-genocide reconstruction policies and peace-building efforts are also briefly explored.

Lastly, 'The Libyan civil war and the rise of the responsibility to protect' is described by Sara Kendall in chapter fourteen. It places the history of the modern Libyan state in a broader context and describes the rise to power of Mu'ammar al-Qadhafi before moving on to describe the 2011 civil war and its aftermath. Knowledge of Libya's history of invasions and colonisation and its status as a major oil exporter is key to understanding the development of the Qadhafi regime, with its limited state structure, regional tensions, and fraught relationship with the West.

Guidelines for Readers

This book combines theoretical approaches to peace and war, as well as case studies on which students will test the theoretical perspectives. The book also contains a list of selected readings and recommended literature for each topic. As for 'Theoretical perspectives':

- *Each chapter* introduces students to the fundamental debates and points of view in the field. It serves to summarise the central concepts students must master, organise the central theme of each chapter, and relate the most important scholarly literature to one another. The final part of the introduction guides students' reading of the selected sources/extracts.
- *Guiding questions* are sets of carefully devised questions that are provided to help students assess their comprehension of the core issues and can be used as the agenda for seminar/lecture discussion.
- *Selected readings* are used as primary or key sources that enable students to grasp the fundamental debates and points of view in the field. Selected readings provide, either explicitly or implicitly, 'answers' to the guiding questions.
- To take the learning process further, a list of *further reading* serves as a guide to find out more about the issues raised within each section topic and help students locate the key academic literature in the field.
- *Case study guiding questions* are sets of carefully devised questions to help students apply their knowledge of each section to the respective case studies, including both inter-state and intra-state conflicts.

As for case study chapters, they provide a short description of the case and address the following questions leading up to the provision of list of further reading at the end of each chapter.

- What was the historical context of the conflict?
- Why did war break out? Which justifications were used to justify armed violence and the use of force in the conflict? How did these justifications and motives develop over time?
- What were the main turning points in the war, and which main actors were involved in the different phases of conflict?
- What are the main human rights violations/war crimes committed, and which main actors were involved (armed forces, state organisations, private armed groups)?
- How did the international community (i.e. states, international and regional organisations, civil society) react to the use of armed force and human rights violations?
- How did the war end?
- What accountability mechanisms were put in place at the end of conflict? Were there accountability gaps?

To conclude, this book provides students with different theoretical approaches to studying peace and war, and allows them to apply learned concepts to several case studies. We hope that this interdisciplinary undertaking will offer a multi-faceted view on the complex topic of peace and war, and allow students to have an open mind regarding opportunities, challenges and controversies around this topic. The book is meant as an introduction to courses on peace and war in liberal arts programmes (thus complementing recent publications such as *The Ashgate Research Companion to War 2012*), and the idea is that other theoretical approaches and case studies can be added in the future. The main goal is to spark many discussions in classrooms and critically evaluate what peace and war mean for different people across various regions.

References

Ashley, R., 1981, 'Political realism and human interests', *International Studies Quarterly* 25(2), 204–36.

Clausewitz, C. von, 2007, *On war*, (trans. M. Howard & P. Paret), M. Howard & P. Paret (eds), Oxford University Press, Oxford.

Galtung, J., 1964, 'An editorial', *Journal of Peace Research* 1(1), 1–4.

———, 1969, 'Violence, peace, and peace research', *Journal of Peace Research* 6(3), 167–91.

Galtung, J., 1981, 'Social cosmology and the concept of peace', *Journal of Peace Research* 18(2), 183–99.

Hall, G. & Kobtzeff, O., 2012, *The Ashgate research companion to war: origins and prevention*, Ashgate, Farnham, Burlington, Vt.

Hindess, B., 2005, 'Politics as government: Michel Foucault's analysis of political reason', *Alternatives: Global, local, political* 30, 389–413.

Laclau, E., 1990, *New reflections on the revolution of our time*, Verso, London.

Levi, M. & Maguire, M., 2002, 'Violent crime', in *The Oxford handbook of criminology*, Oxford University Press, Oxford, pp. 795–843.

Neufeld, M., 1995, *The restructuring of international relations theory*, Cambridge University Press, Cambridge.

The Norwegian Nobel Committee, 2012, viewed 24 February 2013, from http://nobel peaceprize.org/en_GB/laureates/.

Sun, Tzu, 1994, *The art of war*, transl. R.S. Boulder, Westview Press, Boulder.

Yoder, P., 1989, *Shalom: the Bible's word for salvation, justice and peace*, Hodder and Stoughton, London.

PART ONE

THEORETICAL PERSPECTIVES

CHAPTER ONE

PEACE IN HISTORICAL PERSPECTIVE: THE BIRTH OF CONTEMPORARY PEACE MOVEMENTS

Ann Marie Wilson

Introduction

On 15 February 2003, as the US-led invasion of Iraq loomed on the horizon, millions of people took to the streets to voice opposition to what many deemed an unjust war. In over three hundred and fifty cities around the world, an estimated six to ten million people participated in what was to be the largest single day of protest ever organised. National coalitions in dozens of countries coordinated their actions, taking up similar slogans, tactics, and graphic designs. In New York City, a huge banner spanning a stage at the corner of First Avenue and 51st Street summed up the global activists' collective message: 'The World Says No to War'. Two days later, the *New York Times* observed that the 'fracturing of the Western alliance over Iraq and the huge anti-war demonstrations around the world' were 'reminders that there may still be two superpowers on the planet: the United States and world public opinion' (*New York Times* 17 February 2003; Cortright 2008: 172–3).

What made these global protests possible? What motivated activists from so many different parts of the world? And what were the traditions and legacies that shaped their collective efforts? As impressive as this single day of action may seem, it is but a recent episode in a long tradition of transnational protest against militarism and war. To place it in context, this chapter examines the origins of contemporary peace movements from the early nineteenth century to the outbreak of the First World War. The accompanying reading then provides a similar view of the twentieth century. As we shall see, the nature of warfare and the scale of global protest have changed considerably over the last two hundred years. Yet the ideals, strategies, and basic challenges of international peace movements have remained remarkably consistent over time. A look to the past thus sheds light on the opportunities and predicaments facing peace activists in the present day.

1. *Beginnings*

Advocacy for non-violent resolution to conflict has formed part of manifold religious and philosophical traditions around the world (Dietrich 2011). Hinduism, Buddhism, Judaism, Islam, and Christianity all contain principles that advance ideals of peace, even though many of their sacred texts also contain justifications for war. In the West, St. Thomas Aquinas is commonly heralded for establishing the parameters of moderation and proportionality that have come to be associated with 'just war theory', discussed elsewhere in this volume. During the Renaissance, humanist philosophers and theologians such as Erasmus rejected Aquinas' justifications, arguing that war was an unmitigated evil that could and should be prevented. In the seventeenth century, Hugo de Groot declared war to be a violation of universal, natural law and a matter of last resort, to be undertaken only on humanitarian grounds. These ideas were elaborated upon by Enlightenment philosophers such as Rousseau, who likewise deemed war an unnatural perversion, and Kant, who argued that wars could be stopped by the spread of democracy. In the eighteenth and nineteenth centuries, utilitarian philosophers such as Jeremy Bentham and John Stuart Mill argued that increasingly 'civilised' societies would render war unnecessary and infrequent. Building on the free-trade movement of his day, Mill suggested that the extension of global commerce, in particular, would make war obsolete.

Philosophies of peace thus have a long pedigree, but voluntary associations dedicated to peace advocacy did not emerge until the first decades of the nineteenth century. The New York Peace Society, the first known organisation of its kind, was founded by a group of merchants and clergymen in New York City in August 1815. The nearby Massachusetts Peace Society formed in 1816, with members from a similar milieu. More or less simultaneously, a few dozen men convened the Society for the Promotion of Permanent and Universal Peace—also known as the London Peace Society. The first peace societies to form on the European continent were the *Société de la morale chrétienne*, established in Paris in 1821, and the *Société de la paix de Génève*, founded in Switzerland in 1830 (Cortright 2008: 25–9; van der Linden 1987: 1–5, 29–31).

The well-heeled individuals who founded these early associations were responding to the Napoleonic Wars and the related conflict between Great Britain and the United States, which broke out in 1812. On the whole, they were not radical dreamers. Most came from influential families and espoused conservative values, eager to rein in political excesses on either side of the political divides spawned by the French Revolution. In the Anglo-American network in particular, the ideals of early peace advocates combined Christian millennialism with an Enlightenment confidence in human progress. The majority had little interest in creating mass membership organisations, and with few exceptions their organisations rejected participation by women. In 1868, the French peace advocate Frédéric Passy expressed the views of many when he insisted that 'We do not wish to ... overthrow anything, to transform anything', but rather to use '*law and not force* to decide ... not only the condition of individuals and cities but the *condition of nations*' (Cooper 1991: 35; Cortright 2008: 29–30).

Though he expressed a dominant view, Passy spoke at a time when the international peace movement was growing broader and more diverse. British leaders, inspired by the World Anti-Slavery Convention held in London in 1840, hosted the First General Peace Convention in that same city in 1843, welcoming twenty six delegates from the United States and six from Europe. Five years later, in 1848, the Second International Peace Congress sat in Brussels, and the Third met in Paris in 1849. A more radical gathering took place in Geneva in 1867, convened by the newly formed *Ligue international de la paix et de la liberté*. There, over two thousand Swiss, sixteen thousand German, one thousand French, and hundreds of Italian, Russian, British, and Polish citizens represented a lively mix of republican, nationalist, liberal, moderate socialist, and anarchist perspectives. Three years later, a Dutch Peace League formed with twenty six branches. And in November 1889, a lecture tour by William Jones of the British Peace Society inspired the formation of Japan's first peace society, *Nihon heiwa-kai* (Cooper 1991: 22–4, 36; Cortright 2008: 39, 29).

With increasing diversity came intensified debate about strategies and goals. One primary division concerned absolute versus conditional opposition to war. Some early peace advocates, including most British and American Quakers and some Presbyterians and Unitarians, rejected war in any form. David Low Dodge, the first leader of the New York Peace Society, maintained that even defensive war was contrary to the Gospel. He urged his fellows to practice total forbearance, insisting in 1812 that 'The spirit of martyrdom is the true spirit of Christianity' (cited in Ziegler 2001: 30). Noah Worcester and his colleagues in Massachusetts, on the other hand, accepted the possibility of defensive war as a last result—though they, too, believed war subverted human progress and forestalled Christ's millennial return. In continental Europe, most peace advocates favoured a similarly conditional approach, viewing peace as pragmatic good, rather than a moral imperative (Cortright 2008: 31; DeBenedetti 1980: 36).

A second internal debate concerned the breadth of peace demands. As movements for national liberation gripped the European continent, many advocates began to link peace to social justice concerns. The League of Universal Brotherhood, an Anglo-American association founded in 1846 by Elihu Burritt, distinguished itself by seeking out members from rural and working-class communities. It took an absolutist position on peace, while also condemning chattel slavery and demanding economic and racial equality. Mixing peace and justice advocacy was especially common in continental Europe, where liberal republicans, romantic nationalists, utopian socialists, feminists, and Marxist radicals all vied to win support for their particular visions of progress. The platform of France's *Ligue du bien public*, for instance, included demands for workers' collectives, credit societies, freedom of the press and religion, separation of church and state, abolition of capital punishment—even equality of the sexes. Geneva's *Ligue international de la paix et de la liberté* took on a similarly expansive programme. The Italian patriot Giuseppe Garibaldi, who presided over the group's founding conference in 1867, argued that wars would not end until national minorities won their freedom—a process that might require armed conflict (Cooper 1991: 32, 36–8; Cortright 2008: 37).

These ideas troubled conservative figures like Frédéric Passy, who held to the conviction that peaceful means of resolving interstate conflicts were a prerequisite for national liberation and all other forms of social betterment. Echoing John Stuart Mill, Passy argued that liberal economic policies would lead to the expansion of political freedom around the world. By removing the burdens of war and excessive military spending, he insisted, social justice would naturally unfold. His moderate *League international et permanent de la paix* advanced a legalistic agenda that made international arbitration—the adjudication of inter-state conflict through impartial third-party mediators—its centrepiece. 'Friends of peace', he insisted, 'have only one principle in which they can put their trust; it is arbitration...Everything else [must be] subordinated to that single principle' (Cooper 1991: 55).

By the close of the nineteenth century, then, the international peace movement contained a multitude of participants and perspectives. Historians estimate that between 1889 and 1914, approximately three thousand peace advocates were active in Europe and North America, with a smattering of activists spread across Japan, Australia, and Argentina. Coordinating their activities through the International Peace Bureau, established in Berne in 1892, activists employed a variety of tools to broadcast their message. Men and women alike travelled on the lecture circuit. They published countless books, articles, and brochures; lobbied politicians and diplomats at home and abroad; and held annual congresses at which they debated priorities and goals. But activists by no means spoke with a single voice. While some focused on bringing about innovations in international law, others took a more ecumenical approach, linking peace with a range of social justice concerns. And while some rejected violent conflict in all its forms, others veered toward pragmatism (Cooper 1991: 59–60).

In 1901, Émile Arnaud, president of France's *Ligue international de la paix et de la liberté*, coined the term 'pacifism' to refer to the broad body of thought dedicated to finding ways to prevent war. In one stroke, he transformed a varied and often contradictory set of philosophies of peace into a formal 'ism':

> Our great party needs a name; we have no name and this deficiency impedes our progress considerably. We are not passive types; we are not only peace makers; we are not just pacifiers. We are all those but also something more— we are pacifists... and our ideology is pacifism (cited in Cooper 1991: 60).

Arnaud's term caught on quickly, and was officially adopted by the Tenth Universal Peace Congress meeting that year in Glasgow. Thereafter, peace activists around the world began to refer to themselves as 'pacifists' (Cortright 2008: 8–9).

2. *Peace and Justice in The Hague*

One of the most important and surprising episodes in the history of peace activism took place in The Hague in 1899. The previous August, Czar Nicholas II of Russia circulated a diplomatic rescript inviting the nations of the world to a conference to discuss limitations on armaments. The United States recently had won an impressive military victory against Spain, turning heads across Europe. Meanwhile, new rapid-firing machine guns were being adopted by the German, French, and Austro-Hungarian armies. Nervously eyeing these developments, the Russian minister of war wondered how the cash-strapped Russian treasury would be able pay for such an innovation. These concerns prompted the Czar's calculated wish to 'make the great idea of universal peace triumph over the elements of trouble and discord' (cited in Cortright 2008: 41). Wary of the potential political complications of a gathering in the capital of a major power, the Russian government asked the Netherlands to serve as host. With the blessing of the newly crowned, eighteen-year-old Queen Wilhelmina, the Dutch government invited all governments having diplomatic representation at St. Petersburg, plus Siam, Montenegro, and Luxembourg. The ensuing meeting in The Hague was to be the largest diplomatic conference since the Congress of Vienna in 1815 (Cooper 1991: 97; Cortright 2008: 40–1; Davis 1962: 36–53).

Many government leaders and newspaper editorialists reacted suspiciously to the Czar's invitation, but peace activists embraced the gathering as a grand 'peace conference'. In England, the International Arbitration League, the London Peace Society, and other groups held more than one hundred meetings and collected thousands of signatures endorsing the event. Similar enthusiasm swept the United States and the European continent. Women, in particular, raised their voices in support: led by the German feminist Margarethe Selenka, over one million people signed a petition bearing signatures from eighteen countries, including Japan. Pacifists urged their governments to send delegates and insisted that the conference take seriously the wide-ranging proposals that peace societies had been promulgating for decades: disarmament, international arbitration, revisions of the laws and customs of war, intergovernmental unions, and the establishment of permanent international tribunal (Cooper 1991: 97–110; Davis 1999; Kätzel 2001: 46–69; Patterson 1976: 92–110). 'Disdain for our ideas is no longer possible', wrote one determined activist. 'Even if accomplishment does not immediately follow, . . . a beginning will have been made' (Cooper 1991: 102).

The worldwide groundswell of popular support made it difficult for diplomats to avoid the gathering, and in all, twenty six nations sent representatives to The Hague. The conference opened on 18 May 1899 at the Huis ten Bosch, a small summer residence belonging to the royal family. Flags of all nations festooned the route to the palace, and the opening proceedings paid respect to the Netherlands as the 'cradle of the science of international law' where 'for centuries the principal negotiations between European Powers have been conducted' (Scott 1920: 15). For the next several weeks, delegates vigorously debated the laws of war and considered rival proposals for a permanent court of arbitration—all under the watchful eye of an activist community that included France's Emile Arnaud, Germany's Margarethe Selenka, Austria's Baroness Bertha von Suttner, and many others. Although they were not invited to join in the deliberations, peace workers conducted themselves as though they were official members of the congress. In addition to submitting countless petitions, advocates deluged diplomats with technical proposals and resolutions drawn up by peace societies. And like their diplomatic counterparts, they carried out much of their work behind the scenes, at luncheons, banquets, and in private drawing rooms. The Dutch aristocrat and peace advocate Johanna

Waszklewicz-van Schilfgaard was especially helpful in this regard, opening her local salons to statesmen and lobbyists from around the world (Cooper 1991: 72).

Diplomatic historians have tended to downplay the significance of the proceedings at The Hague. The conference achieved little in terms of armaments, as the Germans opposed limits on armies, and the British on navies. The American delegates, led by famed historian of sea power Alfred Thayer Mahan, opposed arms reduction all around. Nevertheless, the conference gave newfound credibility to the cause of peace and international conflict resolution. Though protected by loopholes preserving sovereignty and the right to wage war, participating nations promised to resolve conflicts peacefully. They also agreed to strengthen certain aspects of the Geneva Conventions, which had been devised in 1864 to govern the protection of prisoners and non-combatants in times of war. Finally, the conference successfully created a Permanent Court of Arbitration, consisting of experienced arbitrators who could make themselves available to nations facing disputes (Cortright 2008: 41–3; Davis 1920).

The congress reinvigorated the Dutch peace movement, as it did the international movement as a whole. Soon, continued pressure from peace societies led American president Theodore Roosevelt to call for a follow-up conference in 1907, which drew participation from forty four nations—almost twice as many as the previous twenty six. In the wake of the Russo-Japanese War, this second gathering dealt more seriously with the rules of war at sea, as well as with the rights of neutrals and the protocols for declaring formal hostilities. It also entertained demands from peace advocates—and from the official US delegation—for a worldwide agreement mandating obligatory arbitration and a Court of Arbitral Justice that would be home to a group of justices sitting continuously. Although the conference ultimately rejected these proposals, it did agree to restructure the Permanent Court of Arbitration. In 1913 the Court installed itself in the majestic Peace Palace, constructed specially for this purpose thanks to a behest from the American philanthropist Andrew Carnegie (Cooper 1991: 72, 98).

3. The Legacy of World War I

Despite the optimism of pacifist observers in The Hague, their movement was far too weak politically to prevent the disaster that was to befall Europe in 1914. Moreover, the conflagration nearly destroyed the international peace movement as a whole. Multiple declarations of war, and

especially Germany's invasion of neutral Belgium, made it impossible for
European activists to collaborate freely across national borders. Indeed,
many no longer saw the use. Evincing a bellicose brand of 'patriotic pacifism', activists in Italy, France, and England increasingly argued against
neutrality and returned to old concepts of just war. Many refocused their
energies on mobilising against German militarism, arguing that the world
was neatly divided between those who supported violence and domination, on the one hand, and those who dreamed of peace (but were willing
to take up arms to defend it), on the other. In the United States, legally-
minded defenders of international arbitration at first urged caution, but
eventually supported the war effort. After US entry in the war, the League
to Enforce Peace (LEP), founded in 1915, waged a massive campaign to
defend what they deemed to be a 'war against war'. In Europe, many erstwhile pacifists in the labour and woman suffrage movements suspended
their international interests to focus on the war effort at home (Cooper
1991: 188–92; Cortright 2008: 54).

But where some campaigners gave up the former struggle, others held
fast. A vocal minority of women suffragists played a particularly important role in sustaining international contacts among pacifists during the
war. After the cancellation of the annual meeting of the International
Woman Suffrage Alliance, due to be held in Berlin in June 1915, a small
group of women led by the Dutch doctor Aletta Jacobs met in Amsterdam
to plan an International Congress of Women in The Hague. In late April
1915, despite the many difficulties of wartime travel, over one thousand
women from neutral and belligerent countries gathered there to discuss
strategies for ending the war and implementing a lasting peace. When
the meeting ended, a delegation of women then travelled across Europe
and North America to educate diplomats and heads of state about the
demands of the Congress, which included calls for continuous mediation,
greater democratisation (including the enfranchisement of women), universal disarmament, and the expansion of international courts and intergovernmental organisations. Women from countries represented by the
Congress then formed the Women's International League for Peace and
Freedom, which remains active to this day (Costin 1983: 301–15).

The Women's International League for Peace and Freedom is a prominent example of a contemporary peace organisation that finds its roots
in the First World War, but it is not the only one. In Great Britain in 1915,
Christians who were upset with the pugnacious stance of mainstream Prot-
estant churches formed the Fellowship of Reconciliation (FOR), a group
which soon spread to the United States, where it remains the largest and

oldest interfaith organisation dedicated to peace and social justice. That same year, the American Union Against Militarism (AUAM) was founded to combat the preparedness message being broadcast by erstwhile peace advocates and politicians alike. In 1917, the AUAM established a Civil Liberties Bureau—later the American Civil Liberties Union—to protest conscription, protect the rights of conscientious objectors, and defend the civil rights of critics of the war. And in Netherlands in 1921, European pacifists who had been active during the war created an international federation named Paco—Esperanto for 'peace'—which two years later became the War Resisters League, yet another group that remains active to this day (Cortright 2008: 69–71).

These comparatively radical, antimilitarist organisations, born out of the turmoil and disillusionment spawned by the First World War, represented a turning away from the conservative, legalistic approaches of the most prominent nineteenth-century peace societies. The members of these newer groups tended to view war as the product of imperial conflict and unbridled nationalism, and, more than in the past, their platforms emphasised social justice concerns over and above the values of order and stability. As we shall see in the accompanying reading, these organisations made important contributions to the fight against fascism in Europe, and to later campaigns against nuclear weapons and military conflict in Vietnam. In this way, their legacy shaped the contours of peace activism throughout the twentieth century.

Conclusion

The modern peace movement traces its ideological origins to the intellectual developments of the eighteenth century, and its institutional beginnings to the voluntary associations that began to form after 1815. Subsequently, it developed from a collection of small, comparatively isolated, elite-run societies focussed largely on law, order, and stability, to a much more diverse assortment of organisations oriented around large international conferences and drawing participation from a wide variety of social groups, including woman suffragists, union leaders, lawyers, intellectuals, and a range of social radicals. These activists may have united under the banner of 'peace', but their movement was driven by internal debates regarding such matters as absolute versus conditional opposition to war, the relationship between peace and social justice, and the relative importance of national loyalties.

These controversies have persisted through the twentieth century and beyond. Three extracts listed as selected reading from David Cortright's *Peace: a history of movements and ideas* will trace their evolution since 1914. In the first, he examines the evolution of the international peace movement from the First to the Second World War. In the second, he discusses the campaign for nuclear disarmament during the Cold War. Finally, in the third selection he traces the evolution of peace activism from the Vietnam era to the present day.

Guiding Questions

a. How did peace activists grapple with the debates surrounding appeasement and neutrality on the eve of World War II? How did these experiences reshape the meaning of 'pacifism'?
b. How did nuclear technology alter the stakes of peace activism? How did the peace movement transform itself during the Cold War?
c. How did resistance to conscription shape protest against the war in Vietnam? How was this mode of protest similar and different to later activist responses to the so-called War on Terror?
d. What are the major elements of continuity linking twentieth-century peace movements to those of the nineteenth century? What are the most significant examples of change?

Selected Reading

Cortright, D., 2008, *Peace: A history of movements and ideas*, Cambridge University Press, Cambridge.

1. Chapter 4—pp. 71 (bottom) to 92.
2. Chapter 7—entire—pp. 126–154.
3. Chapter 8—entire—pp. 155–179.

Further Reading

Addams, J., Balch, E.G. & Hamilton, A., 1915, *Women at The Hague: The International Congress of Women and its results*, Macmillan, New York.
Brock, P., & Young, N., 1999, *Pacifism in the twentieth century*, Syracuse University Press, Syracuse.

Cooper, S., 1991, *Patriotic pacifism: waging war in Europe, 1815–1914*, Oxford University Press, New York.

Costin, L., 1983, 'Feminism, pacifism, internationalism and the 1915 International Congress of Women', *Women's Studies International Forum* 5, 301–15.

DeBenedetti, C., 1980, *The peace reform in American history*, Indiana University Press, Bloomington.

Patterson, D., 1976, *Toward a warless world: The travail of the American peace movement, 1887–1914*, Indiana University Press, Bloomington.

Rochon, T.R., 1988, *Mobilizing for peace: The antinuclear movements in Western Europe*, Princeton University Press, Princeton, N.J.

Wells, T., 1994, *The war within: America's battle over Vietnam*, University of California Press, Berkeley.

van der Linden, W., 1987, *The international peace movement, 1815–1874*, Tilleul Publications, Amsterdam.

Case Study Questions

a. Who are the main players involved in this conflict?

b. What is the timeline of the conflict, and what are its major turning points?

c. Which peace leaders and/or peace organisations have responded to this conflict? What actions have they taken, and how have they justified their response?

d. Can you identify any legacies of earlier peace movements in this conflict? Which ideas, strategies, or challenges have carried over?

References

Addams, J., Balch, E.G. & Hamilton, A., 1915, *Women at The Hague: The International Congress of Women and its results*, Macmillan, New York.

Cooper, S., 1991, *Patriotic pacifism: waging war in Europe, 1815–1914*, Oxford University Press, New York.

Costin, L., 1983, 'Feminism, pacifism, internationalism and the 1915 International Congress of Women', *Women's Studies International Forum* 5, 301–15.

Davis, C., 1962, *The United States and the First Hague Peace Conference*, Cornell University Press, Ithaca.

——, 1999, 'Hague Peace Conferences', in H. Richard, (ed.), *The Oxford companion to American military history*, Oxford University Press, Oxford.

DeBenedetti, C., 1980, *The peace reform in American history*, Indiana University Press, Bloomington.

Dietrich, W., (ed.), 2011, *The Palgrave international handbook of peace studies: A cultural perspective*, Palgrave Macmillan, New York.

Kätzel, U., 2001, 'A radical women's rights and peace activist: Margarethe Lenore Selenka, initiator of the first worldwide women's peace demonstration in 1899', *Journal of Women's History* 13 (3), 46–69.

Patterson, D., 1976, *Toward a warless world: The travail of the American peace movement, 1887–1914*, Indiana University Press, Bloomington.

Scott, J.D. (ed.), 1920, *The proceedings of the Hague Peace Conferences: The Conference of 1899*, New York.

van der Linden, W., 1987, *The international peace movement, 1815–1874*, Tilleul Publications, Amsterdam.

Ziegler, V., 2001, *The advocates of peace in antebellum America*, Mercer University Press, Georgia.

CHAPTER TWO

THE CAUSES OF WAR

Niels van Willigen and Benjamin Pohl[1]

Introduction

The question of the causes of war is a classic topic of international relations (IR). In fact, the academic discipline of IR has its origins in the attempt to better understand, and possibly remedy, the origins of war. After summarising recent developments regarding the nature, incidence and consequences of war, this chapter provides an overview of the various explanations that scholars have given in response to the pivotal question of why wars occur. Before addressing that question, however, we need to shortly dwell on the question of what we mean by 'war'.

Perhaps the best known definition of war stems from a Prussian general: Carl von Clausewitz (1780–1831) conjectured that war was simply the continuation of politics by other means (cf. Howard & Paret 1976). War is thus described as the means for political ends and not, for example, as meaningless destruction. This is also reflected in more recent definitions, such as the one by Jack Levy and William Thompson (2010: 5). These authors define war as 'sustained, coordinated violence between political organisations'. Such a broad definition includes many different kinds of war, from pre-modern tribal wars via contemporary civil wars to inter-state wars, but it also delimits three elements in the meaning of 'war'. Following Levy and Thompson's explanation, we will sketch these three elements below.

The first element is the emphasis on 'sustained violence'. The occurrence of (sustained) violence is what distinguishes war from conflict. Non-violent rivalry, threats of violence, and even the limited use of force are insufficient for a conflict to qualify as a war. There is some debate as to exactly how much violence is needed to turn a conflict into war. The best known research projects, the Correlates of War Project (since 1963) and

[1] The authors thank Janne Malkki for his useful comments on an earlier draft of this chapter.

the SIPRI Yearbook (since 1969) use the threshold of one thousand battle-related deaths per year, but this definition is somewhat arbitrary. For example, recent 'wars' such as the one between Russia and Georgia (2008) or between Israel and Lebanon/Hezbollah (2006) would be discounted on the basis that the violence they triggered was insufficiently sustained. Similarly, the 'Cold War' would not qualify because it did not involve sustained violence—at least not in its European manifestation.

The second element is 'between'. This refers to the fact that 'war' requires a pattern of interaction between two or more actors. Violence needs to be reciprocal. If the target of violence does not fight back, it is not a war. We thus exclude events such as the Soviet invasion of Czechoslovakia in 1968, or the Chinese army's intervention against protesters on Beijing's Tiananmen Square in 1989.

The third and final element of the definition centres on 'political organisations'. This brings us back to Clausewitz, as it implies that individuals fight on behalf of a collective that has some form of 'political' objectives, be it a state, an alliance, or a rebel group. Without political direction and purpose, killing a member of another group would not constitute an act of war, but merely homicide (cf. Levy & Thompson 2010).

1. Trends in Warfare

Although war has been a frequent and recurring feature of (international) politics, it has continuously changed. One of the striking characteristics of warfare during the last few decades is the decline of interstate wars and the attendant rise of intrastate (civil) wars. The frequency of interstate wars has continually declined over the past centuries, although the first half of the twentieth century formed an exception to this secular trend (Cashman & Robinson 2007: 1). In fact, countries in the 'developed' world have not conducted direct wars among themselves during the last sixty years. They have, however, been involved in wars against 'developing' countries (for example against Argentina in 1982, or against Iraq in 1991 and 2003) and in internationalised 'intrastate' armed conflicts (e.g. Bosnia in the 1990s or Afghanistan since 2001). Developing countries have also seen only few open interstate wars among themselves; the perhaps most notorious of these taking place between Iraq and Iran during the 1980s.

The decline in interstate wars does not necessarily imply that humanity has become more peaceful. Instead this decline partly reflects the changed way in which organised violence is acted out. For example, states have sought to avoid the negative connotations of 'war' by simply circumvent-ing the practice of officially declaring war—the last time the American Congress did so was during the Second World War. In practice, govern-ments in recent decades often reverted to providing support for 'freedom fighters' against whichever regime they sought to dislodge rather than openly challenging each other. This resulted in a shift from 'interstate' to 'intrastate' war. Intrastate wars have thus often been 'internationalised', meaning they involve actors from beyond the borders of the respective state. Some authors have even warned of a 'coming anarchy' in which state authority generally declines to make way for the mayhem of wide-spread criminal warlordism (Kaplan 1994).

The idea that only the form of warfare may have changed is supported by the finding that the frequency of intrastate wars relative to interstate wars has increased since 1945 (Levy & Thomson 2010: 186). However, whereas armed conflicts continue to be fought today, many of them are below our threshold of one thousand annual battle-related deaths. The 'Human Security Report Project' noted in its last report that the number of such wars has declined from twenty three in 1988 to just five in 2008 (2010: 10–11). Finally, whereas the human toll of recent conflicts such as in Rwanda (1994) or Darfur (since 2003) may invite pessimism, it was the wars between the major powers, especially World War I and World War II that have been the most destructive in recent history. In this respect, we are relatively fortunate to witness an 'era of leading power peace' (Jervis 2002).

In contrast to widely held assumptions, wars have become less deadly in recent decades: 'The average conflict in the new millennium kills ninety percent less people each year than did the average conflict in the 1950s' (Human Security Report Project 2010: 8). The report cites three reasons for this development. First, many contemporary wars are localised and do not feature prolonged engagement by major powers with heavy weapons. Sec-ond, generic public health gains, and particularly increased immunisation coverage, have increased the resilience of more vulnerable populations (many more people used to die from the indirect effects of war, especially disease). Third, the level and scope of humanitarian assistance have sig-nificantly increased, to the extent that mortality in developing countries sometimes decreases during armed conflicts because war leads to greater outside humanitarian engagement than during times of peace (Human Security Report Project 2010: 8).

These trends may raise hopes for those invested into addressing the global challenge of peace. Indeed, comparing the incidence of human violence across history, psychologist Steven Pinker recently argued (sparking much public debate) that we might well be witness to the most peaceful era of humanity (Pinker 2011). Yet not every trend is positive. The number of 'minor' armed conflicts increased over recent years, and there is a risk that some of them might deteriorate into bloodier wars (Human Security Report Project 2010: 8). There has also been a secular trend of increasing military expenditures over the last decade (SIPRI 2011), potentially enabling greater bloodshed in the future. Last but not least, whereas there has not been any direct war between the major powers for six decades, their arsenals continue to feature weapons of hugely destructive power. The possibility of an 'Armageddon' thus persists, and with nine nuclear-armed powers (and counting), a very lethal war might erupt at some point. Therefore, understanding the causes of war is important not least to prevent its occurrence.

2. *Levels of Analysis*

In examining the causes of war, scholars traditionally distinguish three levels of analysis: the individual, the organised group, and the (international) system. This triptych is a useful analytical tool for trying to understand why people fight. It is of course possible to expand the number of levels of analysis by distinguishing between various groups (sub-state groups, states, civilisations) and different systems (dyadic, i.e. between two actors, regional, global). The three levels however correspond to classic treatises in International Relations, such as Kenneth Waltz's *Man, the state, and war* (1959), and are sufficient for a basic understanding of the levels of analysis approach.

The concept of levels of analysis has traditionally been applied to interstate wars. However, we will try to show the parallels and overlap between different strands of academic writing by integrating explanations for intrastate wars into this framework as well. Note that the concept of 'levels of analysis' is an approach rather than a theory. A theory would need to go beyond any level of analysis and propose a logically coherent explanation for a phenomenon such as war. Different theories of IR tend to emphasise different levels of analysis, according to whether they put the blame for war primarily on individual statesmen, state characteristics, or the pressures of the international system. Common sense would of course suggest that all three might have an impact. Yet the different levels of analysis seem to defy *theoretical* integration. We know that actors impact structures and vice versa, but what does that mean regarding the ultimate causes of war? Those interested in this problem may want to read David Singer's (1961) classic analysis of this subject. Here it suffices to say that for a *full* account of the causes of war we need to apply different, parallel levels of analysis—rather than opting for one level or having an integrated theory at hand.

The Individual Level

In trying to explain war, the first level of analysis focuses on the decisions made by individuals. The frequency of warfare in human history obviously suggests that, for a generic explanation of war, we need to go beyond the character of single individuals and look for shared traits. Many observers have found that explanation in human nature. Thomas Hobbes, an important seventeenth century philosopher, famously claimed that man, in the 'state of nature', would find himself in a permanent state of war of all against all. He argues in the *Leviathan* (1651) that, without a disciplining government, human life would be 'solitary, poor, nasty, brutish, and short' (Hobbes 2006: 51). Later, some biologists have similarly traced the occurrence of war to humanity's biological heritage. Nobel Prize-winner Konrad Lorenz thus argued that aggression was an instrumental element of the process of natural selection, and hence part of human nature (cf. Barash & Webel 2009: 99).

However, explaining war by biological determinism would be overly simplistic. Unlike human nature, 'war is a variable, not a constant' (Levy & Thomson 2010: 20). As a group of prominent behavioural scientists concluded in 1986 in the Seville statement, 'biology does not condemn humanity to war. [...] The same species... [that] invented war is capable of inventing peace' (Barash & Webel 2009: 101). Already in 1795, the philosopher Immanuel Kant had similarly argued that perpetual peace was possible and even logical once people applied reason (cf. Doyle 1986: 1159). In short, human nature can cause both peace and war. This implies that the concept of human nature by itself is insufficient for *explaining* either. So, can we then do away with the individual level of analysis?

Not yet. Just because humans might be able to learn that war is not rational at the collective level does not mean that everyone understands it, or that this fact holds true for every individual. Even if humans were not inherently aggressive, many live under circumstances that could plausibly unleash aggression. Lack of opportunities due to poverty, socio-economic inequality, religious and ethnic discrimination or similar grievances might push individuals towards (organised) violence. Moreover, while war often impoverishes many, some also gain from war because it enhances their status or offers them opportunities for gainful employment, smuggling or extortion (Berdal & Keen 1997). Greed may thus also predispose individuals (or groups) to war. The problem, of course, is again that there is more greed and there are more grievances than there is war. Furthermore, other scholars have found that neither greed nor grievances can statistically explain why rebellion breaks out, and that insurgency instead takes place where the 'natural' circumstances facilitate it (Fearon & Laitin 2003)—an argument that can theoretically be extended to all wars. It however falls short of constituting a full explanation and is not really tied to the individual level. Instead, it focuses on opportunities for successful warfare, whatever the causes, and brings in explanations beyond the 'social' sphere, such as physical accessibility.

If such individual-level explanations cast their net too widely, others narrow our focus by looking at one privileged subset of individuals: leaders. Leaders often have an important role regarding the outbreak of war because they usually make the ultimate decision to wage war. Personal factors such as cognitive abilities, psychological characteristics, belief systems and perceptions play an important role in explaining their dispositions and choices. Character traits may cause leaders to misinterpret the risks of (in-)action, their own relative strength, and the likely course and consequences of war. Such individual-level factors can lead to fundamentally flawed cost-benefit analyses. Other leaders may not even try to make a full cost-benefit analysis in the first place, but act and react in egocentric, irrational or pathological ways. In short, individuals and their choices have an enormous influence on the course of history, but human characteristics such as aggression, grievances, greed, or incompetence are so widespread that they often over-determine the cause of war, and do not adequately account for sustained periods of absence of war. To fully understand the occurrence of war, we therefore have to look beyond (powerful) individuals, and instead study the *structures* that enable or constrain war.

The Organised Group Level

When it comes to waging war, the most important organised group in contemporary times is the state. The governments and/or bureaucracies that represent nation-states are the most powerful purposive actors in international politics. The characteristics of states, with respect to their relative power, foreign policy objectives or internal structure thus feature prominently in the academic literature seeking to explain war.

However, in privileging states over other organised groups we should be conscious of the limitations inherent to this approach. Throughout much of human history, states were far less monolithic than their contemporary Western counterparts, and therefore exercised much less of a monopoly on violence. Moreover, many contemporary states are also arenas for, as well as actors in, armed conflicts. Most ongoing conflicts pit a government against one or several rebel groups, meaning that the most important actors are *sub-state* groups. And, even in Western democracies, it is usually only some groups within the state that are involved in warfare, occasionally for reasons other than 'national' interests.

The 2003 US war against Iraq illustrates this: US decisions were subject to substantial bureaucratic struggles within the US administration, and the war was (and became increasingly) contested within US society (Fallows 2004). Moreover, because the war was fought by a professional rather than conscripted army and financed through deficits rather than tax increases, it touched the lives of most US citizens in only a limited fashion. Finally, it is plausible to interpret the Iraq war as a domestic, party political 'wedge strategy' by which the governing party sought to gain advantage by emphasising the national security issues where it enjoyed special credibility, thus enabling it to rally its own partisans and to raid its opponent's electoral base (Snyder, Shapiro & Bloch-Elkon 2009). Analysing the causes of this war, it is thus a shortcut to only look at 'the US position' or 'US national interests'. Despite this caveat, states represent an important analytical category because once a government has decided on war we can usually analyse the state it represents as a largely unified actor that brings important resources to bear.

In trying to explain the occurrence of war, we will look at three state characteristics in particular: relative power, the nature of a state's political system, and domestic politics. Although these characteristics have mainly been applied in order to analyse the behaviour of states, they can also be used to examine the behaviour of groups below or above the state level, such as secessionist rebel groups or interstate alliances.

Relative power shapes states' (and other groups') behaviour in at least two ways. First, power in terms of cultural, economic or military capability increases the ability of states to achieve foreign policy goals, including to wage wars successfully. More power therefore secondly tends to increase the range and scope of foreign policy objectives. Powerful states usually define their interests more broadly, and will have a greater stake in the regional or global order. For that reason, they might see themselves pushed to not only defend narrow national objectives, but also to protect weaker allies, keep sea lanes open, defend humanitarian principles or balance against aggressive states even if the latter do not threaten them directly. With power also comes (perceived) responsibility, which often results in (imperial) overstretch.

The most important contemporary fault line in a state's political system runs between democracies and autocracies. Democratic peace theory (see the chapter on the 'End of war') claims that democratic states behave differently from their authoritarian counterparts, at least when it comes to relations between democracies (cf. Levy & Thomson 2010: 104–17). Empirically, liberal democracies have not fought against each other, although this fact hinges on a narrow definition of 'liberal democracy'. However, liberal democracies are not inherently more peaceful than autocracies. As the US invasion in Iraq and the NATO operation in Libya illustrate, liberal democracies have repeatedly treated autocracies as legitimate targets of intervention. The 'protection' or 'liberation' of foreigners has thus become an additional cause of war.

If the nature of a state's political system has a bearing on the wars it fights, so does the content of its domestic politics. Wars might serve the purpose of diversion by distracting the public from domestic problems or by seeking ideological or electoral profit from fomenting nationalism. The relationship might also be inverted, where a nationalistic public or published opinion pushes leaders into wars they would rather avoid. Moreover, a state's domestic administrative weakness might invite a violent challenge, be it from outside or within. The potential domestic political reasons for war thus link back to the causes of war at the individual level that we discussed earlier: greed, grievance and opportunity.

The Systemic Level

The third level of analysis is the systemic level. System-level theories of war emphasise the constraints on all actors: whatever their intentions, they are periodically pushed into violent confrontation. The best-known systemic theory of international relations is structural realism. Structural realists see war as a 'tragedy' (Mearsheimer 2001) that is the consequence of international anarchy, i.e. the absence of any power above sovereign states that could reliably adjudicate disputes between these sovereigns. For that reason, states (or other groups operating without recourse to higher authority) have to rely on self-help. This reliance causes states to worry about their relative power—as opposed to absolute power. Even if their intentions are peaceful, uncertainty about the future gives states the

incentive to invest in their militaries for the purpose of defending themselves. In turn, this may alarm neighbouring states, which will increase
their defence investment. Ultimately, this makes such investments self-
defeating, because the security of one state spells insecurity for another.

The result is the security dilemma that regularly spurs arms races (Herz
1950). Whereas states can ally with others to balance strong adversaries,
changes in the relative power between states (often as a consequence of
economic and/or technological developments) lead to imbalances and
uncertainty that sometimes result in war. The First World War provides a
particularly vivid illustration of this process. Although structural realists
do not absolve statesmen from their responsibility for war or peace, this
balance-of-power theory carries some fatalistic notions.

Balance-of-power theory remains the most influential system-level
theory for explaining war and conflict, but it has come under sustained
attack in academic writing. On the one hand, scholars have challenged
the empirical reliability of the theory, pointing out that states often do not
behave according to the balancing logic (Schroeder 1994; Wohlforth *et al.*
2007). On the other hand, scholars have attacked the theory's assumptions: we already discussed the phenomenon that liberal democracies
apparently do not need to fear each other, despite the absence of any
world government. Since 1945, interstate territorial conquest has become
delegitimised so that a state's survival is arguably co-guaranteed through
the norms of international society. 'Anarchy' is thus a misleading term for
what should instead be called 'the anarchical society', because it mixes
power competition with ordering principles as embodied in international
law (Bull 1977). More generally, states do not have to use security measures
as a means to compete with other states. In Alexander Wendt's famous
aphorism, 'anarchy is what states make of it' (1992: 395).

Although it is the most influential system-level theory, there are alternatives to structural realism in IR. Many social scientists disagree with
realism's overwhelming concern with state security. After all, apart from
the hierarchical authority exercised by nation-states there is a second
ordering principle in international politics: the free market (Strange
1988). The banking and sovereign debt crises shaking the global economy
since 2008 have recently demonstrated the influence of financial markets
on international politics. Yet what is the link with the causes of war?
Clearly, economic hardship as a result of such crises could induce political leaders to embrace diversionary wars, or to seek to increase their
state's resource base by predation. But for a truly systemic theory, we
might look to Marxism.

Marxism emphasises the primacy of economic forces over the political 'superstructure'. Marxist history is therefore not primarily a history of states or nations, but of class struggles pitting oppressors against the oppressed. Lenin built on Marx' work when he distinguished between 'progressive' wars waged to liberate mankind from feudalism and later capitalism and 'the struggle between the robbers' as he described the First World War (Lenin 1994: 98). According to Lenin's analysis (1915/16), the nation-state had become too small for capitalism, leading to imperialism and therefore to a struggle 'for the artificial preservation of capitalism by means of colonies, monopolies, privileges and national oppression of any kind' (Lenin 1994: 97). In short, Lenin saw this war as a direct result of the global economic interests of the capitalist oppressors, who used war to enhance the exploitation of the oppressed. Although this analysis is certainly flawed in its reduction of conflict to economic interests, it demonstrates the difference between system-level and actor-level analysis: from a Marxist perspective it is not so much individual decision-makers who ultimately cause war, but structural historic forces.

Conclusion

What explains war? We saw that the different levels of analysis stress very different causal mechanisms. Whereas a focus on the individual level tends to overestimate the role of human agency, a system-level analysis tends to disguise the fact that wars are the result of (a series of) discrete decisions. A full understanding of the causes of war will thus necessitate an examination of all levels of analysis, even if they cannot be fused into one theoretically coherent explanation: there is an inherent tension between the explanation that wars come about because great powers are prone to balancing each other, if necessary via preventive war, and the explanation that war came about because an individual leader saw war as the most promising strategy to achieve certain political goals.

This tension also alludes to an important distinction we need to make when explaining war: the distinction between underlying and proximate causes (Brown 2001). Most of the explanations we discussed—from 'human nature' via 'greed', 'grievances' and incentives for diversionary wars to international 'anarchy'—belong to the first category of underlying or permissive causes. They are not sufficient for explaining why a specific war broke out at a specific time. The latter requires knowledge of the proximate causes, i.e. the triggers and decisions that transform a potential for war into actual, sustained, organised violence. Whereas we can point to some generic conditions of human life and social organisation as causing wars in the sense of permitting or facilitating the conduct of war, explaining the causes of particular wars requires understanding the varying, and historically contingent, contexts and motives.

In this chapter we could only offer a very short introduction into the causes of war. There is a large body of literature which deals with this question. The two selected readings below offer an introduction into the literature on civil wars as well as into key interstate conflicts of the past century. Moreover, both the reference list and the list of further readings will help you delve further into the general topic and the debates surrounding specific instances of war.

Guiding Questions

a. Give a definition of war and explain the defining factors.
b. What trends can be identified with respect to interstate wars and intrastate wars?
c. Explain the different levels at which one can analyse the causes of war.
d. What is the merit of the levels of analysis approach?

Selected Reading

Brown, M.E., 2001, 'The causes of internal conflict: An overview', in M.E. Brown, O.R.J. Coté, S.M. Lynn-Jones & S.E. Miller (eds), *Nationalism and ethnic conflict: An international security reader*, pp. 3–25, MIT Press, Cambridge, MA.

Cashman, G. & Robinson, L.C., 2007, *An introduction to the causes of war: Patterns of interstate conflict from World War I to Iraq*, pp. 1–25, Rowman & Littlefield Publishers, Inc., Lanham, MD.

Further Reading

Black, J., 1998, *Why wars happen*, University of Chicago Press, Chicago.

Brown, M.E. (ed.), 1998, *Theories of war and peace: An international security reader*, MIT Press, Cambridge, MA.

Holsti, K.J., 1991, *Peace and war: Armed conflicts and international order, 1648–1989*, Cambridge University Press, Cambridge.

Huntington, S.P., 1996, *The clash of civilizations and the remaking of world order*, Simon & Schuster, New York.

Lebow, R.N., 2010, *Why nations fight*, Cambridge University Press, Cambridge.

Rotberg, R.I., Rabb, T.K. & Gilpin, R. (eds.), 1989, *The origin and prevention of major wars*, Cambridge University Press, Cambridge.

Sobek, D., 2009, *The causes of war*, Polity Press, Cambridge.

Suganami, H., 1996, *On the causes of war*, Clarendon Press, Oxford.

van Evera, S., 2001, *Causes of war: power and the roots of conflict*, Cornell University Press, Ithaca.

Vasquez, J.A., 2009, *The war puzzle revisited*, Cambridge University Press, Cambridge.

Case Study Guiding Questions

a. Which factors have caused the outbreak of war in your particular case study? Try to find an explanation at each level of analysis and weigh which level has been particularly relevant to your case.

b. What are the limits of the level-of-analysis approach for understanding why war has broken out in your particular case study?

References

Barash, D.P. & Webel, C.P., 2009, *Peace and conflict studies*, 2nd edn., Sage, Thousand Oaks, CA.

Berdal, M. & Keen, D., 1997, 'Violence and economic agendas in civil wars: Some policy implications', *Millennium: Journal of International Studies* 26(3), 795–818.

Brown, M.E., 2001, 'The causes of internal conflict: An overview', in M.E. Brown, O.R.J. Coté, S.M. Lynne-Jones & S.E. Miller (eds.), *Nationalism and ethnic conflict*, MIT Press, Cambridge, MA.

Bull, H. 2002 [1977], *The Anarchical society: A study of order in world politics*, 3rd edn., Palgrave, Houndmills.

Correlates of war project, viewed February 28, 2013, from http://www.correlatesofwar.org/.

Cashman, G. & Robinson, L.C., 2007, *An introduction to the causes of war: Patterns of interstate conflict from World War I to Iraq*, Rowman & Littlefield Publishers, Inc, Lanham, MD.

Doyle, M.W., 1986, 'Liberalism and world politics', *The American Political Science Review* 80(4), 1151–69.

Fallows, J., 2004, 'Blind into Bagdad', *The Atlantic*, January 2004.

Fearon, J.D. & Laitin, D.D., 2003, 'Ethnicity, insurgency, and civil war', *The American Political Science Review* 97(1), 75–90.

Herz, J.H., 1950, 'Idealist internationalism and the security dilemma', *World Politics* 2(2), 157–80.

Hobbes, T., 2006 [1651], 'Relations among sovereigns', in P. Williams, D.M. Goldstein & J.M. Shafritz (eds), *Classic readings and contemporary debates in international relations*, Thomson Wadsworth, Belmont, CA.

Howard, M. & Paret, P. (eds), 1976, *Carl von Clausewitz: On war*, Princeton University Press, Princeton.

Human Security Report Project, 2010, 'Human security report 2009/2010: The causes of peace and the shrinking costs of war', Oxford University Press, New York.

Jervis, R., 2002, 'Theories of war in an era of leading-power peace. Presidential address, American Political Science Association, 2001', *American Political Science Review* 96(1), 1–14.

Kaplan, R.D., 1994, 'The Coming anarchy. How scarcity, crime, overpopulation, tribalism, and disease are rapidly destroying the social fabric of our planet', *The Atlantic*, February 1994.

Lenin, V.I., 1994 [1915/16], 'Socialism and war', in L. Freedman (ed.), *War*, Oxford University Press, Oxford.

Levy, J.S. & Thomson, W.R., 2010, *Causes of war*, Wiley-Blackwell, Oxford.

Mearsheimer, J.J., 2001, *The tragedy of great power politics*, W.W. Norton & Co., New York.

Pinker, S., 2011, *The better angels of our nature: Why violence has declined*, Viking, New York.

Schroeder, P., 1994, 'Historical reality vs. neo-realist theory', *International Security* 19(1), 108–48.

Singer, J.D., 1961, 'The level-of-analysis problem in international relations', *World Politics* 14(1), 77–92.

SIPRI (ed.), 2011, *SIPRI Yearbook 2010, Armaments, disarmament and international security*, Oxford University Press, Oxford.

Snyder, J., Shapiro, R.Y., & Bloch-Elkon, Y., 2009, 'Free hand abroad, divide and rule at home', *World Politics* 61(1), 155–87.

Strange, S., 1988, *States and markets*, Continuum, Oxford.

Waltz, K.N., 1959, *Man, the state, and war: A theoretical analysis*, Columbia University Press, New York.

Wendt, A., 1992, 'Anarchy is what states make of it: The social construction of power politics', *International Organization* 46(2), 391–425.

Wohlforth, W.C., Little, R., Kaufman, S.J., Kang, D., Jones, C.A., Hui, V.T.B., Eckstein, A., Deudney, D. & Brenner, W.L., 2007, 'Testing balance-of-power theory in world history', *European Journal of International Relations* 13(2), 155–85.

CHAPTER THREE

BIOLOGY OF WAR

Patsy Haccou

Introduction

The ability to engage in war appears to be uniquely human. Nevertheless, there are clear biological mechanisms at its roots. Biologists are uncovering the evolutionary mechanisms leading to human aggression, collaboration and empathy, while neurophysiological research shows which brain mechanisms are involved. Being aware of these ultimate and proximate factors helps to understand human behaviour better, and may prove to be invaluable if we ever want to be able to mitigate war.

1. *The Evolution of War*

At first sight war appears to be a very human invention. It requires organisation and planning, a strong bond between soldiers, and a clear sense of who is the enemy. Battles between groups of other species have only been observed over territorial issues, are not premeditated, and rarely involve fatal injuries. The only other mammal that behaves in a similar way to us is one of our closest relatives, the chimpanzee. The extremely violent raids against their rivals from neighbouring communities by groups of young male chimpanzees are disturbingly like human team aggression. The question is whether or not they can help us to understand our own wars.

Our other close relative is the bonobo. Recent findings indicate that we are just as closely related to chimpanzees as to bonobos. Genetically, we differ no more than 1.3 percent with either one of these apes (Prüfer *et al.* 2012: 527–31). Our latest common ancestor probably lived about four and a half million years ago; Chimps and bonobos share a common ancestor of one million years ago and their DNA differs by about 1.4 percent. Their behaviour, however, is remarkably different. Whereas chimpanzees can be very violent, bonobos are extremely gentle, peaceful creatures that tend to resolve social conflicts by sexual rather than aggressive acts.

The difference in aggressive behaviour between two such closely related species as the chimpanzees and bonobos illustrates how difficult it is to draw conclusions concerning innate behavioural tendencies on the basis of phylogenetic relatedness. Why do these two species differ so much, and what does this contrast in the behaviour of our relatives imply about our own aggressiveness? The chimpanzee propensity for team aggression may be an ancestral state that has been lost in bonobos but is still present in modern day humans (Potts & Hayden 2010).

Potts and Hayden (2010) argue that the differences in aggressive behaviour between chimps and bonobos are due to the fact that bonobos have a more stable and diverse food supply than chimpanzees. These more benign ecological conditions reduce between-group competition over resources. They argue that chimps as well as humans have an inherited predisposition to team up with (perceived) ingroup members to kill their neighbouring outgroup members. They believe that this predisposition was already present in our historical common ancestors, whereas peaceful bonobo behaviour evolved separately.

Furthermore, they illustrate that the inclination toward team aggression is much lower in females than in males, and argue that this is due to the fact that in our evolutionary history such battles only benefitted males, by enlarging territories and eliminating rivals. Chimpanzees and bonobos both live in fusion-fission societies, where individuals move alone or in small groups of individuals, of which the composition changes constantly. All associations are temporary, except those between mothers and their offspring. Within a territory, however, all groups form one large community, and members of different communities do not mix. During adolescence, young females migrate to other communities, whereas young males stay in their natal group.

While their structures are similar, the social hierarchies of chimp and bonobo communities differ very much. Chimpanzee societies are male dominated, with strong male hierarchies, and coalitions between males. Bonobo societies, on the other hand, are female dominated. After females have migrated, they form strong social bonds with the other females in their new community. Bonobo males derive their social status from their mother's rank (de Waal 1995: 82–88).

According to Potts and Hayden (2010), war is directly tied to the demography of a country in combination with available resources: relative (food) scarcity and a high proportion of adolescent males will increase the probability of conflicts with outgroups. This makes it intimately related to overcrowding; one of the main conclusions is that empowering women, especially giving them the opportunity to control their own reproduction, will dramatically reduce the frequency of such aggressive outbreaks.

2. *The Evolution of Empathy*

Human beings are capable of extremely empathetic behaviour, and recent findings indicate that we have an innate tendency to cooperate with others, even if it involves individual costs and no benefits (Bowles & Gintis 2011). Frans de Waal (2010) argues that the pervasive view that evolution leads to selfishness is not only destructive but also not true. According to de Waal (2010), empathetic behaviour has strong biological roots and can be observed not only in humans, but in other social animals as well.

If you look at empathy 'top down' from the point of view of cognition, it involves understanding another's situation, and being able to put yourself mentally in their place. From this point of view, most people would say that animals are incapable of empathy. If you look at it from a neurobiological point of view (or 'bottom up'), empathy involves being in tune with another and sharing their emotions. The neurophysiological processes involved are motor mimicry and emotional contagion, and some animals are definitely capable of these. For instance, contagiousness of yawning, self-scratching, and neonatal imitating of facial expressions all occur in monkeys. Emotional contagion between familiar individuals has been demonstrated in many mammals, such as mice. de Waal (2010) argues that these abilities probably evolved in connection with parental care in mammals: good care taking implies being able to sense pain, distress, and contentment in babies.

Looking more closely at empathetic behaviour, different levels emerge. Whereas all socially driven monkeys appear to show reconciliatory behaviour after conflicts, consolation only occurs in apes. In this sense, apes appear to be special since they are able to adopt another's perspective (e.g. I know that you know . . .). We thus arrive at the hypothesis that complex empathy requires a sense of *self-identity* (theory of mind). This can be measured with Mirror Self Recognition (MSR). Indeed, empathy and MSR appear to co-emerge in human children at about the age of two. MSR has also been demonstrated in apes, dolphins, and elephants, all species that indeed show complex forms of empathetic behaviour. For instance, de Waal (2010) describes an instance where a bonobo tries to help a wounded bird by spreading out its wings and trying to make it fly again. This requires a highly developed understanding of the perspective of a member of another species.

3. *Are Humans Special?*

In human beings, care taking by alloparents and forming extended families appear to have played a special role that has set us apart from the other apes and enhanced the evolution of social learning and sharing behaviour (Hrdy 2011). Human beings pay much more attention to what others feel and think than any other ape. From a very early age onwards, human children have a much higher tendency to help and share than young of closely related species. Sociocognitive tests show that already at age two human children outperform orang-utans and chimpanzees of all ages with respect to social learning, communication, and theory of mind. Sarah Blaffer Hrdy (2011) argues that these abilities evolved because of alloparental care.

The traditional explanation for the evolution of altruistic social behaviour in humans is based on within-group solidarity in combination with between-group competition. While this argument can explain how within-group collaboration increases once it is already established, it does not explain its origin. Hrdy (2011) argues that the average inter-birth interval in human hunter-gatherer societies is three to four years, whereas in other apes it is four to eight years. Furthermore, even though human babies are bigger at birth, they remain dependent on parental care for much longer than young apes. Thus, human infants are usually not yet independent before the next baby is born. The nutritional input needed for growth and maintenance is such that, even with the help of a mate, a mother would not be able to provide enough resources to rear her child. Alloparental care is thus needed to protect slowly maturing offspring from starvation, and permit the long period of post-weaning dependence in humans.

No apes other than humans show alloparental care. Human mothers readily allow their children to be carried by and taken care of by other familiar individuals, but females of other ape species closely guard their babies and carry them around all the time. For instance, chimpanzees are in continuous contact with their mothers for up to six months of age, and orang-utans have seven years of close maternal care. Alloparental care does occur in more distantly related monkey species, such as marmosets.

The consequence of alloparental care is that children grow up dependent on many others, which is a very 'un-ape' like mode of upbringing.

Hrdy (2011) argues that this generated a selection pressure towards proso-cial behaviour, and empathy evolved as a by-product of such cooperative breeding. As a result, humans are better equipped to cooperate and share with others than any other ape.

4. *The Evolution of Collaboration*

After its original evolutionary establishment, a further increase in within-group altruistic behaviour was probably caused by between-group com-petition (Ridley 1998), although recent results suggest that group hunting might have provided a more important selection pressure towards coop-eration (Bowles & Gintis 2011). Economists have found that in experi-mental games people generally do not act in a self-interested way. Rather than maximising their own payoff, they behave cooperatively. Moreover, many people are even prepared to incur costs in order to punish non-cooperative individuals. The question is how such social norms could ever evolve. To explain this, Bowles and Gintis (2011) use empirical observa-tions of behaviour during games in a range of non-technological societ-ies in Africa, Indonesia, and South America together with mathematical models for gene-culture co-evolution. The experiments show people do not behave in a completely selfish way in any of the examined societ-ies. This indicates that there has been a universal selection pressure on humans to be cooperative. However, the amount that people are prepared to pay to punish others varies between societies, so culture plays a role in this as well.

The models are based on modern hunter-gatherer societies that typi-cally consist of tribes of a few hundred to a few thousand people, where tribes are made up of bands of about seventy-five individuals. This organ-isation probably originated in the Pleistocene era (about ten thousand years ago). Big game hunting appears to have been a crucial factor in the evolution of cooperation, since it requires collaboration between a certain number of adult hunters. According to the models, the genetic variation between such bands would not be large enough to favour within-group cooperation as a result of between-group competition, which is the tra-ditional explanation of the evolution of altruism. Instead, social institu-tions within groups, forcing the more successful hunters to share their food, limited within-group differences in reproductive success to such an extent that group-selection for individually costly acts of cooperation could work. In this way, selection can favour emotions such as shame or guilt that internalise social norms and benefit the group. These findings are consistent with the observations that people in societies with small-scale agriculture are more selfish than big game hunters.

5. *The Mechanisms of Aggression*

When we consider the proximate biological mechanisms underlying aggressive behaviour it is clear that it is a complex phenomenon. Adult aggressive behaviour appears to be affected by genetic, developmental, social, and environmental circumstances (Nelson 2005). In itself, aggression is not an abnormal behaviour. For instance, defending your offspring or vital resources certainly makes sense. What is important is the context in which aggression occurs, and its context-related intensity (Sapolsky n.d.). This is reflected in the neurophysiological underpinnings of aggression, which involve the amygdala as well as the frontal cortex. The amygdala is a part of the limbic system, which, in terms of its evolution, is a much older structure than the frontal cortex. The amygdala is involved in a range of emotional reactions, from fear and anxiety to sensory stimuli. When the amygdala is destroyed, no aggressive behaviour occurs, whereas an overactive amygdala increases aggression (Sapolsky n.d.).

The frontal cortex regulates appropriate, learned, behaviour. It represses undesirable, impulsive, reactions. There is usually an inverse relation between metabolic activity of the two brain structures, indicating that they normally inhibit each other. In comparison to other species, the frontal cortex is the largest and most active in humans. It is involved in learning general rules and behaviour (in relation to rewards). Reduced volume or activity of the prefrontal cortex, either through genetic, developmental, or traumatic factors, often, but not always, leads to increased aggressive behaviour. The activity of the frontal cortex is affected by the neurotransmitters dopamine and serotonin. Animal studies show that low levels of serotonin are associated with more impulsive, aggressive behaviour. Dopamine stimulates the frontal cortex to suppress impulsive reactions that give instant gratification, in order to get a larger reward later.

The role of the frontal cortex in regulating aggressive behaviour indicates that the learned responses to social rules regarding the context of aggression are important. Out-of-context aggressive behaviour can have many different causes. For instance, it may be due to genetic abnormalities, causing a reduced frontal cortex activity, or sensitivity to serotonin. However, it can also be caused by developmental factors, such as social patterns or desensitisation to violence during childhood. Effects of drugs (such as alcohol), hormones (such as testosterone), and environmental triggers (such as overcrowding), appear to depend on predisposition, making already violent individuals more aggressive.

Neurotransmitters, hormones, drugs, psychopharmaca, and external stimuli may all affect the activity of these brain structures and the resulting aggressive behaviour. Their effects, however, are strongly dependent on developmental, learned conditions. What is especially important in connection to war is the relation with perceived ingroups and outgroups. Brain scan research shows that, depending on the context, the amygdala reacts to pictures of individuals that are perceived as 'outgroup members' (Harris & Fiske 2006; Phelps 2001).

Such perceptions appear to be strongly susceptible to developmental conditions and manipulation. For instance, people who grew up in multicultural groups do not show increased amygdala activity in response to pictures of individuals with different ethnicities. There are also dramatic examples of effects of psychological manipulation on aggressive behaviour towards individuals depicted as outgroup members (Zimbardo 2008).

Conclusion

Aggression is a natural behaviour that is essential for survival and successful reproduction. An accurate reaction to potential danger requires being able to recognise danger and to distinguish between friends and foes quickly. Such a reaction to sensory stimuli should therefore be present in all animals, and, accordingly, it is organised by one of the (in terms of its evolution) oldest parts of our brain. With the addition of more recent brain structures, the possibility of overruling instinctive reactions, and learning appropriate contexts for aggressive behaviour evolved. The frontal cortex is the most developed in human beings: therefore we have the highest ability to do this. This implies that we do not need to automatically respond aggressively to perceived outgroup individuals, but also that we are very susceptible to the manipulation of such perceptions. Evolution has also made us capable of extreme empathy towards and cooperative behaviour with our group members. The downside is that there is an association between ingroup altruism and aggressiveness towards outgroup members. Together with our ability to organise and plan, this provides the breeding ground for war. Therefore, being aware of our innate biological mechanisms, and how they can be manipulated is essential in mitigating the

damage of such behaviour. The selected texts describe the evolutionary
factors leading to human aggression (Potts & Hayden) and human social
learning (Hrdy). The lectures by Sapolsky give a thorough overview of the
proximate neurophysiological factors that underlie aggressive behaviour.

Guiding Questions

a. Are there any new concepts or words that you do not know? If so, look
   them up on the Internet.
b. What does the text say about the evolutionary family tree of humans?
c. What are the main conclusions concerning the evolutionary causes of
   human behaviour, and what are the main arguments for them? Can
   you think of any counter arguments?
d. What does the text say about ingroup and outgroup relations?
e. What does the text say about learned contexts of behaviour?

Selected Readings

Hrdy, S.B, 2011, *Mothers and others*, Harvard University Press, Cambridge.

1. Chapter 3, Begin until 'Born in a new milieu', pp. 65–79.
2. Chapter 4, from 'The world as a giving place' until end of chapter,
   pp. 132–141.
3. Chapter 6, from 'Benefits of group membership' until end of chapter,
   pp. 195–208.

Potts, M. and Hayden, T., 2010, *Sex and war*, Ben Bella Books Inc, New York.

1. Chapter 3, from 'The Troop' until 'Hunting', pp. 40–54.
2. Chapter 4, from 'The Importance of population size and structure' until
   'Animal Lessons', pp. 88–95.
3. Chapter 6, from 'Women on the Fring line' until 'Sex and War',
   pp. 129–134.
4. Chapter 11, from 'Virtuous citizens acting in the name of righteous
   causes' until end of chapter, pp. 275–281.
5. Chapter 13, from 'Women waging peace' until end of chapter,
   pp. 328–331.

Sapolsky, R.M. http://www.virtualprofessors.com/stanford-bio-250-human
-behavioral-biology, 25-lecture course on Human Behavioral Biology
(Stanford BIO 250): videos 17–20.

Further Reading

Bowles, S. & Gintis, H., 2011, *A cooperative species: Human reciprocity and its evolution*, Princeton University Press, Princeton.

de Waal, F., 1995, 'Bonobo sex and society', *Scientific American* 272, 58–64.

——, 2006, *Our Inner Ape: The Best and Worst of Human Nature*. Granta Books, London.

——, 2010, *The age of empathy: Nature's lessons for a kinder society*, Three Rivers Press, New York.

——, 2013, *The Bonobo and the Atheist: In Search of Humanism Among the Primates*. W.W. Norton and Co., London.

Kortum, H., & Heinze, J. (eds), 2012, *Aggression in Humans and Other Primates: Biology, Psychology, Sociology*, Walter de Gruyter & Co, Berlin/Boston.

Nelson, R.J., (ed.), 2005, *Biology of aggression*, Oxford University Press, Oxford.

Niehoff, D., 1999, *The Biology of Violence: The Brain, Behavior, Environment and Violence*. Free Press, New York.

Phelps, E.A., 2001, 'Faces and races in the brain', *Nature Neuroscience* 4, 775–6.

Ridley, M., 1998, *The origins of virtue: Human instincts and the evolution of cooperation*, Penguin Books, New York.

Zimbardo, P., 2008, *The Lucifer effect: Understanding how good people turn evil*, Random House Paperbacks, New York.

Case Study Guiding Questions

a. Consider ingroup vs outgroup factors that played a role in the conflict: Were there any manipulations of ingroup and outgroup views? Which historical factors contribute to the cultural ingroup-outgroup views?

b. What is the demographic structure of the different parties involved?

c. What is the position of women in the different parties?

d. What are culturally accepted contexts for aggression in the different parties?

e. Does the conflict involve contested resources? If so, which ones, and how do they relate to perceived survival chances?

References

Bowles, S. & Gintis, H., 2011, *A cooperative species: Human reciprocity and its evolution*, Princeton University Press, Princeton.

de Waal, F., 1995, 'Bonobo sex and society', *Scientific American* 272, 58–64.

———, 2010, *The age of empathy: Nature's lessons for a kinder society*, Three Rivers Press, New York.

Harris, L.T. & Fiske, S.T., 2006, 'Dehumanizing the lowest of the low: Neuroimaging responses to extreme out-groups', *Psychological Science* 17, 847–53.

Hrdy, S.B., 2011, *Mothers and others*, Harvard University Press, Cambridge.

Nelson, R.J., (ed.), 2005, *Biology of aggression*, Oxford University Press, Oxford.

Phelps, E.A., 2001, 'Faces and races in the brain', *Nature Neuroscience* 4, 775–6.

Potts, M. & Hayden, T., 2010, *Sex and war*, Ben Bella Books Inc., Dallas.

Prüfer, K. *et al.*, 2012, 'The bonobo genome compared with the chimpanzee and human genomes', *Nature* 486, 527–31.

Ridley, M., 1998, *The origins of virtue: Human instincts and the evolution of cooperation*, Penguin Books, New York.

Sapolsky, R.M., http://www.virtualprofessors.com/stanford-bio-250-human-behavioral-biology 25-lecture course on Human Behavioral Biology (Stanford BIO 250).

Zimbardo, P., 2008, *The Lucifer effect: Understanding how good people turn evil*, Random House Paperbacks, New York.

CHAPTER FOUR

JUST WAR THEORY

Laurens van Apeldoorn

Introduction

It is often said that 'just war theory' is the dominant intellectual tradition in the ethics of war. The ethics of war is a subfield of philosophy aimed at providing a systematic investigation of the normative principles that apply to conduct in warfare. In identifying just war theory as the dominant position in this field, the term is usually used to refer to a loosely connected body of philosophical reflection that can be traced back to philosophers of Greek and Roman antiquity, scholastic theologians such as Thomas Aquinas (1225–1274), Francisco de Vitoria (1492–1546), Francisco Suarez (1548–1617), Alberico Gentili (1552–1608), and (early) modern philosophers such as Hugo Grotius (1583–1645), Samuel von Pufendorf (1632–1694), Emerich de Vattel (1714–1767), and Immanuel Kant (1724–1804). These thinkers stake out measured defenses of the permissibility of resorting to war, and for that reason, just war theory is often contrasted with realism and pacifism—realism, very roughly, being the view that moral concerns have no place in the subject of warfare—that, in Thucydides words, 'the strong do as they wish and the weak suffer as they must', and pacifism being the view that resorting to war can never be morally justified. Between these extremes just war theory is thought to establish a middle ground. Like realism it recognises that warfare is a 'necessary evil' and can therefore sometimes be morally justified. On the other hand it acknowledges, like pacifism, that warfare has many morally reprehensible consequences and ought to only be pursued as a last resort.

As several commentators have recently pointed out, however, the indiscriminate use of the term 'just war theory' is potentially misleading (Haggenmacher 1992; Reichberg 2008). They argue that we should instead identify two general approaches or 'paradigms' within the tradition, which they call the 'just war' and the 'regular war' paradigm respectively. Although authors in the tradition often do not fall neatly into either category, the internal consistency of the paradigms can be brought out clearly enough to help us better understand the nature of the debate. This is in part due to a closely related distinction: the evaluation of warfare can be divided into two fundamentally distinct issues. On the one hand, there is a set of issues related to the decision to use force. Such considerations are commonly referred to with the Latin phrase *jus ad bellum*—the rightfulness of resorting to war. On the other hand, there is a set of issues related to conduct in war. Once the fighting has started one might ask what is permitted, required, or forbidden in the conduct of hostilities. These are so called *jus in bello* considerations—rightfulness in war.[1] The just war paradigm is centrally concerned with whether the resort to force is just or lawful and is therefore most closely associated with *jus ad bellum*. The regular war paradigm, conversely, primarily focuses on *jus in bello*.

1. *The Just War Paradigm*

A canonical example of the just war paradigm can be found in the work of Thomas Aquinas, the thirteenth century Catholic theologian and philosopher. Aquinas identifies 'just cause' as one of three conditions that must hold to justify waging an offensive war. 'A just war', Aquinas writes, 'is customarily described as one that avenges wrongs, when a nation or state has to be punished, for refusing to make amends for the wrongs inflicted by its subjects, or to restore what it has seized unjustly' (Aquinas 1920: IIaIIae.40.1). A just cause for war is the redress of some past wrong by another party. In a just war there will therefore be always one party (a state or political community) that has acted unjustly and is therefore liable to an attack.

The two other conditions for a just war are first that the war is initiated by a legitimate authority and is publicly announced, and secondly that it is fought with the 'right intention'. With regard to the former, Aquinas argues that this is so because war is aimed at redressing injustices. If an individual seeks to right an injustice it is possible to pursue his or her cause within the institutions of the state. Political communities themselves, however, have no such avenues open to them. That is why in order to secure justice and protect the common good, legitimate political authorities must have the right to declare war. With regard to the latter condition Aquinas argues that a war is unjust if waged with

---

[1] One can also distinguish a third set of issues, *jus post bellum*, justice in the peace settlement but that falls outside of the scope of this introductory chapter. See for example Bass (2004).

an intention other than to correct the wrong that has been committed. Personal enrichment or vengeance can never be an appropriate aim in warfare (Aquinas 1920: IIaIIae 40.1).

Aquinas is not very explicit about the kinds of wrongs that constitute a just cause. He distinguishes obliquely between requirements of defensive and offensive war. Defensive war, or self-defence, is legitimate and can be pursued by individuals as well as the state. 'For if his sole intention be to withstand the injury done to him, and he defend himself with due moderation, it is no sin' (Aquinas 1920: IIaIIae.41.1). Offensive war, however, does not merely consist of the defending one's interests against an attack, but aims for the punishment or rectification of some wrong.

This distinction between defensive and offensive war is taken up by Thomas de Vio, better known as Cajetan (1468–1534), in his commentary on Aquinas. He maintains that while a private person is free to 'repel force by force', only the state is also allowed 'to exact revenge for injuries to itself or its members—not only against its subjects, but also against foreigners' (Cajetan 2006: 242). This punitive right forms the basis for the legitimacy of offensive wars, for, as he points out elsewhere, if 'this were not the case, since an equal has no empire (*imperium*) over his equal, all wars would be unjust with the exception of defensive ones' (Cajetan 2006: 248).

The Spanish philosopher and theologian Francisco de Vitoria also follows Aquinas' distinction between defensive and offensive war. In his work *On the law of war* we find an explicit discussion of the kinds of considerations that are a just cause for offensive wars. A 'difference of religion' cannot be a just cause, and neither can the 'enlargement of empire' or 'the personal glory or convenience of the prince' (De Vitoria 2006: 313). Harm or injury, in the form of physical injury, stolen or damaged property, or breach of territorial integrity, is the only just cause for offensive warfare. But the response must be proportional; 'it is not lawful to persecute those responsible for trivial offenses by waging war upon them' (De Vitoria 2006: 314). This is what in more recent times has come to be known as the proportionality condition, which can be summarised by the idea that the good to be achieved by war must outweigh the harm.

In more recent restatements of the just war paradigm, the emphasis has come to lie squarely on one particular wrong, namely the act of aggression. Whereas the above-mentioned philosophers are primarily concerned with analysing and justifying offensive wars, modern day just war theories generally identify defence against aggression as the only just cause for war. The prime example of this tendency is Michael Walzer's famous *Just and unjust wars* (1977), which will be discussed in greater detail below.

Regardless of the way in which 'just cause' is characterised, what is particular about just war theories is that waging a war is seen as analogous to the imposition of a punishment for a crime. In a war combatants are considered to be in a morally asymmetrical relationship, with one party fighting a just war and another party acting unlawfully by being guilty of a crime. 'On this conception, the unrighteous adversary was not even deemed a belligerent; he was merely the rebellious object of armed coercion' (Reichberg, Syse & Begby 2006: 227). This has consequences for the way in which *jus in bello* considerations are treated. The rights of combatants *in bello* are directly derived from the justness of their cause. The party who acts unjustly in fighting a war, conversely, has no right to conduct hostilities, not even in self-defense.

The asymmetric characterisation of *jus in bello* is reflected in the writings of the above mentioned philosophers. Aquinas does not say much about how to conduct hostilities although he intimates that even fighting a just war binds one to observing some principles, as there are 'certain rights of war and covenants, which ought to be observed even among enemies'.[2] However, those who go into battle against a party that has just cause have no *in bello* rights, they have no recourse to self-defense and are 'guilty of strife and commit sin' (Aquinas 1920: IIaIIae.41.1). De Vitoria engages more extensively with the question 'what may be done in the conduct of a war', setting out various *jus in bello* conditions. A warring party that has justice on its side may do everything that is necessary to secure the public good; it may also reclaim all the losses caused by the perpetrator as well as the costs of the war, and perhaps above all, it may 'do everything in a just war which is necessary to secure peace and security from attack' (De Vitoria 2006: 315). Further he maintains that one may plunder and enslave innocent persons in so far that this may be necessary to ensure victory. And he also allows for the execution of enemy combatants if they would otherwise form a threat. But these rights and obligations are only meant to apply to the actions of just parties. Others have no *in bello* rights due to the injustice of their cause.

2. *The Regular War Paradigm*

While the just war paradigm focuses primarily on identifying *jus ad bellum*, the regular war paradigm focuses on *jus in bello* considerations.

---

[2] While discussing the permissibility of ambushes in a just war (Aquinas 1920: IIaIIae.40.3).

Central to the structure of regular war theories is the idea that the relationship between warring parties is symmetrical—that each party in the conflict has an equal status with corresponding rights and duties. These theories are called 'regular' in the sense that war is understood to be conducted in accordance with certain accepted or adopted 'regulations', standards, or norms.[3] Instead of focusing on the question 'who in a conflict has 'just cause', the warring parties are formally placed on an equal footing, 'as in a dual' (Haggenmacher 1992: 435) and have therefore access to the same rights and prerogatives *in bello*.

Raphael Fulgosius (1367–1427) is sometimes said to have been the first to state the regular war paradigm's central principles. The question Fulgosius asks is: 'how is it that the one who wages an unjust war acquires the ownership of the things he captures through his unjust action?' (Fulgosius 2006: 228–9). Those thinkers working within the just war paradigm would deny that one acquires ownership of things captured unjustly. But Fulgosius asks this question in a commentary on ancient Roman law where the legal effects of war did generally apply, irrespective of just cause. Fulgosius responds that this is due to the uncertainty about who is right and who is wrong in a war. There is no common judge to decide on the question. Instead, he writes, we must 'let war be the judge' (Fulgosius 2006: 229). What matters, he reiterates is that the war is 'public', that is, that it 'was declared by someone who could do so, that is, an independent nation or an independent king'. Besides that, there is no 'inquiry into the cause for which the war was begun, nor about whose cause is just' (Fulgosius 2006: 229).

Like Fulgosius, Alberico Gentili aims to draw out the implications of the conception of law found in the writings of Roman jurists, and like Fulgosius he accepts what just war theorists strenuously deny: that war may be waged justly on both sides. This claim seems to be based on epistemological considerations—considerations that can also be found in De Vitoria, which shows the difficulty of neatly placing authors in either paradigm.[4] Because it is often hard, if not impossible, to know whose cause in a conflict is just we must instead 'aim at justice as it appears from man's standpoint' (Gentili 2006: 374). From our perspective it often

---

[3] 'Regular' as in 'conformable to some accepted or adopted rule or standard; or made or carried out in a prescribed manner; recognized as formally correct' (Reichberg 2008: 16).

[4] For example, de Vitoria writes that, 'it may happen that one side has justice on its side, and other side falsely, but in good faith, believes it is right: then the war is also just for the other side, because they wage war in good faith and are hence excused from sin' (de Vitoria 2006: 322).

appears that both contending parties have a just cause. It is therefore best to grant the rights of war to both sides in all cases except those where the injustice of a cause is clearly evident.

Emerich de Vattel is particularly noteworthy among the various thinkers that in subsequent centuries further elaborated this regular war paradigm. A Swiss philosopher and diplomat, Vattel develops a detailed theory of belligerent rights and obligations in his most famous work *The law of nations*. Like other proponents of the regular war paradigm he embraces the idea of a just cause but denies its practical relevance (Vattel 2006: 512). He advances a powerful consequentialist argument for the separation of *jus ad bellum* and *jus in bello*. If belligerent rights are dependent on having a just cause, and 'each Nation claims to have justice on its side', then 'the contest will become more cruel, more disastrous in its effects, and more difficult of termination'. Rather, while sovereigns are bound by considerations of just cause in conscience, in the public consideration 'war in due form, as regards its effects, must be accounted just on both sides' and all laws of war apply to belligerents in equal measure. This is the 'voluntary Law of Nations', embraced by the tacit consent of all, and 'established from necessity and for the avoidance of greater evils' (Vattel 2006: 515).

3. *Michael Walzer*

In contemporary debates about the ethics of warfare no other book has had the impact of Michael Walzer's *Just and unjust wars*. Written with the aim of bringing consistency to common sense moral judgements as well as drawing on established international law, it can be read as an attempt to combine elements of both the just war and the regular war paradigm.

On the one hand, Walzer defends the importance of strong *jus ad bellum* requirements for legitimate warfare. He maintains that 'any use of force or imminent threat of force by one state against the political sovereignty or territorial integrity of another constitutes aggression and is a criminal act' (Walzer 2006: 62). Conversely, it is the act of aggression, and the act of aggression only, that warrants taking up arms—either by the victim in self-defence or any other member of the international community in aid of the assaulted party. More specifically he identifies the following *jus ad bellum* principles, which together amount to an account of what is a just cause for war:

1) Any use of force or imminent threat of force by one state against the political sovereignty or territorial integrity of another constitutes aggression and is a criminal act.
2) Aggression justifies two kinds of violent response: a war of self-defense by the victim and a war of law enforcement by the victim and any other member of international society.
3) Nothing but aggression can justify war.
4) Once the aggressor state has been militarily repulsed, it can also be punished. (Walzer 2006: 60–61)

Walzer admits that several amendments must be made to the equation of just cause with self-defense against the crime of aggression. In particular he argues that the very values that underlie the principles above seem to require that we sometimes disregard the territorial integrity and political independence of states. The prime example of this is what is often called humanitarian intervention. When states are involved in massive violations of human rights the appeal to political independence seems to lose its force, and waging a war to aid those in need can be considered just (Walzer 2006: 101). Another example is assistance to secessionist movements, which Walzer takes to be appropriate if the democratic character of the movement is established. In short, while Walzer allows exceptions to the general rules, he approvingly quotes De Vitoria who maintains that 'there is a single and only just cause for commencing a war, namely, a wrong received' (Walzer 2006: 62). Walzer grounds these claims ultimately in the rights of individuals. States have these rights of territorial integrity and political sovereignty because their citizens have the right to defend themselves, freely associate and determine their lives as they see fit.

On the other hand he also embraces a number of *jus in bello* principles largely taken from international law. In particular he defends the moral equality and symmetrical rights of combatants and the inviolability of non-combatant immunity. These are what he calls principles of the 'war convention' (Walzer 2006: 151). He further emphasises the principles of necessity and proportionality in the conduct of hostilities that demand that the harms are necessary means to the victory and the end of hostilities that are appropriately weighed 'against the contribution that mischief makes to the end of victory' (Walzer 2006: 129). Echoing Vattel, and in conformity with the structure of the regular war paradigm, Walzer maintains that these *in bello* 'rules of war are made obligatory by the general consent of mankind'. They are the answer of human kind to the realities of warfare: 'Only because there is no escape from hell, it might be said, have we laboured to create a world of rules within it' (Walzer 2006: 47). Walzer thus identifies the following *jus in bello* conditions:

5) Symmetrical liability of combatants ('symmetry thesis')
6) Non-combatant immunity
7) Utility and proportionality

The *jus ad bellum* and *jus in bello* principles are strictly independent ('independence thesis'), so that *in bello* considerations apply regardless of the justice or injustice of the belligerent's cause for resorting to war. As Walzer writes:

> *Jus ad bellum* requires us to make judgements about aggression and self-defense; *jus in bello* about the observance or violation of the customary and positive rules of engagement. The two sorts of judgement are logically independent. It is perfectly possible for a just war to be fought unjustly and for an unjust war to be fought in strict accordance with the rules. (Walzer 2006: 21)

For example if a soldier fighting in an aggressive (and therefore unjust) war kills another soldier, it is not considered murder, even though his side of the conflict has no just cause.

Much of the subsequent work on the ethics of war has grappled with the implications of Walzer's view. Walzer has been criticised both on historical and on systematic grounds. With regard to the former, Walzer has been faulted for claiming that the independence thesis and the symmetry thesis are central elements of traditional just war theory (Reichberg 2008: 193). Indeed, the previous discussion has shown that many important proponents of the just war paradigm explicitly denied both. With regard to the systematic aspects of his view it can be argued that Walzer brings together elements of the just war paradigm and the regular war paradigm in a marriage that is not an altogether happy one.

Accordingly, several contemporary theorists have shown the fragile stability of Walzer's theory. David Rodin argues that the independence thesis leads Walzer to a striking paradox: An aggressive war as a whole is a crime (given Walzer's principle 1), but each individual act in the conduct of hostilities that together makes up this crime are entirely lawful (given principle 5). 'Such a war, the just war theory seems to be saying, is both just and unjust at the same time' (Rodin 2002: 167). Jeff McMahan follows the proponents of the just war paradigm in denying the symmetry thesis. He argues that one only becomes liable to an attack if one is responsible for an unjustified act of aggression. Simply by posing a threat to someone, for example, one does not give others the right to self-defense. Otherwise the 'police would forfeit their right not to be attacked by criminals they justifiably threatened. The correct criterion of liability to attack in these cases is not posing a threat, nor even posing an unjust threat, but moral responsibility for an unjust threat' (McMahan 2008: 21–2). Thus, McMahan denies that the symmetry thesis can be defended and instead follows Aquinas, Cajetan and others in maintaining that *jus in bello* is dependent on the justice of one's cause.

Conclusion

The selected reading include extracts from Michael Walzer's *Just and unjust wars*. In the passage from chapter four we find a defense of the *jus ad bellum* conditions summarised above. In the extracts from chapters eight and nine Walzer outlines the *jus in bello* conditions. This introduction has shown that *jus ad bellum* and *jus in bello* considerations can be understood as deriving from two intellectual traditions—the just war paradigm and the regular war paradigm respectively. It is this division that explains the difficulty at the heart of Walzer's theory. The 'dualism of *jus ad bellum* and *jus in bello*', Walzer rightly points out, 'is at the heart of all that is most problematic in the morality of war' (Walzer 2006: 21).

Guiding Questions

a. Why can only aggressive war create a just cause for war? Or, in Walzer's words, why does the concept of aggression have a special place in the theory of war?
b. How does Walzer derive the rights and obligations of states? Do you think his argument is successful?
c. Walzer denies that the killing in war of one soldier by another is analogous to killing in society. Why? According to Walzer, what are the differences?
d. 'Simply by fighting, whatever their private hopes and intentions, they have lost their title to life and liberty, and they have lost it even though, unlike aggressor states, they have committed no crime' (Walzer 2006: 136; see also Walzer 2006: 144 footnote). Why? Do you agree?
e. Do you think that Walzer's *jus in bello* and *jus ad bellum* requirements can be consistently unified in one theory?

Selected Reading

Walzer, M., 2006, *Just and unjust wars* (4th ed.), Basic Books, New York.

1. Chapter 4 (pp. 51–55, 58–59, 61–64)
2. Chapter 6 (pp. 86–91, 101–108)
3. Chapter 8 (pp. 127–133, 135–137)
4. Chapter 9 (pp. 138–146, 151–156)

Further Reading

Haggenmacher, P., 1992, 'Just war and regular war in sixteenth century Spanish doctrine', *International Review of the Red Cross*, 434–45.

Luban, D., 1980, 'Just war and human rights', *Philosophy and Public Affairs* 9(2), 160–81.

McMahan, J., 2008, 'The morality of war and the law of war', in D. Rodin & H. Shue (eds), *Just and unjust warriors*, pp. 19–43, Oxford University Press, Oxford.

——, 2009, *Killing in war*, Clarendon Press, Oxford.

Nagel, T., 1979, 'War and massacre', in M. Cohen, T. Nagel & T. Scalon (eds), *War and moral responsibility: A philosophy and public affairs reader*, pp. 3–24, Princeton University Press, Princeton.

Norman, R., 1995, *Ethics, killing and war*, Cambridge University Press, Cambridge.

Reichberg, G.M., Syse, H., & Begby, E. (eds), 2006, *The ethics of war*, Blackwell, Oxford.

Reichberg, G.M., 2008, 'Just war and regular war: Competing paradigms', in D. Rodin & H. Shue (eds), *Just and unjust warriors*, pp. 193–213, Oxford University Press, Oxford.

Rodin, D., 2002, *War and self-defense*, Clarendon, Oxford.

Rodin, D., 2008, 'The moral inequality of soldiers: Why jus in bello symmetry is half right', in D. Rodin & H. Shue (eds), *Just and unjust warriors*, pp. 44–68, Oxford University Press, Oxford.

Walzer, M., 2006, *Just and unjust wars*, 4th edn., Basic Books, New York.

Case Study Guiding Questions

a. Which justifications were used to justify the resort to arms? Did they conform to Walzer's *jus ad bellum* conditions (conditions 1–4)?

b. Identify the various actors in the conflict. Do you think that their resort to warfare was morally justified? Why?

c. Which justifications were used to justify the conduct in war? Did they conform to Walzer's *jus in bello* conditions (conditions 5–7)?

d. For each of the actors in the conflict, do you think that the conduct of the hostilities was morally justified? Why?

References

Aquinas, T., 1920, *Summa theologiae*, transl. The English Dominican Fathers, Burns, Oates, and Washburne, London.

Bass, G.J., 2004, 'Jus post bellum', *Philosophy and Public Affairs* 32(4), 384–412.

Cajetan, 2006, 'Summula', in G.M. Reichberg, H. Syse & E. Begby (eds), *The ethics of war*, pp. 240–50, Blackwell, Oxford.

De Vitoria, F., 2006, 'On the law of war', in G.M. Reichberg, H. Syse & E. Begby (eds), *The ethics of war*, pp. 288–332, Blackwell, Oxford.

Fulgosius, R., 2006, 'In primam Pandetarum partem Commentariam', in G.M. Reichberg, H. Syse & E. Begby (eds), *The ethics of war*, pp. 227–30, Blackwell, Oxford.

Gentili, A., 2006,'On the law of war', in G.M. Reichberg, H. Syse & E. Begby (eds), *The ethics of war*, pp. 371–7, Blackwell, Oxford.

Haggenmacher, P., 1992, 'Just war and regular war in sixteenth century Spanish doctrine', *International Review of the Red Cross*, 434–45.

Luban, D., 1980, 'Just war and human rights', *Philosophy and Public Affairs* 9(2), 160–81.

McMahan, J., 2008, 'The morality of war and the law of war', in D. Rodin & H. Shue (eds), *Just and unjust warriors*, pp. 19–43, Oxford University Press, Oxford.

McMahan, J., 2009, *Killing in war*, Clarendon Press, Oxford.

Nagel, T., 1979, 'War and massacre', in M. Cohen, T. Nagel & T. Scalon (eds), *War and moral responsibility: A philosophy and public affairs reader*, pp. 3–24, Princeton University Press, Princeton.

Norman, R., 1995, *Ethics, killing and war*, Cambridge University Press, Cambridge.

Reichberg, G.M., Syse, H., & Begby, E. (eds), 2006, *The ethics of war*, Blackwell, Oxford.

Reichberg, G.M., 2008, 'Just war and regular war: Competing paradigms', in D. Rodin & H. Shue (eds), *Just and unjust warriors*, pp. 193–213, Oxford University Press, Oxford.

Rodin, D., 2002, *War and self-defense*, Clarendon, Oxford.

Rodin, D., 2008, 'The moral inequality of soldiers: Why jus in bello symmetry is half right', in D. Rodin & H. Shue (eds), *Just and unjust warriors*, pp. 44–68, Oxford University Press, Oxford.

Vattel, E., 2006, 'Law of nations', in G.M. Reichberg, H. Syse & E. Begby (eds), *The ethics of war*, pp. 504–17, Blackwell, Oxford.

Walzer, M., 2006, *Just and unjust wars*, 4th edn., Basic Books, New York.

CHAPTER FIVE

LAW OF WAR

Yih-Jye Hwang and Lucie Cerna[1]

Introduction

Public international law distinguishes itself from private international law in different ways. Private international law is a 'body of rules of the domestic law of a State that is applicable when a legal issue contains a foreign element, and it has to be decided whether a domestic rule should apply foreign law or relinquish jurisdiction to a foreign court' (Aust 2010: 1). Public international law instead is identified as 'laws of nations', derived from various sources including treaties, international customs, the general principles of law, judicial decisions and the teachings of the most highly qualified publicists of the various nations (Statute of the International Court of Justice, Article 38:1; Aust 2010: 5). The aim of this chapter is to very briefly introduce the reader to two distinctive fields of public international law related to war and peace: namely, *jus ad bellum* and *jus in bello*, and three subfields of public international law: namely the United Nations system, International Criminal Law and International Humanitarian Law.

The nineteenth and twentieth centuries saw the codification of *jus ad bellum* and *jus in bello*. The former, *jus ad bellum*, is essentially concerned with the question of when it is right to resort to armed force—wherein the idea of 'just war' is replaced by a general ban on the use of force under international law. The latter, *jus in bello*, is a consideration of what is acceptable in using force—wherein international law sets out certain rules to be respected by all parties in warfare. Those codifications, among others, have been best presented in the creation of the United Nations (UN), the International Military Tribunal sitting at Nuremberg and the International Military Tribunal for the Far East in Tokyo, the Universal

[1] This chapter is developed from the lectures given by Carsten Stahn, Director of Grotius Centre at Leiden University. Our sincere thanks to Carsten Stahn for giving us lots of interesting food for thought. We are also grateful to Sara Kendall for helpful comments on this chapter. Any remaining errors are of course our own.

Declaration of Human Rights (UDHR) of 1948, and Four Geneva Conventions (GC) of 1949. The statute of the International Criminal Court, established by an international treaty on 1 July 2002, further codifies and defines forms of *jus in bello* such as crimes against humanity, genocide, and war crimes, and advances the codification of the *jus ad bellum* crime of aggression.

This chapter is divided into three main parts. Firstly, it examines how the idea of 'sovereignty as responsibility' influences moral and legal obligations of states and the international community, and what consequences its violation may entail. Secondly, it explores the development of the concepts of humanitarian intervention and responsibility to protect (R2P). Finally, the chapter looks at institutions and mechanisms that have been created to sanction violations of the laws and customs of war.

1. *Towards a Legal Ban of Warfare: Jus ad bellum in the Twentieth Century*

As discussed in the chapter on peace movements by Ann Marie Wilson (see chapter one), one of the most important episodes in the history of peace movements took place in The Hague. The Hague Peace Conference of 1899 attempted to place restrictions on the unqualified right to wage war, although the outcome of the conference proved to be disappointing. 'It included promises by the assembled nations to resolve conflicts peacefully, but these were hedged with loopholes that preserved national sovereignty and the right to wage war' (David 2008: 42). The second Hague Peace Conference was held in 1907, and the peace supporters again had high hopes for it. Yet the proposal for obligatory arbitration over international disputes among states was rejected. Despite those disappointments, the Hague Peace Conference, in the words of Sandi E. Cooper, contributed to a 'gradual growth of the spirit of peace' (David 2008: 42).

In the aftermath of the First World War several attempts were made to make the use of force by states unlawful. First of all, in the Treaty of Versailles (1919) the idea to prevent future wars was put forward through the creation of the League of Nations, whose Covenant stated that member states shall settle all of their disputes through two organs peacefully: the political organ (i.e. the League Council) and the judicial organ (i.e. The Permanent Court of International Justice). The Covenant however did not abolish the right of states to resort to war. Instead, members of the League promised themselves protection against 'external aggression' directed against Members of the League (Article 10). Any war or threat of war became a matter of concern to the 'entire League' (Article 11). Moreover, member states agreed to settle disputes 'primarily through peaceful settlement' (Article 12).

It is worth noting that there were loopholes in the Covenant. Firstly, the limitations under the Covenant applied only in relation between Members of the League. They did not curtail freedom in relation to non-League members. Secondly, in the absence of a unanimous report by the Council, Members of the League retained the right to take any action that they considered necessary for the maintenance of rights and justice. Thirdly, war remained a means to enforce certain claims, as it could be started against a state that failed to comply with an award, decision or recommendation after three months (Article 12). The Briand-Kellogg Pact (or The Pact of Paris), signed on 27 August 1928, closed some of the gaps of the Covenant. It made war illegal after the League's peace settlement facilities had been exhausted. Article 1 of the Pact renounced warfare, condemning 'recourse to war for the solution of international controversies'. Freedom to go to war was still preserved between contracting and non-contracting parties.

The UN Charter instituted a new global order in which war is prohibited as an instrument of state policy. Instead, a collective security system was put into place—that is, the exclusive power of the Security Council to use force in maintaining security and peace. Article 2(4) of the UN Charter states that:

> All members shall refrain in their international relations from the threat or use of force against the territorial integrity or political independence of any state, or in any other manner inconsistent with the Purposes of the United Nations.

One point should be stressed in the above-mentioned statement: prohibition is limited to states. There is no explicit reference to the prohibition of the use of force by non-state actors, and internal violence within a state is, in principle, not covered in this prohibition.

Moreover, the UN Charter addresses a states' inherent right to self-defence against an 'armed attack'. It states:

> Nothing in the present Charter shall impair the inherent right of individual or *collective* self-defence if an armed attack occurs against a Member of the United Nations, until the *Security Council* has taken measures necessary to maintain international peace and security (Article 51, emphasis ours).

Here the prerogative of the Security Council in the UN system (UNSC) is underlined. The UNSC acts on behalf of UN Members and has the primary responsibility to maintain international peace and security. Article 24(1) states that:

> In order to ensure prompt and effective action by the United Nations, its Members confer on the Security Council primary responsibility for the maintenance of international peace and security, and agree that in carrying out its duties under this responsibility the Security Council acts on their behalf.

Decisions of the UNSC under Chapter VII are binding to UN members (Article 25), which differs from the League of Nations as it could only recommend that states apply force against an aggressor.

In short, the UNSC determines the existence of a threat or breach of peace or an act of aggression, and the right to collective self-defence that mandates a non-attacked state to intervene with armed force for the benefit of the attacked state should be under the supervision of the UNSC. However, the powers of the UNSC are not defined in an exhaustive fashion. This leaves room to interpret Chapter VII as an ongoing, active process (such as with the creation of ad-hoc tribunals for Rwanda and the former Yugoslavia). Moreover, several problems are still unsolved such as pre-emptive self-defence, the duration of self-defence, and the exclusion of attacks by non-state actors.

2. Humanitarian Intervention and Responsibility to Protect

Up until the 1990s, the use of force by states, except for self-defense, was illegal apart from military interventions for humanitarian purposes authorised by the UNSC. Since the end of the Cold War, the consensus over the illegality of the use of force crumbled in the face of massive violations of human rights that occurred in Yugoslavia and some African states (such as Rwanda). While the UN system proved itself unable to react in a prompt and appropriate manner to halt the mass violation of human rights from occurring, public opinion, especially in the West, called for their governments to do something when humanitarian emergencies take place. Lawyers, international relations theorists, philosophers, and policy makers alike contended that it was time to enlarge the scope of the legitimate use of force in order to put an end to what appeared to be a growing list of human rights violations. All of these have led to the resurgence of the idea of humanitarian intervention in the post-Cold War era.

The term humanitarian intervention is defined as 'the use of armed force by either a state, a group of states, or an international organisation to address widespread suffering or death among civilians in another state affected by grave violations of human rights' (Badescu 2011: 9). It should be noted that humanitarian intervention is not a new phenomenon; it has its historical basis in nineteenth century, when the British intervened in support of the Greek revolt against the Ottoman Empire in the 1820s. Since then, the manifestation of humanitarian intervention has varied over the course of history and the topic of humanitarian intervention has been a hotly contested topic in academic discussions.

One the one hand, the practice of humanitarian intervention is explicitly forbidden in the UN Charter that was widely accepted during the Cold War because it is an infringement of sovereignty. Article 2(7) of the UN Charter states:

> Nothing contained in the present Charter shall authorize the United Nations to intervene in matters which are essentially within the domestic jurisdiction of any state or shall require the Members to submit such matters to settlement under the present Charter; but this principle shall not prejudice the application of enforcement measures under Chapter VII.

On the other hand, scholars argue that the society of states needs to resort to the armed force in order to stop systematic, severe and widespread violations of human rights and humanitarian law despite the illegality of such practice in light of the UN Charter. The chief argument upheld, as Nicholas J. Wheeler succinctly put it, is that, 'law can be the servant of particular interests rather than an expression of the general will. In these circumstances, a space opens up between legality and legitimacy' (Wheeler 2000: 3). The practice of humanitarian intervention therefore becomes an issue concerned with legitimacy rather than legality: it is considered illegal, but legitimate, by some commentators.

The catchphrase 'illegal but legitimate' resonated in the Kosovo Report, a work of the Independent International Commission on Kosovo—the members of this Commission were not appointed by any governmental or non-governmental organisation but participated solely in their personal capacities in an attempt to reflectively study the lessons to be learned from the Kosovo conflict (The Independent International Commission on Kosovo 2000: 21). The report argues that NATO military intervention was illegal yet legitimate: illegal because it had no prior authorisation by the Security Council, legitimate because it liberated people from massive human rights violations, after all realistic diplomatic efforts has been exhausted (186). In addition, the report also suggests two valid triggers of legitimate military interventions. The first is 'severe violations of international human rights or humanitarian law on a sustained basis', while the second is 'the subjection of a civilian society to great suffering and risk due to the "failure" of their state, which entails the breakdown of governance at the level of the territorial sovereign state' (193).

A concept akin to humanitarian intervention is the notion of 'responsibility to protect' (R2P). The R2P is 'a political catchword', and 'some of the propositions are grounded in established concepts of international law' (Stahn 2007: 102). The notion is explicitly articulated as the result of the 2005 World Summit. Paragraph 138 defines the term as follows:

> Each individual State has the responsibility to protect its populations from genocide, war crimes, ethnic cleansing and crimes against humanity. This responsibility entails the prevention of such crimes, including their incitement, through appropriate and necessary means. We accept that responsibility and will act in accordance with it . . .

As such, this crime-based notion manifests a shift from 'right to intervene' to 'responsibility to protect' in the context of genocide, crimes against humanity and war crimes. Moreover, it is important to note that R2P is not an automatic right to use armed force. It focuses on measures other than 'use of force' such as prevention, criminal justice, or sanctions, and is coordinated within the UN system. Paragraph 139 makes this characteristic of R2P clear:

> The international community, through the United Nations, also has the responsibility to use appropriate diplomatic, humanitarian and other peaceful means, in accordance with Chapters VI and VIII of the Charter, to help to protect populations from genocide, war crimes, ethnic cleansing and crimes against humanity. In this context, we are prepared to take collective action, in a timely and decisive manner, through the Security Council, in accordance with the Charter, including Chapter VII, on a case-by-case basis and in cooperation with relevant regional organizations as appropriate, should peaceful means be inadequate and national authorities are manifestly failing to protect their populations from genocide, war crimes, ethnic cleansing and crimes against humanity.

Overall, as discussed above, the codification of *jus ad bellum* in the twentieth century sees the transition from just war to illegal war except for self-defence and military interventions under the UN mandate. Humanitarian intervention and R2P came to the fore since the 1990s as the existing UN system failed to protect people from mass violations of human rights. However, humanitarian intervention and R2P still rely on willingness and ability of the UN Security Council to pass appropriate resolutions.

3. *Atrocity Crimes*

Following the discussion about R2P which aims to protect populations from genocide, ethnic cleansing, and crimes against humanity and war crimes,[2] this section will briefly introduce the aforementioned four categories of international crimes, identified in the two most important lists of international crimes, namely the 1945 Charter of the Military Tribunal at Nuremberg and the 1998 Rome Statute of the ICC.

The word genocide was coined in 1944 from the root words *genos* (Greek, family, tribe, or race) and *-cide* (Latin, killing). The concept is however ancient since the practices of genocide can be traced back to distant millennia (Kuper 1981: 9). In 1946, Resolution 96(I) of the UN General Assembly declared genocide as an international crime. In 1948, the Convention on the Prevention and Punishment of the Crime of Genocide (CPPCG) was adopted, which is intended to protect the rights of a group to survival and human diversity in times of war and peace. The term is defined in the CPPCG as 'any of the following acts committed with intent to destroy, in whole or in part, a national, ethnical, racial or religious group', such as: (a) Killing members of the group; (b) Causing serious bodily or mental harm to members of the group; (c) Deliberately inflicting on the group conditions of life calculated to bring about its physical destruction in whole or in part; (d) Imposing measures intended to prevent births within the group; (e) Forcibly transferring children of the group to another group. As such, crimes of genocide constitute the deliberate destruction of a stable and permanent group of people with a focus of its membership by birth. Accordingly, social and political groups are excluded in the CPPCG as a target of genocide.

Another crime that is frequently confused with 'genocide' is 'ethnic cleansing'. Ethnic cleansing has been defined as the elimination of an unwanted group from a society (or certain territories), either murderous ethnic cleansing (e.g. genocide) or non-murderous cleansing (e.g. forced migration). According to Mann (2005: 3) ethnic cleansing is essentially a modern phenomena because it is 'the dark side of democracy', which 'has always carried with it the possibility that the majority might tyrannize minorities, and this possibility carries more ominous consequences in certain types of multiethnic environments'. Ethnic cleansing belongs to

---

[2] The category 'war crimes' includes 'crime against peace'.

a broader category of atrocity crimes, crimes against humanity, a 'widespread and systematic attack directly against the civilian population' either in time of peace or in time of war (The Statute of the ICC). Examples of crimes against humanity, listed in Article 7 of the Statute of ICC, include murder, extermination, enslavement, deportation, imprisonment, torture, rape, sexual slavery, enforced prostitution, forced pregnancy, enforced sterilisation, enforced disappearance of persons, the crime of apartheid, and other inhumane acts of a similar character intentionally causing great suffering, or serious injury to body, mental or physical health.

The crime of aggression (or crimes against peace) was for the first time charged at Nuremberg and Tokyo, described as 'the supreme international crime':

> The charges in the Indictment that the defendants planned and waged aggressive wars are charges of the utmost gravity. War is essentially an evil thing. Its consequences are not confined to the belligerent states alone, but affect the whole world. To initiate a war of aggression, therefore, is not only an international crime; it is the supreme international crime differing only from other war crimes in that it contains within itself the accumulated evil of the whole. (Nuremberg War Crimes Tribunal Judgement 1946)

The central source of justification in both tribunals is the Kellogg-Briand Pact of 1928, an international agreement in which signatory states including Germany and Japan promised not to use war to resolve international disputes.

There has been an enormous amount of controversy about crimes against peace as international crimes. Among others, those two *ad hoc* tribunals were established by the Allied powers that had won the war, rather than a free-standing international criminal court, thereby fuelling the charge that such tribunals were merely victor's justice. The ICC has thus been seeking a mechanism for international trials for the crime of aggression. One of most important attempts was the ICC Review Conference on the International Criminal Court, upheld in Kampala, Uganda in 2010. Delegates representing states from around the world amended the Rome Statute to define the crime of aggression, and to agree on conditions to which the jurisdiction will be triggered. The final agreement reached at the review conference differentiated the 'act of aggression' from 'crime of aggression'. The act of aggression is that which *the state* commits:

> [The] use of armed force by a State against the sovereignty, territorial integrity or political independence of another State, or in any other manner inconsistent with the Charter of the United Nations. (Article 8*bis*)

The crime of aggression instead is the act committed by *the individual*:

> [the] planning, preparation, initiation or execution, by a person in a position effectively to exercise control over or to direct the political or military action of a State, of an act of aggression which, by its character, gravity and scale, constitutes a manifest violation of the Charter of the United Nations. (Article 8*bis*)

Thus, the presumption of state aggression is strongly in favour of state sovereignty, as Larry May noted. He subsequently defines state aggression as 'the first use of violent force by one State against another State that jeopardizes basic human rights, which has not been initiated in self-defense or defense of other innocent states, is not provoked, and has not been authorized by the United Nations' (May 2008: 208).

Whereas the crime of aggression is intimately related to *jus ad bellum*, the war crimes introduced below are related to *jus in bello*. It is important to note that the question whether a war is just or unjust, legal or illegal shall not affect the obligations under *jus in bello*, that is, the equal application of international humanitarian law. In other words, the judging of acts within war can be dissociated from its cause: Soldiers face one another as moral equals (see chapter four by Laurens van Apeldoorn). There are, however, a number of restraints with regard to the means in which warfare is conducted. The idea is that in times of armed conflict some peacetime rules are superseded by practices of laws of war, and killing of combatants is permitted among parties to the conflict (understood as combatant's privilege). *Jus in bello* therefore focuses on humanity rather than the just cause of armed force; its application is tied to factual criteria (i.e. existence of conflict). The purpose of *jus in bello* is hence to balance 'military necessity' with 'principles of humanity'. Violating laws or customs of armed conflict are categorised as 'war crimes', which are significant in today's international humanitarian law.

Most laws of armed conflict can be found in multilateral treaties. These treaties can be roughly divided into two (though not mutually exclusive) main episodes of codification of *jus in bello*: the 'Hague Law' and the 'Geneva Law'. The 'Hague Law' constructed the rules on how hostilities can be conducted in a lawful manner. The Hague Conventions of 1899 and 1907 contain rules concerning permissible methods and means of warfare. In other words, as Article 22 of 'Regulations Respecting the Laws and Customs of War on Land' notes, 'the right of belligerents to adopt means of injuring the enemy is not unlimited' (The Hague Convention, 1907). The 'Geneva Law' is intended to regulate the treatment of non-combatants, protecting persons not (or no longer) taking part in hostilities. The Geneva Law was first adopted in 1864, in parallel to the founding of the International Committee of the Red Cross that originally aimed to safeguard the welfare of prisoners of war (POWs) as well as civilians in occupied territories.

The Four Geneva Conventions (GC) of 1949 focus on international armed conflicts, protecting the sick and wounded in the field (GC I), the wounded, sick and shipwrecked at sea (GC II), regulating the status and protection of prisoners of war (GC III), and codifying the protection of civilians in armed conflict (GC IV). Moreover, it is noted that the Four GC mainly deal with armed conflicts between states. Common Article III of the four Geneva Conventions merely regulates minimum standards for 'armed conflict not of an international character' (i.e. civil wars). The legal distinction between international and internal armed conflicts was narrowed afterwards. Additional Protocols I and II to the GC's in 1977 adapted the law to changing circumstances and new forms of conflict through additional protocols. Additional Protocol I updated the protection of persons in international armed conflict, including wars of national liberation, and Additional Protocol II expanded the provisions of Common Article III and establishes comprehensive regulations for internal armed conflict, but does not criminalise violations.

Furthermore, some of the humanitarian laws became customary international law binding upon all states. The Martens Clause, which was first taken up in the Hague Conventions and later in the GC, specifies that because an act of war is not prohibited by an international treaty does not mean that it is permitted:

> Until a more complete code of the laws of war has been issued, the High Contracting Parties deem it expedient to declare that, in cases not included in the Regulations adopted by them, the inhabitants and the belligerents remain under the protection and the rule of the principles of the law of nations, as they result from the usages established among civilized peoples, from the laws of humanity, and the dictates of the public conscience.

On the other hand, states are still bound by those rules even when they do not sign those treaties:

> Civilians and combatants remain under the protection and authority of the principles of international law derived from custom, from the principles of humanity and from the dictates of public conscience.

While a complete analysis of various types of war crimes of armed conflict in multilateral treaties—including aforementioned laws together with the 1980 Weapons Convention, the 1997 Ottawa Convention on the Prohibition of Land Mines, and the 1998 Rome Statute of the International Criminal Court—is beyond the scope of this chapter, certain key principles deserve mention below. These principles are:

1) Reciprocity: A state is not obliged to apply the provisions of a humanitarian law treaty in the hostilities if its adversary is not a party to the treaty (but do not include those which are based on customary law);

2) Non-reciprocity: Once a humanitarian law treaty is binding upon states on both sides in the hostilities, one side in an armed conflict violates humanitarian laws does not justify the other side's disregard of that law;

3) Protection of non-combatants: Civilians, prisoners of war and persons out of combat such as wounded, sick, shipwrecked, persons who have surrendered are to be spared from harm;

4) Principle of distinction: Combatants must distinguish between fighters and civilians, and between military objectives and civilian targets. Attacks against the civilian population and civilian targets are prohibited. This principle also applies to the civilians not taking direct part in hostilities;

5) Principle of proportionality: Combatants must take measures to avoid superfluous injury or unnecessary suffering. Weapons and methods of warfare that cause unnecessary suffering are prohibited. Examples of weapons treaties include poison, biological weapons (1972), chemical weapons (1993), landmines (1997) and cluster munition (2008). Prohibited means encompass starvation, acts that spread terror among the civilian population, and use of child soldiers. It is however noted that the use of nuclear weapons as last resort for self-defence is not prohibited.

Conclusion

The chapter has discussed two fields of public international law related to war and peace: *jus ad bellum* and *jus in bello,* as well as three subfields of public international law: the UN system, international criminal law and international humanitarian law. It is evident that the field of law of war has advanced considerably beyond *jus ad bellum* and *jus in bello.* Human interventions and R2P have evolved in recent years especially since the existing laws/conventions and the UN system have been inefficient in protecting human lives in wars and civil conflicts, as well as in holding responsible actors accountable. However, it is important to highlight that the current system still has several weaknesses. For instance, it is not always clear when exactly and with what means the international community is supposed to intervene in conflict areas. While the international community might be more ready to intervene and protect lives than in the 1990s, it does not always do so on time. In addition, willingness to intervene also varies across conflict areas. The UNSC is able to pass resolutions for interventions more easily for some countries than for others. Whereas the law of war provides an overarching framework, political, economic and social aspects can also play an important role.

Guiding Questions

a. What are the UN's current regulations on the use of force, and to what extent do they meet the challenges of the post-Cold War world, in particular facing the demands of addressing humanitarian emergencies?

b. What are the doctrines of 'humanitarian intervention' and 'responsibility to protect'? How are they connected to violations of the law of war and peace, and what are their main principles? How can the legal constraints on the use of force and respect for state sovereignty be reconciled with the international community's willingness and readiness to take action in such instances?

c. What are 'war crimes'? Which institutions and mechanisms exist to hold perpetrators of violations accountable? Who can be held accountable, and how?

Selected Reading

Abass, A., 2004, *Regional organisations and the development of collective security: beyond Chapter VIII of the UN Charter*, pp. 109–114; 119–139.

The Independent International Commission on Kosovo, 2000, *The Kosovo report: conflict, international response, lessons learned*, pp. 290–298, Oxford University Press, Oxford.

Evans, G., 2008, 'The responsibility to protect: an idea whose time has come...and gone?' *International Relations* 22, 283–298.

van Schaack, B. & Slye, R., 2007, 'A concise history of international criminal law', Santa Clara University Legal Studies Research Paper No. 07-42.

Further Reading

Badescu, C.G., 2011, *Humanitarian intervention and the responsibility to protect security and human rights*, Routledge, London.

Fleck, D., 2008, *The handbook of international humanitarian law*, Oxford University Press, Oxford.

Jones, A., 2006, *Genocide: A comprehensive introduction*, 2nd edn, Routledge, London.

Kalshoven, F. & Zegveld, L., 2011, *Constraints on the waging of war: An introduction to international humanitarian law*, 4th edn, Cambridge University Press, Cambridge.

Mann, M., 2005, *The dark side of democracy explaining ethnic cleansing*, Cambridge University Press, Cambridge.

May, L., 2008, *Aggression and crimes against peace*, Cambridge University Press, Cambridge.

Stahn, C., 2007, 'Responsibility to protect political rhetoric or emerging legal norm?', *American Journal of International Law*, 101, 99–120.

Thakur, R., 2006, *The United Nations, peace and security: From collective security to the responsibility to protect*, Cambridge University Press, Cambridge.

Case Study Guiding Questions

a. What are the main human rights violations committed, and which main actors were involved (armed forces, State organs, private armed groups)? What labels were used to describe those violations, i.e. 'war crimes', 'genocide', 'crimes against humanity', 'aggression'?

b. How did the international community (i.e. states, international and regional organisations, civil society) react to the conduct of hostilities?

c. What accountability mechanisms were put in place or would you advise for a peace strategy?

References

Legal Documents

The Hague Convention of 1899, http://www.icrc.org/ihl.nsf/INTRO?OpenView [accessed 21 February 2013]

The Hague Convention 1907, http://www.icrc.org/ihl.nsf/intro/195?OpenDocument [accessed 21 February 2013]

The Covenant of the League of Nations, http://avalon.law.yale.edu/20th_century/leagcov
.asp [accessed 21 February 2013]

Briand-Kellogg Pact 1928, http://avalon.law.yale.edu/20th_century/kbpact.asp [accessed
21 February 2013]

Charter of the United Nations, http://www.un.org/en/documents/charter/index.shtml
[accessed 21 February 2013]

Statute of the International Court of Justice, http://www.icj-cij.org/documents/index
.php?p1=4&p2=2&p3=0 [accessed 21 February 2013]

Nuremberg War Crimes Tribunal Judgement 1946, werle.rewi.hu-berlin.de/IMTJudgment
.pdf [accessed 21 February 2013]

Convention on the Prevention and Punishment of the Crime of Genocide, http://untreaty
.un.org/cod/avl/ha/cppcg/cppcg.html [accessed 21 February 2013]

The Geneva Conventions of 1949 and their Additional Protocols, http://www.icrc.org/eng/
war-and-law/treaties-customary-law/geneva-conventions/index.jsp [accessed 21 February 2013]

Rome Statute of the International Criminal Court, http://untreaty.un.org/cod/icc/statute/
romefra.htm [accessed 21 February 2013]

2005 World Summit Outcome, General Assembly resolution 60/1 of 16 September 2005
(responsibility to protect: paragraphs 138–139), http://www.un.org/ga/search/view_doc
.asp?symbol=a/res/60/1 [accessed 21 February 2013]

The ICC Review Conference on the International Criminal Court, http://www.iccnow
.org/?mod=review [accessed 21 February 2013]

Secondary Sources

Aust, A., 2010, *Handbook of international law* 2nd edn, Cambridge University Press,
Cambridge.

Badescu, C.G., 2011, *Humanitarian intervention and the responsibility to protect: Security and
human rights*, Routledge, London.

Clapham, A., 2003, 'Issues of complexity, complicity and complementarity: From the
Nuremberg Trials to the dawn of the new International Criminal Court', in P. Sands
(ed.), *From Nuremberg to The Hague the future of international criminal justice*, pp. 30–68,
Cambridge University Press, Cambridge.

Cortright, D., 2008, *Peace: A history of movements and ideas*, Cambridge University Press,
Cambridge.

The Independent International Commission on Kosovo, 2000, *The Kosovo Report: Conflict,
international response, lessons learned*, Oxford University Press, Oxford.

Kuper, L., 1981, *Genocide: Its political use in the twentieth century*, Penguin, Harmondsworth.

Mann, M., 2005, *The dark side of democracy: Explaining ethnic cleansing*, Cambridge University Press, Cambridge.

May, L., 2008, *Aggression and crimes against peace*, Cambridge University Press,
Cambridge.

Stahn, C., 2007, 'Responsibility to protect: Political rhetoric or emerging legal norm?',
American Journal of International Law 101(1), 99–120.

Wheeler, N.J., 2000, *Saving strangers: Humanitarian intervention in international society*,
Oxford University Press, Oxford.

CHAPTER SIX

THE ECONOMICS OF WAR

William Hynes

Introduction

Economics is fundamentally about human behaviour—it is about choices in a world of resource constraints. It is about rationality and maximising welfare, and the gains of trade and co-operation. This would seem to put it at odds with war—a zero-sum game—which is about the worst aspects of human interaction and the costs of violent competition. War is difficult to square with rationality, but nations have passions as well as interests (Offer 1989). Of course we assume that war is counter-productive and futile from an economic point of view—it is even irrational. But when Azar Gat (2006) set out to unravel the 'riddle of war', he found that on the contrary—war is not an irrational act of passion or about the emotional acts of the battlefield. Rather, war is often fundamentally about economics, welfare maximisation and resulting aggression from a competition for resources. As Keynes (1919) argued, the great events of history are often due to secular changes in the growth of population and other fundamental economic variables. Yet these factors can escape attention from contemporary observers owing to their gradual character. The causes of war are too easily attributed to 'the follies of statesmen or the fanaticism of atheists' (Keynes 1919: 15). Economics offers one perspective on war—an important one in analysing and understanding conflict. Its explanatory approach puts less emphasis on accidents of history or the actions of prominent actors—instead it stresses the role of markets, the importance of resources, the conditions which predispose nations and peoples to war. While economic factors are important, they require human agency—economic factors do not declare war on their own (Offer 1989).[1]

---

[1] An edited volume by Garfinkel and Skaperdas (2012) examines how the tools of economics can be fruitfully used to advance understanding of conflict and also how explicitly incorporating conflict into economic analysis can add substantively to understanding of observed economic phenomena.

While inter-state warfare is much less common, violent internal conflict still affects those areas which have not been integrated into the global economy.[2] Factors such as 'need, creed and greed' are all important sources of conflict increasingly found in the developing world; civil wars, rebellions, etc. are strongly related to limited state capacities, weak institutions and low opportunity cost of fighting (Collier & Hoeffler 2004). Therefore conflict is strongly linked to development and the establishment of credible and strong institutions. Greed or economic motivations tend to be more significant in sustaining, prolonging and transforming conflict. Wars over natural resources happen but this is not a consistent cause of conflict, although resources may help to finance conflict (Woodrow Wilson International Centre for Scholars 2001).

War is economics by other means, as Hirshleifer (2001) puts it, 'there are two main methods of making a living...the way of production and exchange versus the way of predation and conflict' (Hirshleifer 2001: 1). This rather mercantilist view of the world regards military power as both a means and an end of economic activity—wars can be fought for economic advantage, while economic policy puts in place the means of war—for power and plenty (O'Rourke & Finlay 2007).

This chapter proceeds as follows. Section 1 looks at the rationality of war and examines if war can have economic benefits. Section 2 then considers the costs of war and discusses how these can be difficult to estimate. The costs and benefits help explain the decision to go to war. Section 3 analyses the short and long term legacies of war in terms of institutional change, economic ideas and social policies. The final section asks, if given the changes in the global economy, do economic factors make war impossible or at least irrational from an economic point of view?

1. Is War Rational? Can War Improve the Economy?

Economics predicates whether war will occur as wars are based on a calculation of the costs and benefits, the incentives and the risks. Though throughout history, the costs have proved rather difficult to assess a priori—with benefits often being over-estimated and costs under-estimated. Gunderson (1974) examined the origins of the American Civil War and estimated the expected utility of Southern secession from the

---

[2] Counting all countries and years since 1950, the average yearly prevalence of civil conflict is about 7%, with a peak of more than 12% in 1991 and 1992 (Besely & Persson 2008).

Union. Archival sources indicate that the decision to secede was not based on costs versus the expected payoffs. It is clear that societies are not very good at estimating the costs of war. Lindley and Schildkraut (2006) test the rationality of decisions in war. In large inter-state wars the initiator won 55% of the time based on seventy nine large interstate wars between 1815 and 1991. Since 1945, only one third of initiators win, yet despite declining win rates, states initiate wars at an increasing to steady rate over time; 'states are not learning that war increasingly does not pay' (Lindley & Schildkraut 2006: 1). So why do they do it? It seems that just as individual choice is fallible, states make decisions to go to war based on miscalculation and misperception. In the past, careful calculations affected decisions in war. For example, there were strong economic causes of both World War I and World War II.

Supply and demand, incentives and how markets work are important dimensions of war. Offer (1989) suggests that it was agricultural resources which determined the outcome of World War I and not access to weaponry or financial resources—it was 'not a war of steel and gold but of bread and potatoes' (Offer 1989: 1). Overseas resources, the security of sea lanes and the economics of blockades affected the war plans of the great powers and influenced their decision to go to war. Both Germany and Britain became dependent on foreign sources of food and industrial raw materials in the decades leading up to the First World War. Thus access to markets gave Britain a decisive edge and goods played a critical role in Germany's collapse, which in turn affected the motivation of the military. However Britain had assumed that the threat of a blockade would be a sufficient deterrent but this was not visible enough to Germany. The logic of markets meant that economies were not self-sufficient and relied on the gains from trade. Bloch regarded the economic factor as the dominant and decisive element in Europe—'You cannot fight unless you can eat, and at the present moment you cannot feed your people and wage a great war' (Bloch 1899: 109).

Adam Tooze (2006) argues that the German invasion of the Soviet Union in World War II was inevitable because of German concerns about the backwardness of its agriculture and the lack of abundant raw materials and land resources which both the United States (US) and the British Empire had at their disposal. Ultimately, the failure to capture new resources meant that Germany was eventually overwhelmed. Gordon (2008) argued that the solution to Germany's agricultural problem was not acquiring more land for existing German farm population but rather by making existing land more efficient through mechanisation and encouraging rural-urban migration.

Economic resources and organisation can play a major role in determining the outcome of wars. Take the case of World War II: an explanation for allied victory is that the German economy was overwhelmed by the combined economic strength of the US, the United Kingdom and the Union of the Soviet Socialist Republics. War can be the ultimate stimulus for an economy. Poast (2006) discussed this in his *Iron Law of War* which states that war is good for the economy: In order to wage war, the government must raise resources—armies and weaponry. This creates employment and opportunity driving up consumption and investment and therefore national income. As long as the negative fallout of war can be avoided or minimised, an economy can grow rapidly. It is speculated that the large government expenditures of World War II in the US finally ended the Great Depression. US GDP soared to unprecedented levels with an average growth of over 9% every year between 1938 and 1945. It was helped, of course, by the fact that the war was fought 'over there'. The US had the economic strength, technology, mass production techniques and natural resources to wage war on a massive scale. It used its resources efficiently to overwhelm its enemies while its output potential was not diminished or degraded by enemy bombing. Figure 1, based on data estimated in Harrison (2000) shows the expansion of GDP compared to other World War II combatants. The GDP of Russia fell following German invasion, but rebounded. While for Germany and Japan, output was insufficient to wage the war successfully.

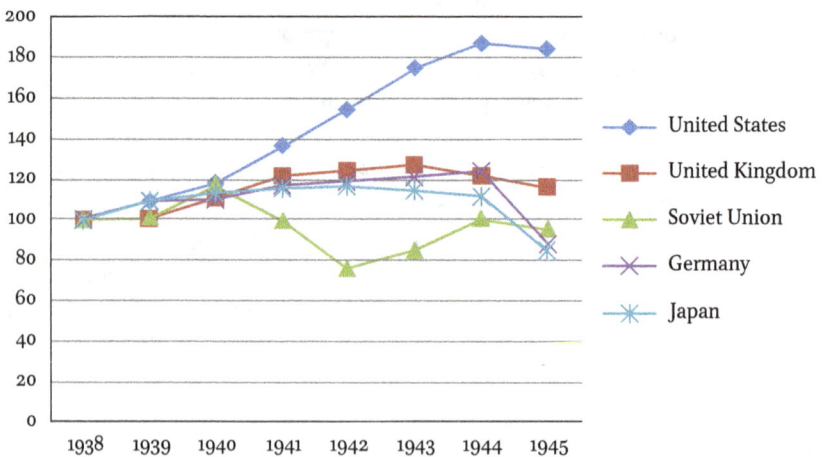

Source: Harrison (2000)

Figure 1. Wartime GDP of Main Combatants

2. *Estimating the Costs of War*

The examples above indicate that estimating the costs of war is seldom accurate. Edwards (2010) reviews war cost forecasts and suggests that increasing the frequency and transparency of such forecasting would be useful in guiding policy. Planners generally have a poor record of estimating costs accurately. Furthermore, Kapstein (2003) pointed out that economics is both illuminating and important as an analytical tool and calls for even more of it in the study of national security. Yet economics has been rather poorly employed in assessing the merits of war in recent prominent conflicts. According to Nordhaus (2002), the costs of the Vietnam war were underestimated by 90% by the Pentagon—the planners assumed it would end by 1967. Moreover, these estimates only included the budgetary costs—indirect costs such as inflation, economic instability and civil unrest and a weakening of the authority and credibility of the US government at home and abroad were not taken into account.

Nordhaus (2002) also notes that the costs of war are often ignored when war is debated, and yet the commission of war is only viable if the costs in dollars and especially blood are acceptably low. Public opinion is increasingly important and Glaeser (2006) notes that wars are often quite popular with citizens who stand to gain little materially. Joseph Stiglitz (2008) has examined the economic costs of the Iraq War and found that original estimates of expenditures understated the war's true costs such as lifetime healthcare and disability payments to returning veterans, replenishment of military hardware and increased recruitment costs (Bilmes & Stiglitz 2008). Far from the war costing 50–60 billion USD as originally envisaged, the cost to the US alone (and not to other countries through military expenditures and higher prices of oil) was probably in the trillions of dollars. Indeed Bilmes and Stiglitz released a book in 2008 called the *Three trillion dollar war*.

However, containment, not going to war and 'peace' also have their respective costs. Davis, Murphy and Topel (2009) estimate that the present value costs of containment (including costs for containing the Iraqi regime until it ultimately fell) would have been in the 400 to 600 billion dollar range. Thus, the choice of the better strategy—to contain or to go to war—is unclear ex ante because one does not dominate the other. Hess (2009) states 'what we can say is that whereas war is costly, "peace" is not cheap either, and it may not even be all that peaceful' (Hess 2009: 5).

3. *The Economic Legacy of War*

Wars can have a major impact on economics as well. Rockoff (2005) reviewed the mobilisation and financing of US involvement in World War I and concluded that the shift in the landscape of ideas about economics and the proper role of the government in economic affairs was the most significant long-term economic outcome of the war. The success of the wartime economy built up confidence in central planning as a way to solve economic problems.

The tax system is also a product of wars. For the US, according to Poast (2006), taxes helped pay for 30% of the cost of World War I and 47% of the cost of World War II. In anticipation of a European war, the US initiated an income tax, initially to tax the rich but eventually extended. Tax Withholding, i.e. removing taxes from pay checks monthly rather than once a year was part of the resource mobilisation effort during World War II. The rest of the costs for the war were funded through debt—a series of bonds were offered. Demand for these bonds was high so interest rates were low—in affect patriotism led to affordable debt and helped lower the cost of war (Rockoff 2005).

Wars can also have important social consequences—some of the great societal transformations heralding social progress have occurred after wars. Women were given the vote after World War I, the United Kingdom established the National Health Service after World War II. War has had an impact on crime—outbreaks often led to a fall in crime, while the end of war often caused a large increase. But periods of violence do not necessarily lead to crimes of violence. Crime caused by social tension diminishes in times of upheaval and chaos such as war (Wilson 1985: 610). Wars can disrupt labour markets and legitimise violence (or at least decrease the threshold for committing violent acts). After the Napoleonic Wars and World War I, millions of demobilised soldiers struggled to reintegrate; many were unemployed and poor. The post-war slump further aggravated the situation. From 1810–1820 soldiers were paid off by being given surplus horses—which some then used in highway robbery (Gattrell 1994). Hay (1982) explained theft in the eighteenth century in this way, attributing its levels to cycles of war and peace. However there is some dispute about war as a causal factor of crime surges, though it seems that economic conditions and wars, and consequent unemployment, inflation and food availability are linked.

By Way of Conclusion

O'Rourke and Finlay (2012) look at the issue of war, trade and natural resources. They find that while students of economics may have had little to say about war, students of war have generally recognised that competition over scarce resources, particularly natural resources, has been the underlying cause of war from the emergence of humanity itself to the present day (O'Rourke & Finlay 2012: 3). O'Rourke and Finlay (2012) look at war and trade as two seemingly contradictory aspects of humanity (conflict in the one case and cooperation in the other) that are inextricably intertwined throughout the entire course of history. Yet trade has changed the nature of war and now makes war increasingly unlikely with conflicts left to those regions disconnected from the global market place.

Globalisation has changed the calculus of war. The world's economies are increasingly interconnected, driving up the costs of war. A world economy of Walmart, McDonald's and globally integrated supply chains with a free flow of investment and trade make war unthinkable. Globalisation has eroded the supremacy of the nation state and constrained the ability of political agents to wage war. Ultimately money helped do what nuclear weapons failed to do—to make war less likely.

However there is no room for complacency. Economic tensions can lead to protectionism and war in the economic sphere is rarely confined to this realm. Also preventing trade through economic sanctions is often used to weaken enemy states without resorting to violence, although the distributional and humanitarian consequences of sanctions can have unpredictable consequences and can often strengthen the powers that they were meant to undermine.[3]

Economics brings a realism to the discussion of war, a compelling if sometimes disheartening approach to how people actually perceive and pursue their interests (Offer 1989: 20). Bloch in an article titled 'Is war now impossible?' written in 1889 felt that the nature of trade meant that if war was possible at all, it was only possible with the price of suicide. History

---

[3] Hufbauer, Schott, Elliott and Oegg (2007) provide a comprehensive analysis on economic sanctions since World War I. They review 116 cases and conclude that sanctions are of limited utility in achieving foreign policy goals that depend on compelling the target country to take actions it stoutly resists. However in some cases sanctions have helped to achieve modest policy goals (Hufbauer, Schott, Elliott & Oegg 2007: 92).

and economic logic has shown time and again that just because war is not rational, does not mean it is not possible.

Chapter 1 of Paul Poast's *The economics of war* presents the economic theory underpinning the Iron Law of War—the idea that fighting wars can provide a boost to an economy (if the war is not fought on that country's soil). This theory will lead to the creation of a four-point scheme for evaluating the economic impact of war. Avner Offer's Introduction: economic and social interpretation of the First World War in *The First World War: An agrarian interpretation* (1989) offers a superb overview of the economic interpretations of war. It looks at the links between wars and rationality, the origins of wars in economic and social forces and reviews the literature in the context of the First World War.

Guiding Questions

a. How has the calculus for war changed in the last 60 years?
b. Why are actors so poor at estimating the costs of war?
c. Under what circumstances might the economic consequences of war be positive?
d. Is inter-state war more or less likely in the future?

Selected Readings

Offer, A., 1989, *The First World War: An agrarian interpretation*, Clarendon Press, London. Introduction: economic and social interpretation of the First World War, pp. 1–20.

Poast, P., 2006, *The economics of war*, McGraw Hill, New York. Chapter 1.

Further Reading

Broadberry, S. & Harrison, M. (eds), 2005, *The economics of World War I*, Cambridge University Press, Cambridge.

Collier, P. & Hoeffler, A., 2004, 'Greed and grievance in civil war', *Oxford economics papers* 56(4): 563–95.

Garfinkel, M. & Skaperdas, S. (eds.), 2012, *The Oxford handbook of the economics of peace and conflict*, Oxford University Press, London.

Harrison, M., 2000, *The economics of World War II: Six great powers in international comparison*, Cambridge University Press, Cambridge.

Hess, G.D., 2009, *Guns and butter: The economic causes and consequences of conflict*, MIT Press, Cambridge and London.

Keynes, J.M., 1919, *The economic consequences of the peace*, MacMillan, London.

Le Billon, P., 2005, *Geopolitics of resource wars: Resource dependence, governance and violence*, Frank Cass, London.

O'Rourke, K. & Finlay, R., 2007, *Power and plenty: trade, war, and the world economy in the second millennium*, Princeton University Press, Princeton.

Stiglitz, J. & Bilmes, L., 2008, *The three trillion dollar war*, W.W. Norton and Co., New York.

Tooze, A., 2006, *The wages of destruction: The making and breaking of the Nazi economy*, Allen Lane: London.

Case Study Guiding Questions

a. Were there economic motivations behind the war in your case study? What role did resources play?

b. Globalisation binds nations together through economic interdependence. Why have market forces and economic forces not prevented war in your case study?

c. Does economic supremacy determine the outcome of war?

References

Azar, G., 2006, *War in human civilization*, Oxford University Press, Oxford.

Besely, T. & Persson, T., 2008, 'The incidence of Civil War: theory and evidence'. *NBER working papers 14585*, National Bureau of Economic Research, Cambridge, MA.

Bilmes, L., Stiglitz, J.E., 2008, *The three trillion dollar war: The true cost of the Iraq conflict*, WW Norton & Co., New York and London.

Bloch, I.S., 1899, 'Is war now impossible', being an abridgment of: *The war of the future in its technical, economic & political relations*, Richard: London.

Collier, P. & Hoeffler, A., 2004, 'Greed and grievance in civil war', *Oxford economics papers* 56(4): 563–95.

Davis, S.J., Murphy, K.M. & Topel, R.H., 2009, 'War in Iraq versus containment', in G.D. Hess (ed.), *Guns and butter: The economic causes and consequences of conflict*, pp. 203–70, MIT Press, London and Cambridge.

Edwards, R., 2010, 'A review of war costs in Iraq and Afghanistan', *NBER Working Paper No. 16163*, National Bureau of Economic Research, Cambridge, MA.

Garfinkel, M. & Skaperdas, S. (eds), 2012, *The Oxford handbook of the economics of peace and conflict*, Oxford University Press, Oxford.

Gattrel, V.A.C., 1994, *The hanging tree: Execution and the English people 1770–1868*, Oxford University Press, Oxford.

Glaeser, E., 2006, 'The political economy of warfare', *NBER working paper No. 12738*, National Bureau of Economic Research.

Gordon, R., 2008, 'Did economics cause World War II?', *NBER Working Paper No. 14560*, National Bureau of Economic Research, Cambridge, MA.

Gunderson, G., 1974, 'The origins of the American Civil War', *Journal of economic history* 34(4), 915–50.

Harrison, M., 2000, *The economics of World War II: Six great powers in international comparison*, Cambridge University Press, Cambridge.

Hay, D., 1982, 'War, death and theft in the eighteenth century: The record of the English courts', *Past and Present* 95, 139–46.

Hess, G.D., 2009, *Guns and butter: The economic causes and consequences of conflict*, MIT Press, Cambridge and London.

Hirshleifer, J., 2001, *The dark side of the force*, Cambridge University Press, New York.

Hufbauer, G.C., Schott, J.J., Elliott, K.A. & Oegg, B., 2007, *Economic sanctions reconsidered*, 3rd edn., Petersen Institute, Washington, D.C.

Kapstein, E.B., 2003, 'Two dismal sciences are better than one: Economics and the study of national security', *International Security* 27(3): 158–87.

Keynes, J.M., 1919, *The economic consequences of the peace*, Macmillan & Co., London.

Lindley, D. & Schildkraut, R. 2006, 'Is war rational? The extent of miscalculation and misperception as causes of war', American Political Science Association Conference, Philadelphia.

Nordhaus, W., 2002, 'The economic consequences of a war with Iraq', in C. Kaysen, S.E. Miller, M.B. Malin, W.D. Noordhaus & J.D. Steinbruner (eds), *War with Iraq: Costs, consequences, and alternatives*, pp. 51–86, American Academy of Arts and Sciences, Cambridge, MA.

O'Rourke, K., Finlay, R., 2007, *Power and plenty: Trade, war, and the world economy in the second millennium*, Princeton University Press, Princeton.

O'Rourke, K. & Finlay, R., 2012, 'War, trade and natural resources: a historical perspective', in M. Garfinkel & S., Skaperdas (eds), *The Oxford handbook of the economics of peace and conflict*, pp. 557–84, Oxford University Press, Oxford.

Offer, A., 1989, *The First World War: An agrarian interpretation*, Clarendon Press, London.

Poast, P., 2006, *The economics of war*, McGraw Hill, New York.

Rockoff, H., 2005, 'Until it's over, over there: The US economy in World War I', in S. Broadberry & M. Harrison (eds), *The economics of World War I*, pp. 310–43, Cambridge University Press, Cambridge.

Wilson, C., 1985, *A criminal history of mankind*, Panther, London.

Woodrow Wilson International Centre for Scholars 2001, *The economics of war: The intersection of need, creed and greed: A conference report*, Washington D.C.

CHAPTER SEVEN

THE REPRESENTATION OF WAR IN LITERATURE, FILM AND NEW MEDIA

Corina Stan

Introduction

The Cambridge companion to war writing edited by Kate McLoughlin (2009) offers a suggestive synthesis of the ways literary scholars have approached the representation of war: under 'Poetics', studies cohere around particular time-periods or major conflicts, pointing to possible periodisations (pre-modern, modern, postmodern) and focusing on specific national literatures (in this case, British and American). This editorial decision mirrors the consecrated focus of scholarly monographs on national literatures (Krimmer 2010), a focus sometimes narrowed down to particular genres (Goldensohn 2003). Under 'Themes', readers can identify common concerns across textual traditions and periods, such as the idea of war, the credibility of war-reporting, or narrative involvement.[1] Finally, the section 'Influences' identifies echoes of biblical and classical texts traversing various writings about war, taking readers back to some of the oldest representations of conflict, showing their enduring value.

The more recent collective volume *Fighting words and images: Representing war across the disciplines* (2012) broadens the scope of inquiry to encompass other cultures and media, including print, painting, sculpture, architecture, television, film and photography. The editors of this first interdisciplinary study of war-representations have found it fit to group the articles under headings such as 'Silences', 'Perspectives', 'Identities', 'Aftermaths'; the list of contributors, some of them scholars in the field of war studies, includes a useful up-to-date bibliography of relevant sources.

As my brief overview of these two sources suggests, there is no shortage of scholarly literature on the representation of war in fiction, film and other media: the diligent student will easily find her or his way through

---

[1] McLoughlin used this organising principle in her own ambitious monograph *Authoring war. The literary representation of war from the* Iliad *to Iraq* (2010).

the well-signposted maze of companions, books, articles, and journals, whether interested in engaging with the representation of a specific war, with a belligerent period in the history of a particular country, or with a cross-disciplinary approach to a more abstract idea or theme related to war. Rather than attempt here even the most modest of analyses of the representation of historical wars in *all* national literatures, cinema, other media, and of the scholarly work interpreting them, in this chapter I will offer an interlude—an opportunity to pause and reflect on what we learn about war when we interrogate the premises, peculiarities, and challenges posed by its representation in various media.

Simply put, what does it mean to *represent* war? If there are as many wars as participants, and given the antagonistic nature of war, *whose story* is told, and *what version* of a war has more visibility in the public eye is no trivial matter. Representation, it is worth remembering, refers not only to the act of transforming an experience into discourse (in this sense we speak of mimetic representation, conveyed by the German *Darstellung*), but also to the foregrounding of certain actors involved, often at the expense of others (this is the political sense of the word, *Vertretung*). The experience of war itself poses challenges to representation; whether it is short vignettes or Tolstoy's epic *War and peace* (1869) or, closer to us, Jonathan Littel's controversial 900-page *The kindly ones* (2006), a significant number of factors come in the way of putting the experience of war into words. McLoughlin enumerates them aptly:

> logistical difficulties; censorship and self-censorship; squeamishness (on the part of the writer, publisher and reader); the particular difficulties involved in conveying physical pain; the inhibiting psycho-physiological effects of trauma; moral considerations ranging from exploitation of others' suffering to voyeurism to sadism; an absence of sympathetic response; ethical-aesthetic factors such as taste, sensibility and responsibility. (McLoughlin 2007: 17)

Often, representing war becomes writing about the difficulties of the task, a meta-commentary on the genre, and a gesture that historicises the practice while inscribing it in a lineage of works that have already gained their place in the literary pantheon. McLoughlin goes as far as to say that not only is there a veritable anxiety of influence when it comes to war writing, but that representations often fall back onto previous narratives, deferring authority to an ur-representation ultimately as old as social life itself.

This deferral suggests an affinity between the representation of war and post-structuralism, a school of critical thought from the 1960s that dominated for decades the field of literary studies and critical theory.

Post-structuralist thinkers drew attention to the discursive mediation of experience, claiming that, ultimately, we do not have direct access to reality, and that everything in the world is a 'text': that is, something to be read, decoded, interpreted.[2] 'There is no *outside the text*', Jacques Derrida famously claimed. Another thinker associated with post-structuralism, Michel Foucault, tirelessly showed in his work that we are produced as individuals by the discourses that dominate the social, cultural and political structures of which we are a part. 'Deconstruction' is thus central to the agenda of a hermeneutic of suspicion: we need to be aware of how structures of power transform reality into discourses that we might be inclined to accept unthinkingly because they are presented to us as natural. If the idea of such complex determinations sounds compelling—we will see in what follows that a war, for instance, is a deeply ideological construct—, the critique of post-structuralism, highlighting the dilution of its real social and political potential in a realm of indecision and relativity, is worth acknowledging, too. For instance, if the human body can indeed be symbolically regarded as a site of ideological inscription (an individual belonging to a sexual or racial minority has his or her difference symbolically marked, so to speak, on his or her skin), it is important not to obscure the concrete reality of experience, such as, in the context of war, suffering and trauma. Literature, film and other media help us understand the complex ways in which war is construed in public discourse, thus enabling our critical thinking, and reveal what it means to experience such a traumatic event from the intimate perspective of its participants, thus appealing to our ethical sense.

These considerations will frame my discussion of a film, a novel, and a blog. Alain Resnais' *Hiroshima mon amour*, based on a screenplay by Marguerite Duras, is the story of a French actress and a Japanese architect who come to terms with their respective experiences of World War II. The film invites reflection on the notion of 'representation' by pondering the effects on the two main characters of the clash between the subjective memory of events and the record sanctioned by political authorities

---

[2] They did not invent this idea, of course; in 'On truth and lies in an extra-moral sense' (1873) the German philosopher Friedrich Nietzsche wrote: 'A mobile army of metaphors, metonyms, and anthropomorphisms—in short, a sum of human relations which have been enhanced, transposed, and embellished poetically and rhetorically, and which after long use seem firm, canonical, and obligatory to a people: truths are illusions about which one has forgotten that this is what they are; metaphors which are worn out and without sensuous power; coins which have lost their pictures and now matter only as metal, no longer as coins'.

or the vestiges present to public consciousness. A similar gap is explored in Ken Saro-Wiwa's novel *Sozaboy*, narrated in an idiosyncratic language meant to convey the experience of postcolonial oppression that lies at the root of the conflict. Finally, the blog *Baghdad burning* brings us closer to our time, broadening the scope of representation by taking into account its readers' reactions and expectations: it sketches not life in the trenches and in prisoner camps like *Sozaboy*, but the everyday lives of civilians affected by a war of 'liberation' that they experience as a foreign invasion.

1. *Hiroshima, mon amour*

The way in which Alain Resnais' initial project, a documentary about the A-bomb, made its way into *Hiroshima, mon amour* (1959), speaks to the self-reflexive nature of the film: one of the two main characters, interpreted by Emmanuelle Riva, is a French actress who has come to Hiroshima, the annihilated city of World War II, to make a film about peace. Here she has a short but most meaningful affair with a Japanese architect who helps her remember and deal with the relics of her own painful past. The film famously opens on the image of two naked bodies embracing each other, while the voice-over signals the major inadequacy that we are encouraged to ponder:

> – *You have seen nothing at Hiroshima. Nothing.*
> – *I have seen everything. Everything.*

The juxtaposition of these two contradictory statements introduces a paradox central not only to the film, but also to any act of remembering: we try to *re-member*, to piece together the past because it haunts us, and by the same gesture, we replace it with its re-presentation, achieving a sense of closure. The opening sentence, uttered by a male voice, denies the possibility of imagining the enormity of Hiroshima's nuclear destruction. The woman's response indicates that she has seen everything that has become public proof of that destruction in museums, newsreels, or the survivors' gestures of unveiling: that is, all the traces that signify that destruction, that signify the absence of what is irretrievably lost. This disjunction between what really happened and what is represented triggers the woman to work through the long silenced trauma of her youth, the *madness* of having loved during World War II a German man, then an 'enemy' of her country. For this, she was publicly humiliated, shorn, and then locked up in a cave by her embarrassed parents.[3] The tension between the *nothing* and the *everything* of Hiroshima brings to consciousness the poignant disconnect between her love for the German man and the humiliating interpretation of their relationship in official discourse: a case of immoral collaboration with the enemy. Just as Hiroshima only exists, in the film, as a signifier of annihilation, her own love story resurfaces in memory from under erasure by official laws and public discourse.

The film traffics in bodily symbols and its narrative follows closely a logic of correspondence and substitution: the Japanese man makes it possible for the unnamed French woman to relive her past story by representing the German lover and thus helping to bury him, symbolically, once and for all. Displacement, however, does not mean erasure: the narrative of the film advances by way of a game of relays of images and symbols connecting the past and the present; Nevers, the hometown of her shame, and Hiroshima; the German lover and the Japanese one. Strikingly, many of these images are partial objects, often body parts—hands, hair, eyes— that bespeak a nostalgia for a lost wholeness and finitude, while marking absence and intimating a symbolic community of suffering: images of hands, for instance, punctuate the narrative, the beautiful hands of the Japanese man recalling, in a flashback, the dead hand of the German lover, and connecting to her 'useless' hands grabbing the walls in the cave, but also to the mutilated hands of Hiroshima's victims. Hair is also the index of a lack, of a physical and emotional amputation: there is anonymous hair exhibited at the museum, shown in close-up, hair falling off the head of a silent Japanese woman, hair pushed away to reveal a mutilated forehead, hair cut off as a punishment and humiliation in Nevers. Eyes, both averted glances and indiscrete gazes that revel in the sensational, look mutely at the blurring of boundaries between the familiar and the unimaginable, normality and madness, the human and the inhuman. The film also alludes to the reversal of values during war, measuring the consequences of a 'state of exception': a 'doubtful morality' becomes 'doubting the morality of others'.

---

[3] By having a relationship with a German soldier, the French woman had made herself guilty of 'horizontal collaboration', a form of 'national indignity' as defined by laws that were passed in France in 1944. Ironically, prostitutes were regarded more leniently, since they did not hurt France 'in its soul' (their relationships with German soldiers were not emotional, the argument went, their engagement with them remaining on a physical level).

The film is a meditation on the difficulty of representing war, its destruction and trauma, and on the complicated process of making peace with the past. The end of the film suggests that the work of mourning is lengthy and can take unpredictable detours. At best, suffering can achieve a kind of formal closure, be resolved—after war broke down the tenuous relationship between language and the world—in the identification of names with new realities: 'Your name', says the French woman to the Japanese architect, 'is Hiroshima'. Nameless throughout the film, the man comes to represent for her the experience of loss and its difficult healing, while she acquires, in his eyes, the symbolic name of her town—'And your name is Nevers. Nevers in France'—perhaps as an intimation of the hope that her story will *never* repeat itself.

2. *Sozaboy*

The image of an individual swept by the chaotic machinery of a war, a machinery far in excess of his or her capacity to grasp it, is perhaps the best illustration of another, more abstract predicament: that of a person caught up in the complex interstices of dogmas, ideologies, or bureaucratic apparatuses. *Sozaboy*—'soza' means 'soldier' in the idiosyncratic language in which Ken Saro-Wiwa wrote his 1985 novel—is both a young man who struggles to understand a world dominated by confusing powers, and an ignorant participant in a war that dehumanises all involved. That the main character goes by *sozaboy* rather than by his own name, Mene, suggests the universality of his situation, and this effect is enhanced by Saro-Wiwa's choice not to reference explicitly the Nigerian Civil War of 1967–1970 (also known as the Biafran War) during which the story is set. As William Boyd aptly remarks in the introduction, 'there were no clear-cut heroes or villains in this conflict, and culpability can be equally distributed'; moreover, the multiethnic composition of Nigeria's population made it difficult for individuals of various ethnic groups to side with one or the other of the main opponents in the conflict, hence the inevitable impression of 'fighting another man's war'.[4] This last point is worth considering as perhaps more generally valid even in contexts where nationalist

---

[4] 'The British government's support [because Nigeria had gained independence only in 1960, and Britain still had interests there]—material and diplomatic—was firmly behind the Federal Government, led by General Gowon, and against the secessionist eastern states, known as Biafra, led by General Ojukwu' (Boyd 1994 [1985]: n.p).

discourse offers a more compelling motivation to those who fight: sooner or later, perhaps all soldiers wonder—Sozaboy's story suggests—*why* they are so intimately involved in a conflict that causes massive destruction and loss of human lives.

Ken Saro-Wiwa's subtitle, 'a novel in rotten English', surreptitiously makes a related claim. The author's note explains that the language is:

> a mixture of Nigerian pidgin English, broken English and occasional flashes of good, even idiomatic English. This language is disordered and disorderly. Born of a mediocre education and severely limited opportunities, it borrows words, patterns, and images freely from the mother-tongue and finds expression in a very limited English vocabulary. To its speakers, it has the advantages of having no rule and no syntax. It thrives on lawlessness, and is part of the dislocated and discordant society in which Sozaboy must live, move and have not his being. (Saro-Wiwa 1985: n.p.)

In creating such a language, the author conveys very powerfully that English is the dominant idiom of the coloniser, and as such, it does not have the capacity to represent the specificity of the minority's experience: it is the 'lawlessness' on which this idiosyncratic 'rotten English' thrives. This predicament supposedly reflects—and, importantly, makes ironic—the ideological manipulation of its speakers by dominant powers that have no regard for moral principles or, as it turns out, human lives.

Sozaboy's perplexity in pondering the justification of war is funny not only because of his naivety and ignorance, but also because it exposes the simplistic polarisation of forces in a conflict:

> the man was speaking ... [using] big big words that I cannot understand. But every time he will be calling that Enemy. I begin to fear this Mr. Enemy you know. Because I am thinking he must be strong man pass Hitla sef. Otherwise why is everyone talking about him? Even the Chief Commander General is fearing this man. Why? Even sef, why all of us will join hand to kill him. Does he have many heads? What is wrong with him? 'E get stronghead? Or did he call another man's wife? Why does everybody want to kill him? And why they will train plenty people to kill him? (Saro-Wiwa 1985: 78)

Why indeed? A primary school drop-out, Mene has the modest ambition to get his driver's license and drive the lorry owned by the villagers of Dukana that they have called 'Progress'. A civil war erupts after a military coup brings about even worse corruption than before, and the young man is persuaded to join 'the soza' by his girlfriend and the elders of the village, who interpellate him into an ideological position that aligns manhood, reliability as a member of the community, and suitability as a husband. The story follows Mene in the trenches, as a POW and then in refugee camps; he wanders through the war-ravaged country in search of his mother and wife. The poignancy of the novel, as the following passage suggests, lies in the brutal juxtaposition of his naïve expectations and the shocking destruction of war:

> And you know as we used to look up every time when the plane pass because it is a very wonderful thing to see this canoe sailing in the sky through the air. . . . So as we were still looking at the plane as it came to pass round and round the camp, I saw that plane drop something. 'E dey me like say the plane dey shit and I begin laugh. But my laugh no reach my belly because that thing from the plane just land near we camp and I hear very very big noise which come carry me for air thruway for ground. Then I hear Bullet shouting 'Bomb! Bomb! Take cover! Take cover!' (Saro-Wiwa 1985: 110)

Graphic descriptions of the destruction follow, with details of the gruesome spectacle of body-parts scattered everywhere, his friend and guide through the war, dead, and Sozaboy's bearings irretrievably lost. This is when he begins to realise that he was deceived into joining the army, into believing that the war was fought for honourable reasons. 'Oh, foolish man', he says in one of the frequent moments when he speaks to himself, 'na who send me make I go join soza?' (Saro-Wiwa 1985: 111).

In the last part of the story, Saro-Wiwa skilfully deploys two strategies for dismantling the polarisation of forces (the 'good', the 'Enemy'). Firstly, by having Mene inadvertently join the enemy camp and then desert, out of an overwhelming fear, disgust, and homesickness, the author portrays war as equally absurd from both sides. Secondly, Sozaboy encounters in his wanderings a protean character that he refers to as Manmuswak, who successively appears as a friend, an ally, an enemy, a care-taker, and a member of an adverse firing-squad who almost kills him. 'Manmuswak', the glossary of terms at the end of the novel clarifies, means 'man must live (eat) by whatever means'. And this principle, Mene's story implies, governs the ultimate logic of war—a very different logic, indeed, from the one he had entertained at the beginning:

> And I come say to myself that oh my God, war is very bad thing. War is to drink urine, to die and all that uniform that they are giving us to wear is just to deceive us. And anybody who think that uniform is fine thing is stupid man who does not know what is good or bad or not good at all or very bad at all. All those things that they have been telling us before is just stupid lie. (Saro-Wiwa 1985: 113–4)

This radical reappraisal of his initial beliefs, shaped by those around him, speaks, yet again, to the tremendous disconnect between the actual experience of war and the image sold to him by others (quite literally sold, ironically, since he had bribed his way into the army). In a last address to the reader, he poignantly bids farewell, suggesting that he could not distance himself more from the common perception of war that he had believed in: 'I was thinking how I was prouding before to go to soza and call myself Sozaboy. But now if anybody say anything about war or even fight, I will just run and run and run and run and run. Believe me yours sincerely'. Although the young man survives, there is no place for him to resume his life; the valediction at the close of the novel is a farewell not only to the reader, but also to a world that has lost its candor.

3. *Baghdad Burning*

Baghdad Burning, the blog of a 24-year old Iraqi woman, debuted on 17 August 2003 with an unusual self-introduction: 'I survived the war. That's all you need to know. It's all that matters these days anyway' (riverbendblog.blogspot.nl). Her name, profession, hobbies, dreams or life-projects become irrelevant as a prolonged 'war of liberation' replaces the everyday and its reassuring repetition of gestures, rituals, encounters, with experiences that are frustrating, disorienting and scary: 'jolted into reality with the sound of a gun-shot, explosion, or yelling. You sit up, horrified and panicked, any dream or nightmare shattered to oblivion. What can it be? A burglar? A gang of looters? An attack? A bomb? Or maybe it's just an American midnight raid?' (17/08/2003). Riverbend records her compatriots' rude awakening to a life of fear, a life that requires guerrilla warfare skills: 'I can tell you how far away [the shooting] is. I can tell you if it's a pistol or machine-gun, tank or armored vehicle, Apache or Chinook...I can determine the distance and maybe even the target. That's my new talent. It's something I've gotten so good at, I frighten myself. What's worse is that almost everyone seems to have acquired this new talent...young and old' (21/08/2003). Everyone has also learnt to deal with water shortages, scarcity of everyday essentials and precarious electricity (thus intermittent or no air conditioning on impossibly hot days and nights, and so on). And yet, no amount of courage or resilience helps civilians accept the daily violence, kidnappings, raids, killings: Riverbend says repeatedly that she can never feel safe on the street, and therefore cannot leave the house unaccompanied by one or two male relatives, whereas before she used to have a job at an IT company. To those who followed her blog as she wrote it, perhaps the most unnerving was the occasional silence, eventually explained in stories of blackouts, fear, chronic tired-ness, or business.

It is remarkable that at twenty four, the young woman who calls herself Riverbend has such an informed and lucid outlook on the war; for clearly, she is a very keen observer not only of what she sees around herself, but also of people, media reports and political discussions everywhere. River-bend deconstructs the ideology of 'liberation' providing context about life before the war, crucial moments in the Gulf War, the various presidential candidates forming the 'puppet council' that supposedly represented the Iraqi people, the various ethnic and religious groups and their interac-tions. She also explains how certain tendencies were radicalised in the course of the war, inadvertently empowering religious fanatics. She speaks of loss of sovereignty, economic disaster, and the disempowerment of the Iraqi people. Importantly, in response to comments on her blog from vari-ous readers, she debunks generalities and stereotypes, articulating lucidly and unapologetically her position: 'I'm going to set the record straight, once and for all. I don't hate Americans, contrary to what many people seem to believe. Not because I love Americans, but simply because I don't hate Americans, like I don't hate the French, Canadians, Brits, Saudis, Jor-danians, Micronesians, etc. It's that simple. I was brought up, like millions of Iraqis, to have pride in my own culture and nationality' (22/08/2003). Riverbend's dignity is obviously matched only by her desire to reach out and connect with people who are willing to take with her the measure of the reality—rather than mediated representations—of war. Her most recent entry as I write, dated 9 April 2013, follows a six-year hiatus during which readers familiar with her blog worried about her fate, speculated about her whereabouts, while some even doubted the authenticity of her professed identity. 'And what happened to Riverbend and my family?', she asks in this last entry, acknowledging the curiosity her silence generated. Evaluating the gloomy lessons of ten years of conflict since 'the fall of Baghdad', she expresses frustration and anger at the situation in the Arab world—like many other families, hers fled to Syria in 2007, and they have been displaced twice since then—but also gratitude and a sense of hope: 'For those of you who have been asking about me and wondering how I have been doing, I thank you. "Lo khuliyet, qulibet..." Which means "If the world were empty of good people, it would end". I only need to check my emails to know it won't be ending any time soon'.

Conclusion

'When a war is ended', writes Tim O'Brien in *Going after Cacciato*, 'it is as if there have been a million wars, or as many wars as there were soldiers' (O'Brien 1988: 191). The multitude of perspectives O'Brien refers to conceals as many wars *within* each individual who has experienced the shattering of his or her sense of self, life-experience, and values. As we have seen in the texts discussed, one of the effects of war is the breakdown of the tenuous link between words and the world—hence the effort to represent war requires finding a way to suture these realities, to reconnect them somehow. It means trying to bring order—if only the linearity of discourse—into the chaos of destruction, senselessness, and trauma. If there are, indeed, as many wars as there are participants, it means there is no end to the war's representation; one can only continue to read—hereafter, for instance, Böll's poignant short story 'Stranger, bear word to the Spartans we…', an excerpt from *Sozaboy*, and O'Brien's memorable 'How to write a true short story'—, and pay attention to the ways conflicts are represented today. Literature, film and (some) new media help us bridge the gap between the *millions* of statistics and the affecting singularity of individual experiences. It is the latter, I believe, that give us the true measure of what war means.

Guiding Questions

a. What does 'representation' refer to? Are the different meanings of representation related?
b. What are some of the challenges posed by the representation of war?
c. How would you describe the contribution of literary texts, personal accounts, and films to your understanding of the phenomenon of war?
d. What is deconstruction? How can we relate it to the representation of war?

Selected Reading

Böll, H., 1950, 'Stranger bear word to the Spartans we…' Available from http://cristina-ann.blogspot.nl/2011/02/stranger-bear-word-to-spartans-we-by.html.

Brien, T., 2009, 'How to tell a true war story', in *The Things They Carried*, Mariner Books, pp. 64–82.

Saro-Wiwa, K., 1995, *Sozaboy*, Pearson, Longman Publishing Group, White Plains, New York, pp. 92–127; 182–7.

Further Reading

Primary Sources

Here are a few famous texts of fiction, drama, and poetry that students interested in the representation of war might want to read. I am listing them in alphabetical order by author, with the initial publication date (many have been reprinted several times). This list is of course not exhaustive:

Alcott, L.M., *Hospital sketches* (1863)
Aldington, R., *Death of a hero* (1929)
Auden, W.H. & Isherwood, C., *Journey to a war* (1973)
Bao Ninh, *The sorrow of war* (1991)
Barker, P., *The ghost road* (1996)
Barbusse, H., *Under fire: the story of a squad* (1926)
Brecht, B., *Mother Courage and her children* (1941)
Defoe, D., *Memoirs of a cavalier, or a military journal of the wars in Germany and the wars in England from the year 1632, to the year 1648* (1720)
Graves, R., *Goodbye to all that* (1929)
Greene, G., *The quiet American* (1955)
Hašek, J., *The good soldier Švejk* (1923)
Hemingway, E. *A farewell to arms* (1929)
Homer, *The Iliad*
Junger, E., *Storm of steel* (1920)
Littell, J., *The Kindly ones* (2006)
Mailer, N., *Why are we in Vietnam?* (1967)
O'Brien, T., *Going after Cacciato* (1978) and *The Things they carried* (1990)
Orwell, G., *Homage to Catalonia* (1938)
Owen, W., *The Collected poems of Wilfred Owen* (1965)
Remarque, E.M., *All quiet on the Western front* (1920)
Saint-Exupéry, A., de *Pilote de guerre* (1942)
Sassoon, S., *The War poems of Siegfried Sassoon* (2010)
Sebald, W.G., *The rings of Saturn* (1999)
Shakespeare, W., *Henry V* (1599)

Stein, G., *Wars I have seen* (1984)
Sterne, L., *The life and opinions of Tristram Shandy* (1767)
Thucydides, *History of the Peloponnesian War*
Tolstoy, L., *War and peace* (1869)
Virgil, *The Aeneid*
Vonnegut, K., *Slaughterhouse-five* (1969)
Wiesel, E., *Night* (1958)

Secondary Literature

Allan, S., Zelizer B., 2004, *Reporting war: Journalism in war time*, Routledge, London and New York.
Baraban, E.V., Jaeger, S. & Muller, A., (eds), 2012, *Fighting words and images: Representing war across the disciplines*, Toronto University Press, Toronto.
Baudrillard, J., 1994, *The Gulf War did not take place*, (trans. P. Patton), Power Publications, London.
Chatman, S., 1978, *Story and discourse: Narrative structure in fiction and film*, Cornell University Press, Ithaca.
Friedlander, S., 1992, *Probing the limits of representation: Nazism and the 'Final Solution'*, Harvard University Press, Cambridge MA.
Goldensohn, L., 2003, *Dismantling glory: Twentieth-century soldier poetry*, Columbia University Press, New York.
LaCapra, D., 2003, *Writing history, writing trauma*, Johns Hopkins University Press, Baltimore.
McClatchy, J.D., 2005, *Poets of the Civil War*, Library of America.
McLoughlin, K., (ed.), 2009, *The Cambridge companion to war writing*, Cambridge University Press, Cambridge.
——, 2011, *Authoring war. The Literary representation of war from the Iliad to Iraq*, Cambridge University Press, Cambridge.
Seaton, J., 2005, *Carnage and the media: The making and breaking of news about violence*, Penguin, London.
Steiner, G., 1969, *Language and silence*, Penguin, Hardmondsmith.
Taylor, I. & Taylor, A., (eds), 2004, *The Secret annexe: An anthology of the world's greatest war diarists*, Canongate, Edinburgh.
Taylor, J., 1998, *Body horror: photojournalism, catastrophe and war*, Manchester University Press, Manchester.
Virilio, P., 1989, *War and cinema: The Logistics of perception*, Verso, London.

Case Study Guiding Questions

a. How do various participants in wars understand the ideological under-
    pinnings of the conflict?
b. How does war impact the everyday life of civilians?
c. What are some strategies adopted by filmmakers in the representation
    of war?

References

Baraban, E.V., Jaeger, S. & Muller, A., (eds), 2012, *Fighting words and images: Representing war across the disciplines*, Toronto University Press, Toronto.
Duras, M., 1961, *Hiroshima mon amour*, Grove Press, New York.
McLoughlin, K. (ed.), 2009, *The Cambridge companion to war writing*, Cambridge University Press, Cambridge.
——, 2011, *Authoring war. The Literary representation of war from the Iliad to Iraq*, Cambridge University Press, Cambridge.
Riverbend, *Baghdad burning*, riverbendblog.blogspot.nl.
Saro-Wiwa, K., 1995, *Sozaboy. A novel in rotten English*, Pearson, Longman Publishing Group, White Plains, New York.

CHAPTER EIGHT

END OF WAR

Niels van Willigen and Jessica Kroezen

Introduction

This chapter delves into the question of how wars end. Or, to put it differently, this chapter is about how peace is established. We first discuss what peace actually is. Is it sufficient to define peace as the mere absence of war? Or do we need a more elaborate definition in order to grasp the meaning of peace? The chapter then proceeds with a discussion of the democratic peace thesis, which holds that democracies are unlikely to fight one another. Whether or not this is true, this conviction has inspired (mainly Western) states and international organisations to pursue and support democratisation policies targeted at autocratic regimes and conflict-ridden societies (Clinton 1994). The dominance of the idea that liberal democracy fosters peace is reflected in the many peace operations that have been organised by the United Nations (UN). Therefore, in the third and last part of this chapter we explain what these missions entail and how they have been influenced by the end of the Cold War.

1. What is Peace?

Peace as the absence of war would be the most straightforward answer to this question. The Oxford English Dictionary provides the following definition of peace: 'freedom from or the cessation of war' (1993). Peace as the absence of war or violent conflict can be understood as 'negative peace' (Galtung 1996: 61). It is important to realise that in a state of negative peace, there may still be animosity between the former belligerents and the underlying conflict may often continue unabated. Conflict, therefore, is not synonymous with war or violence.

Conflict itself is not the problem. Conflict can be managed or resolved in parliaments and in other democratic institutions. This is what happens in any peaceful liberal democracy, in which conflicts about how best to organise society are abundant. This is also what happens in international politics where many conflicts are managed or resolved peacefully through mediation, negotiation and judicial settlement. Understood in this way, the management of conflict—and the search for compromise and consensus— is synonymous with politics (Heywood 2002: 9–10).

An example of an international conflict that did not involve warfare is the Cold War. From 1945 to 1991, the United States (US) and the Soviet Union were entangled in a fierce ideological, political and economic conflict. Although the Cold War witnessed so-called proxy wars in Korea, Vietnam and a few other places, the US and the Soviet Union never fought each other directly. Therefore the Cold War was characterised by a negative peace in which the superpowers managed issues using political tools including deterrence, but also bilateral and multilateral diplomacy rather than military force. When conflict management or conflict resolution fails and military force is used to fight out differences, one speaks of *armed* or *violent* conflict. Armed conflict becomes a war when it involves organised, large-scale violence (see the chapter 'Causes of war' for a definition of war).

Negative peace as the absence of war or armed conflict is only part of the story. Peace can also be conceptualised as 'positive peace' (Galtung 1996: 61). Positive peace is much more difficult to define than negative peace. It is often associated with the concept of justice, as is illustrated by the following textbook definition:

> Positive peace refers to a social condition in which exploitation is minimized or eliminated and in which there is neither overt violence nor the more subtle phenomenon of underlying *structural violence* [sic]. It denotes the continuing presence of an equitable and just social order, as well as ecological harmony. (Barash & Webel 2009: 7)

The term structural violence was coined by Galtung and entails a form of violence that is not physical, or committed by or directed towards a specific actor (as is the case when belligerent forces fire weapons at each other). Instead, the violence is indirect and embedded in a specific social structure. Galtung (1996: 197) describes structural violence as 'avoidable insults to basic human needs, and more generally to *life* [sic]'. Slavery is an example of this, as are other situations in which human beings are deprived of basic human rights, such as racial discrimination and oppression. The definition is very broad and even includes poverty, disease and environmental degradation. All three are considered to be violence because they inhibit the development and well being of human beings (Barash & Webel 2009: 8). Therefore, positive peace can only exist when structural violence is absent. The assumption behind this is that factors like social injustice and exploitation are key causes of (armed) conflict. That is why positive peace is often associated with solid, stable or sustainable peace. Whereas negative peace easily reverts into war, this is not the case with positive peace. Negative peace can be concluded by reaching an armistice between belligerents; an armistice puts a stop to the violence, but does not address the root causes of the armed conflict. As a result, violence often reoccurs. The achievement of positive peace, in the form of a comprehensive peace agreement which goes beyond a mere armistice, for example, would prevent this as it implies that structural violence, seen as a key cause of conflict, will have been addressed. That being said, positive peace is difficult to achieve and should be seen more as an ongoing process than a discrete outcome.

2. *The Democratic Peace Thesis*

The concepts of positive and negative peace can be applied to societies at a national level, but also to international society. Whereas many countries enjoy at least a negative peace domestically, in international society the attainment of peace (of any kind) is more problematic. The history of the world is rife with warfare and armed conflict. Nonetheless, the overall majority of states currently enjoy at least a negative peace situation. How is peace established in international society? One thesis that attempts to answer this question is the democratic peace thesis.

Democratic peace theorists claim that democratic states are not inherently peaceful, but that they will act peacefully towards each other. This claim is supported by empirical evidence because no democracies have fought against each other. The claim may be contested based on the fact that an interpretation of the empirical evidence depends on one's chosen definition of 'democracy'. The empirical evidence in support of democratic peace theory is strongest when it involves consolidated liberal democracies. A liberal democracy is a democracy in which basic human rights and fundamental political freedoms are respected. In that sense, liberal democracy differs from electoral democracy in which John Stuart Mill's 'tyranny of the majority' might lead to infringements upon fundamental political freedoms (Diamond 1999: 10; Mill 1989: 8). A democracy is consolidated when it will not easily revert to autocracy. In other words, when democracy has become 'the only game in town' (Linz & Stepan 1996: 5).

In addition to empirical contestation, the democratic peace thesis could be criticised for lacking a coherent theoretical explanation. In other words, the exact causes of democratic peace are contested. Two camps of democratic peace theorists can be distinguished: the first claims that democratic institutions constrain politicians in their military ambitions (Bueno de Mesquita *et al.* 1999). The costs of war are paid by the population and, in a democracy, a rational population would only vote for war as a last resort. That makes political leaders sensitive to public support (or the lack thereof) and therefore restrictive in their use of force. The second group emphasises the importance of democratic norms and culture, which makes citizens and politicians alike restrictive in using military force to settle differences (Maoz & Russett 1993). These two groups of theorists are not the only ones offering explanations of the absence of war between democracies: other theorists argue that democracies do not fight each other due to economic interdependence (Keohane & Nye 1977), cultural proximity (Henderson 1998), and the existence of an international balance of power (Rosato 2003).

Nonetheless, the democratic peace thesis has become quite influential among the Western foreign policy elite. The logic is: if democracies do not fight each other, international society would benefit from the presence of as many democracies as possible. In 1989, in his famous article 'The end of history', Fukuyama argued that the end of the Cold War meant the victory of liberal democracy. Liberal democracy was the logical outcome of a historical process in which other ideologies, including communism and fascism, had lost (Fukuyama 1989). Fukuyama realised that it would take time for liberal democracy to spread around the world, but he claimed it would be an unstoppable process. Critics attacked Fukuyama's theoretical assumptions as well as his empirical arguments (Burns 1994). There is much to say about the extent to which Fukuyama was right or wrong, but that is beyond the scope of this chapter. What we would like to emphasise here is that (mainly Western) policymakers were eager to support democratisation worldwide. The transition from autocracy to (consolidated) democracy, however, did not necessarily imply less armed conflict. Whereas democracies tend not to fight each other, democratising states, i.e. states experiencing the transition towards democracy, seem particularly vulnerable to violent conflict (Snyder 2000). One could therefore ask the normative question: can the objective of democratic peace justify the risks of war as a result of democratisation efforts?

3. *Peace Operations*

The risk of violent conflict associated with the democratisation process might be mitigated by the presence of a well-organised and effective peace operation in an at-risk area. Additionally, democratisation has become a key aspect of peace operations—the assumption that democracy is a necessary component of positive peace is implicit in the long-term objectives of these missions. Peace operations have only become more prevalent and more relevant to maintaining international peace and security since the first mission was deployed in 1948. More personnel are currently deployed in peace operations across the world than ever before, an upward trend that began in the early 1990s (Bobrow & Boyer 1997; Fortna 2008; Fortna & Howard 2008; Regan 2002). Though there is no official consensus on what the term 'peace operation' means, it refers generally to the following types of activities: conflict prevention/peacemaking; peacekeeping; peace enforcement; and peacebuilding (Bellamy & Williams 2010). Each of these will be discussed in more detail below in terms of historical context. While there has been some evolution in peace operations over time, all types of these operations continue to be deployed today.

After the First and Second World Wars ended, the international community (i.e. the Great Powers that were victorious in these wars) sought to reinforce its desire to prevent a recurrence of total warfare by establishing the UN as the guardian of peace and security in the international system. In order to carry out this task, a number of conflict management tools at the international community's disposal were specified in the UN Charter—some more clearly stated than others. These tools included diplomatic and mediation (peacemaking) strategies for resolving conflicts as well as some less clearly defined, but seemingly more coercive strategies. Peacemaking and conflict prevention include the non-coercive conflict management activities provided for under Chapter VI of the United Nations Charter. These activities included diplomatic efforts to resolve conflicts between belligerents and mediation, involving the presence of a neutral third-party mediator in peace negotiations between belligerents to assist the parties in reaching an agreement. Peacemaking activities can be carried out by individual states, regional organisations, non-governmental organisations or prominent individuals at the behest of the belligerents or of the UN itself.

What soon became clear was that peacemaking strategies alone were not sufficient in all cases and that more efficient and pragmatic tools of conflict management were required. In some cases, strategies were needed in order to help end violent conflicts as quickly as possible and to assist in keeping the very fragile peace produced by a cease-fire. Though peacekeeping is not mentioned by name anywhere in the UN Charter, it emerged as an accepted practice during the Cold War era, with its legal foundation falling somewhere between Chapters VI and VII of the Charter—in an imaginary Chapter VI ½: a means of dispute settlement not quite as pacific as diplomacy, but not entirely coercive either.

Peacekeeping, as it was originally envisioned, was intended to be applied to *interstate* conflicts, or conflicts between independent states, in which the warring parties had reached a cease-fire or a preliminary peace agreement and had formally requested the help of a UN peacekeeping force to find a lasting solution to the conflict at hand. The role of the peacekeeping operation was to interposition itself between the warring parties, usually along a border or demilitarised zone, in order to monitor an existing cease-fire arrangement and ensure that neither side defaulted on their agreement. Keeping the tentative negative peace created by a cease-fire arrangement was seen as an essential step in promoting lasting peace as it served to mitigate the risk associated with (one-sided) adherence to the cease-fire perceived by the belligerents.

This type of operation, often referred to as 'traditional' peacekeeping, involves the presence of lightly armed (or unarmed) military personnel along a demarcated line between two warring states that have reached a temporary cessation of hostilities. Peacekeepers are tasked with monitoring and/or supervising a cease-fire and are *not* authorised to use force except in self-defence, and only then as a last resort. That peacekeepers are *not* equipped for combat is seen as essential to guaranteeing the neutrality and impartiality of the peacekeepers, a key aspect of traditional peacekeeping. 'Traditional' peacekeepers, easily identifiable on the battlefield by their blue UN helmets, do not take part in combat and are protected from attack under international law. Member states of the United Nations voluntarily contribute personnel, materiel and other resources to these operations.

Peacekeeping operations of this nature were carried out during the Cold War era, but these missions were few in number, authorised only infrequently due to the great power competition in the UN Security Council (UNSC) (Fortna 2008). In the years following the end of the Cold War, however, there was a significant increase in the number of peace operations that were deployed, particularly those carried out under the auspices of the United Nations. Not only was it easier for the permanent members of the UNSC to agree to authorise a peace mission in this era, but post-Cold War processes of decolonisation also led to an increase in the number of civil wars (intrastate conflicts), which in turn increased the demand for peace operations. It became increasingly clear, however, that traditional peacekeeping—designed for conflicts in the Westphalian state system *between* sovereign states—was not appropriate for application in conflicts *within* states, between governments and rebel groups, in which fighting may or may not have ceased prior to the arrival of peacekeepers and in which one or both parties to the conflict may not have consented to the presence of the peace operation. The application of traditional peacekeeping in civil war amounted to putting a square peg in a round hole and had disastrous consequences in several situations including that of the Rwandan genocide.

In an effort to remedy this problem, more robust, militarised peace operations were deployed to ongoing intrastate conflicts. Authorised under Chapter VII of the Charter, peace enforcement missions enjoy a broader mandate than 'Chapter VI ½' missions and are often tasked with civilian protection, security provision and other activities that involve the use of force to achieve strategic objectives. In stark contrast to traditional peacekeeping, enforcement missions may or may not have the consent of the belligerents (thus violating the principle of non-intervention) and troops on the ground are not required to maintain neutrality in a strict sense. Often the protection of civilians as a mandate necessarily implies choosing sides. Due to the robust and complex nature of these missions, regional organisations such as the North Atlantic Treaty Organization (NATO) are often tasked with providing troops and command and control. Alternatively, a *coalition of the willing and able* under the leadership of a great power (often the United States) may be asked (or may volunteer) to do the job.

Increasingly often, intrastate conflicts have taken place in the context of weak or absent state institutions, resulting in high numbers of civilian casualties and have been relatively more intense, bloody and intractable than interstate conflicts (Licklider 1995; Miall 1992). Peace operations are often deployed not only to keep or enforce negative peace, but also to (re-)create stable political institutions and engage in post-conflict reconstruction more generally, in an effort to guarantee peace in the long term (i.e. positive peace). In this context, the military instrument is used increasingly often to achieve political ends. Peacebuilding includes post-conflict activities aimed at creating the conditions for positive peace. These tasks consist of the creation of democratic political institutions, reconstruction of infrastructure, and monitoring elections, for example. Peacebuilding is often included as a component of the mandate of modern 'post-Westphalian' peace missions (Bellamy & Williams 2010). These combined efforts are known as multidimensional missions.

In spite of the conflict management tools at the international community's disposal as described above, there remains a great deal of contention as to whether or not peace operations actually make a difference. A universal definition of peace operation success also does not exist—is the achievement of negative peace sufficient? Or is positive peace the only acceptable outcome? Moreover, many studies have found that civil wars are particularly intractable and are fairly likely to recur in a given time period (Collier, Hoeffler & Soderbom 2008; Fortna 2004; Walter 2002). Still others argue that a decisive victory of one party in the conflict is more likely to produce stable peace over the long term than a negotiated settlement (Call 2008). The role that peace operations play here in terms of war recurrence is also not entirely clear. Some authors contend that there are aspects of a mission that may make it more or less successful, such as the credibility of the mission (Walter 2004). Nonetheless, the role that peace operations play in the pursuit of peace (negative or positive) remains the focus of many current studies of conflict management.

Conclusion

Peace proves to be a complex and somewhat contested concept. From the very definition of what peace is to how it can be achieved, the concept remains a focal point of academic study and a concept that is of undeniable practical importance. This chapter has presented working definitions of both negative and positive peace in an effort to provide a foundation upon which to understand and problematise peace. In addition, we have discussed the democratic peace thesis, its assumptions and the influence it has had on the way in which the international community deals with armed conflict. Finally, we discussed the evolution of peace operations over time, their characteristics and have touched upon the ongoing debate as to whether or not peace operations help or hinder the pursuit of lasting peace. The body of literature on the 'end of war' is very extensive. The two selected readings below offer merely a short introduction to the literature on peace. To further expand your knowledge of the topic, a list of further readings is added. In addition to the reference list, this is a good start to exploring the issue of peace.

Guiding Questions

a. Define negative peace and positive peace and explain the characteristics of both concepts.
b. What does the democratic peace thesis entail? What did Francis Fukuyama mean by 'the end of history' and how does this concept relate to the democratic peace thesis?
c. Which types of peace operations can be distinguished? What are the major differences between them, and how effective are they?

Selected Readings

Bellamy, A.J. & Williams, P.D., 2010, *Understanding peacekeeping*, 2nd edn., Polity, Cambridge. Chapter 1: Peace operations in global politics, pp. 13–41.

Ray, J.L., 1998, 'Does democracy cause peace?', *Annual Review of Political Science* 1, 27–46.

Further Reading

Doyle, M.W., 1983, 'Kant, liberal legacies, and foreign affairs part 1', *Philosophy and Public Affairs* 12(3), 205–35.

——, 1983, 'Kant, liberal legacies, and foreign affairs, part 2'. *Philosophy and Public Affairs* 12(4), 323–53.

Fortna, V.P., 2008, *Does peacekeeping work? Shaping belligerents' choices after civil war*, Princeton University Press, New Jersey.

Fukuyama, F., 1992, *The end of history and the last man*, The Free Press, New York.

——, 1995, 'Reflections on the end of history, five years later', *History and Theory* 34(2), 27–43.

Kupchan, C.A, 2011, *How enemies become friends: The sources of stable peace*. Princeton University Press, Princeton.

Mansfield, E.D. & Snyder, J., 2005, *Electing to fight*, MIT Press, Cambridge.

Paris, R., 1997, 'Peace-Building and the limits of liberal internationalism', *International Security* 22(2), 54–89.

——, 2010, 'Saving liberal peacebuilding', *Review of International Studies* 36(2), 337–65.

Ungerer, J.L. 2012, 'Assessing the progress of the democratic peace research program', *International studies review* 14(1), 1–31.

Case Study Guiding Questions

a. How have the different actors involved in your specific case study tried to build peace?
b. Did peacebuilding lead to the end of war? If not, why not?
c. What role does (liberal) democracy play in ending the war in your specific case study? If it does not play any role: why not?

References

Barash, D.P. & Webel, C.P., 2009, *Peace and conflict studies*, Sage Publications, Los Angeles.
Bellamy, A.J. & Williams, P.D., 2010, *Understanding peacekeeping*, 2nd edn., Polity, Cambridge.
Bobrow, D.B. & Boyer, M.A., 1997, 'Maintaining system stability: Contributions to peacekeeping operations', *The Journal of Conflict Resolution* 41(6), 723–48.
Bueno de Mesquita, B., Morrow, J., Siverson, R. & Smith, A., 1999, 'An institutional explanation of the democratic peace', *The American Political Science Review* 93(4), 791–807.
Burns, T., 1994, *After history? Francis Fukuyama and his critics*, Littlefield Adam Quality Paperbacks, Lanham, MD.
Call, C.T., 2008, 'Knowing peace when you see it: Setting standards for peacebuilding success', *Civil Wars* 10(2), 173–94.
Clinton, W., 1994, *State of the Union 1994 (25 January)*, viewed 21 November 2012, from http://www.presidency.ucsb.edu/ws/index.php?pid=50409.
Collier, P., Hoeffler, A. & Soderbom, M., 2008, 'Post-conflict risks', *Journal of Peace Research* 45(4), 461–78.
Diamond, L., 1999, *Developing Democracy: Toward Consolidation*, The Johns Hopkins University Press, Baltimore.
Fortna, V.P., 2004, 'Does peacekeeping keep the peace? International intervention and the duration of peace after civil war', *International Studies Quarterly* 48, 269–92.
——, 2008, *Does peacekeeping work? Shaping belligerents' choices after civil war*, Princeton University Press, Princeton.
Fortna, V.P. & Howard, L.M., 2008, 'Pitfalls and prospects in the peacekeeping literature', *Annual Review of Political Science* 11, 283–301.
Fukuyama, F., 1989, 'The end of history?', *The National Interest* 16, 4–18.
Galtung, J., 1996, *Peace by peaceful means*, Sage Publications, London.
Henderson, E.A., 1998, 'The democratic peace through the lens of culture, 1820–1989', *International Studies Quarterly* 42(3), 461–84.
Heywood, A., 2002, *Politics*, Palgrave Macmillan, Basingstoke, UK.
Keohane, R.O. & Nye, J.S., 1977, *Power and interdependence: World politics in transition*, Little, Brown and Company, Boston and Toronto.
Levy, J.S., 1989, 'Domestic politics and war', in R.I. Rotberg & T.K. Rabb (eds), *The origin and prevention of major wars*, pp. 79–99, Cambridge University Press, London.
Levy, J. S. & Thompson, W.R., 2010, *Causes of war*, Wiley-Blackwell, Malden and Oxford.
Licklider, R., 1995, 'The consequences of negotiated settlements in civil wars, 1945–1993', *American Political Science Review* 89(3), 681–90.
Linz, J.J. & Stepan, A., 1996, *Problems of democratic transition and consolidation*, Johns Hopkins University Press, Baltimore.
Maoz, Z. & Russett, B., 1993, 'Normative and structural causes of democratic peace, 1946–1986', *American Political Science Review* 87(3), 624–38.

Miall, H., 1992, *The peacemakers: Peaceful settlement of disputes since 1945*, St. Martin's, New York.

Mill, J.S., 1989 [1859], 'On liberty', in S. Collini (ed.), *J.S. Mill. On liberty and other writings*, Cambridge University Press, Cambridge.

Regan, P.M., 2002, 'Third-Party interventions and the duration of intrastate conflicts', *The Journal of Conflict Resolution* 46(1), 55–73.

Rosato, S., 2003, 'The flawed logic of the democratic peace', *American Political Science Review* 97(4), 585–602.

Snyder, J., 2000, *From voting to violence: Democratization and nationalist conflict*, W.W. Norton & Company, New York.

Thompson, D., (ed.), 1993, *The Oxford dictionary of current English*, Oxford University Press, Oxford.

Walter, B.F., 2002, *Committing to peace: The successful settlement of civil wars*, Princeton University Press, Princeton.

——, 2004, 'Does conflict beget conflict? Explaining recurring civil war', *Journal of Peace Research* 41(3), 371–88.

PART TWO

CASE STUDIES

CHAPTER NINE

THE YUGOSLAV WARS

Francesco Ragazzi

Introduction

As the International Criminal Tribunal for the former Yugoslavia (ICTY) prosecutes the last main protagonists of the Yugoslav wars Ratko Mladić and Radovan Karadžić,[1] the conflicts in former Yugoslavia finally transition from newspapers to history books. The bloodiest European conflicts since World War II leave a profound mark on the post-war societies there, as well as on many institutions that govern contemporary international relations. The European Community (EC, now European Union), the United Nations (UN) and its peacekeeping operations, the North Atlantic Treaty Organization (NATO), among others, have all been transformed by the wars in former Yugoslavia. Under the label of 'Yugoslav wars', this chapter covers (1) the Ten Days War, in which Slovenia gained independence from the Yugoslav Federation, (2) the war between Croatia and the Yugoslav Federation, (3) the war in Bosnia-Herzegovina, (4) the war in Kosovo, and (5) the war in Macedonia. However, the main focus will be on three of these wars: Croatia, Bosnia and Kosovo, as these conflicts have had the largest political implications, and have generated the most academic debate.

While they were taking place, the Yugoslav wars were often described in the press as tribal, barbaric and devoid of rationality. According to this view, they were supposedly the result of ancient hatreds and long-kept feudal animosities. In this chapter, I will show that this point of view, which has always been widely contested by historians, political scientists and specialists of the conflict, has to a great extent prevented early interventions on the part of foreign governments in the conflict. It has also helped the supporters of 'ethnic cleansing'—the systematic assassination or forced displacement of populations on the basis of their ethnicity—in carrying out their deed undisturbed. This chapter therefore covers not only

---

[1] See the state of current cases here: http://www.icty.org/action/cases/4.

the facts, but the diverse interpretations (also called narratives) of these facts by the different actors in the war. As in any major conflict, there is not one truth about the wars in Yugoslavia. Not only are the actors of the conflict divided, so is the academic community. Rather than choose one single position, and based in great part on the colossal work of Sabrina Ramet, *Thinking about Yugoslavia* (2005), this chapter will show different positions, the political consequences of these positions, and provide further references to dig deeper into the various arguments presented here.

The remainder of the chapter is divided in seven sections. First, we will revisit the historical context of the conflict. Second, we will review the reasons and multiple justifications for the war. The next five sections will consider in chronological order the different conflicts in Slovenia, Croatia, Bosnia-Herzegovina, Kosovo and Macedonia.

1. *The Historical Context*

The Socialist Federation of Republics of Yugoslavia—the official name of Yugoslavia—was a federation of states, which emerged from the Second World War in 1946.[2] It was a socialist country, but it was emancipated from Soviet Union control as Josip Broz Tito, the leader of the Communist Party of Yugoslavia, had managed to carve for its country a third space between the Capitalist West, Communist East, leading the 'Non-Aligned' movement, along with India's leader Nehru and Indonesia's leader Soekarno (Rajak 2009).

In 1946, Yugoslavia was a relatively young country. For centuries, the Slavic-speaking people of the South of Europe were divided between two empires. Slovenes and Croats were under the domination of the Austro-Hungarian Empire, while Bosniaks, Serbs, Montenegrins, Albanians and Macedonians were ruled by the Ottomans. These people were reunited for the first time in 1918 in the Kingdom of Serbs, Croats and Slovenes (which also includes Albanians and Macedonians). The country changed its name to the Kingdom of Yugoslavia in 1929. The name Yugoslavia (*Jugoslavija*) is a creation, from *Jug*- which means 'South' and -*slavija* meaning the land of Slavs, Yugoslavia therefore literally means 'the Land of South Slavs'.

Contrary to the 'ancient hatreds' argument, which dates the opposition between Serbs and Croats to the middle ages, the Second World War

---

[2] It was officially called the Federal People's Republic of Yugoslavia until 1963.

is the first real episode of confrontation between nationalist movements from each side. The separatist Nazi-puppet Croatian Independent State, formed in 1941 under the leadership of Ante Pavelić, established a regime of terror for Jews, Roma and Serbs. In Serbia, the Četnik movement of Draža Mihailović committed atrocities. The massacres committed by both sides, among other factors, favoured the victory of the Communist Party of Yugoslavia—which is not exempt from its share of war crimes—and the establishment of Socialist Yugoslavia after World War II. Noel Malcolm (2002: 68) estimates that two hundred and fifty thousand people were killed by Tito's partisans immediately following the end of the war.

During the socialist period (1946–1990), despite the initial massacres and the repression of political dissidents, Yugoslavs enjoyed more freedoms than their Eastern bloc neighbours. In 1948, Tito broke the ties with Stalin—who had been an ally until then—and turned towards the West. In 1966, the borders were opened, and Yugoslavs acquired the right to travel abroad. They could buy a limited number of foreign goods, and the youth could follow the cultural and musical trends of the West. Yugoslavia developed its own path to socialism, through 'self-management'. However, after a few successful years of development, the Yugoslav economic system proved unsustainable, and needed international help to survive.

Up until the mid-1980s, Yugoslavia was divided into six republics and two autonomous provinces, with different ethnic compositions in which each nation had different legal statuses. Slovenians were the constituent nation of the Socialist Republic (SR) of Slovenia. SR Croatia, composed in a majority by Croats (77.9%),[3] had an important Serbian minority (12.2%), but both peoples shared the status of constituent peoples. SR Bosnia-Herzegovina was composed of Croats (17.3%), Muslims (later called Bosniaks, 43.6%) and Serbs (31.3%), who enjoyed the same status. Serbs were the constituent people of SR Serbia, although the republic comprised the Autonomous Province of Kosovo, mostly populated by Albanians (82.2%), and the Autonomous Province of Vojvodina, where Serbs represented only half the population (57%), along with Hungarians (16.9%) self-proclaimed Yugoslavs (8.39%) and other minorities. SR Montenegro was the Republic of Montenegrins, and SR Macedonia the republic of Macedonians—understood as Slav Macedonians. In Macedonia, the Albanian population,

---

[3] All figures are taken from the 1991 Population Census of Yugoslavia.

although it constituted around one third of the population, did not enjoy the same status as the majority group.[4]

Pacified ethnic relations were an important concern of Tito and the socialist government that ruled under the slogan of 'brotherhood and unity'. Throughout the period, an increasing number of people married outside their ethnic group, and the few marginal individuals within the Party and in the broader civil society who held nationalist views were silenced, jailed or forced to live in exile (Ragazzi 2009). The most important manifestation of nationalism culminated in 1971 in Croatia, during what came to be known as the 'Croatian Spring' (in reference to the Prague Spring of 1968), in which claims for more democracy were intermingled with claims for more Croatian cultural and linguistic autonomy. The movement was repressed but some of the demands were later accommodated, and ethnic tensions scored low in opinion polls until the mid-1980s.

3. *Why did the War Break Out?*

The death of Tito marked the end of the single man-lead dictatorship in 1980 and revealed the weaknesses of the federal system. The federal presidency was a collective composed of eight people (each republic and autonomous province has a representative), with Tito at its head. With the death of Tito, the head of the presidency was elected every year on a rotational basis. But no one emerged as a strong new leader and the different republics started to drift in their own, separate directions.

In 1986, a key turning point arrived; Slobodan Milošević, a young member of the party, was elected as the head of the League of Communists of Serbia (the Serbian branch of the Yugoslav Communist Party). In 1987 in Kosovo, during clashes between Serbian protesters and the police, Milošević broke with the League's 'brotherhood and unity' anti-nationalist stance when he declared support for Kosovo Serbs against the Kosovo Albanian authorities. In 1987–8, Milošević maintained his grip on power through what was defined as the 'anti-bureaucratic revolution'. It consisted mainly of organising 'spontaneous' meetings that promoted Serbian nationalism. Legitimised by these meetings, Milošević revoked the autonomous status of the provinces of Kosovo and Vojvodina and centralised power in Belgrade, a measure that took effect in 1990.

---

[4] See map 1 'Making The History of 1989', viewed 24 February 2013, from http://chnm .gmu.edu/1989/items/show/170.

In the meantime, tensions were rising between Belgrade and the other republics. In 1989, the Slovenian and Croatian authorities supported the Kosovo miners against Milošević's anti-bureaucratic revolution. In retaliation, Serbia boycotted Slovenian products in its stores. At the 14th Congress of the League of Communists of Yugoslavia in 1990, the Slovenian and Croatian delegations left in protest over Milošević's actions.

The tension reached a new level with the first democratic elections organised in Yugoslavia in 1990. With the fall of the Berlin wall, the pressure from the Soviet Union disappeared, and many in Yugoslavia believed that democratic elections could save the country. In most republics, the nationalist parties won, and the consequences were immediate. In Croatia, Franjo Tuđman, the leader of the Croatian Democratic Union (HDZ), was elected on a nationalist platform. Serbian minorities in Croatia, worried by the references to the Independent State of Croatia of World War II in Tuđman's speeches, rallied behind Serbian nationalist movements in Croatia. This marked the beginning of the 'Tree-log revolution', a revolt led by organisations from the Serbian minority in Croatia which consisted initially in blocking roads with tree-logs (Lampe 2000: 369). The Croatian government pursued its nationalist agenda by demoting Serbs from the status of 'constituent people', which they had until then to one of 'minority'. A few months later, Slovenia held a referendum for independence; 88.5% of the voters were in favour. In the meantime, in Belgrade, students and progressive movements organised massive demonstrations against Milošević and his aggressive policies, but the protest was severely repressed. After a few months of negotiations between the heads of states of the various republics, Slovenia and Croatia declared their independence in June of 1991. Large-scale conflict was about to break out.

Why did the war break out? Croatian nationalists blamed the conflict only on Milošević's policies, when they did not simply blame Serbs as a whole. Many among the Serbian population in Croatia blamed it on Tuđman's nationalist rhetoric. Nationalist Serbs in Serbia blamed Albanian nationalism in Kosovo. Others blamed it on Tito, who died and left an unmanageable country in a dire economic situation. But what are the *causes* of the war?

Scholars are still divided on this issue. Some point to the importance of the 1981 strike in Kosovo (Magaš 1993), others insist on the role of the international context, and in particular the breakup of the Soviet Union (Allcock 2000), others, finally, point to the importance of economic factors in creating scapegoats and fuelling ethnic mobilisation (Woodward 1995). Building on these studies, scholars such as Sabrina Ramet (2005) have argued that the war indeed was caused by a multiplicity of factors. They pointed out additional factors, such as the fact that the federal system is based on ethnicity; the role of specific personalities (such as Tuđman, Milošević and other key players), the weak Yugoslav institutional structure and in particular problems of legitimacy. They argued all these elements were interrelated, and that it is therefore misleading to single one out.

The first armed conflict in the territory of former Yugoslavia—Slovenia— lasted only a few days. After the declaration of Slovenian independence on 25 June, Milošević ordered the Yugoslav People's Army (JNA) to occupy the border posts. Slovenian police as well as the Slovenian Territorial Defense units countered the JNA's activities, leading to limited exchanges of fire in various areas of the newly independent Republic. It is estimated that during the ten days the conflict lasted, less than one hundred people died, including military and civilian casualties. The war ended on 7 July 1991, when the authorities in Belgrade recognised Slovenian and Croatian independence respectively and agreed on a timetable to withdraw their forces. The conflict in Slovenia ended not because of a Slovenian military victory but due to Belgrade's loss of interest in the fate of the Slovenian Republic. There was no substantial Serbian minority, and the tensions in Croatia came quickly to attention, both at the political and military levels.

3. *The War in Croatia (1991–1995)*

The war in Croatia had a much more complex development and resolution, in great part due to the politicisation of the Croatian and Serbian ethnic identities within the country itself by three main actors: (1) the authorities of the newly established Croatian state, (2) the Yugoslav authorities and the Federation's People's Army (JNA), and (3) the local Serbian minority political and paramilitary organisations.

The conflict took its immediate roots a few months before Croatia's and Slovenia's declaration of independence. On 16 March 1991, Serbian organisations in Croatia, mostly based in the Krajina region, declared their own independence from the SR Croatia, and rapidly proclaimed their wish to be unified with Serbia. Tuđman's government responded with force. The Krajina Serbian organisations had the backing of the JNA—officially impartial in the conflict, but de-facto a supporter of the Serbian secession— and the clash rapidly turned into a confrontation between Croatian forces and the JNA. The Serbian rebellion quickly extended to other areas of

Croatia, and by 1992, about one third of the Republic of Croatia was under the control of the Serbian separatists, in what would be called Republic of Serbian Krajina (RSK). Unable to change the situation militarily, the Croatian government agreed to an unfavourable ceasefire in January 1992 (one third of the territory was beyond its control), and a peacekeeping force of the UN, the United Nations Protection Force (UNPROFOR) was deployed. From then on and until 1995, only sporadic military operations took place on Croatian territory, and the heart of the conflict moved to Bosnia-Herzegovina. With the end of the conflict in BiH in July–August 1995, the Croatian Amy launched two major military attacks—Operation Flash and Operation Storm—to regain control over the Serbian areas of its territory from the RSK authorities, who no longer had the support of Milošević and the JNA. The operations were successful, and by the end of the summer of 1995, most of the territories—except for Eastern Slavonia, were under Croatian control. The war ended with an overwhelming victory on the Croatian side, even through the economic and social situation of the conquered zones were dire in 1995. The Erdut Agreement of 12 November 1995 made the Croatian victory official and scheduled the return of Eastern Slavonia to Croatia after two years.

The shelling of the city of Dubrovink and the martyrdom of the city of Vukovar are two strong symbols of the war. It is estimated that twenty thousand people died in the conflict, fifty two thousand are still disabled as a result of the conflict, and between three hundred thousand and five hundred thousand people were displaced, mostly ethnic Croats dislodged from Serbian areas in 1991–1993, and ethnic Serbs in reconquered areas in 1995. An entire generation affected by the war suffers from Post-Traumatic Stress Disorder (PTSD). The war also left a country in dire economic conditions, with an economy heavily burdened by military expenditure. Other negative outcomes of the war concern landmines: approximately two million mines were laid during the war, of which about two hundred and fifty are still in the ground.[5]

The beginning of the war in 1991 in Croatia coincided with the first Gulf War and the collapse of the Soviet Bloc. In a period of troubled international equilibrium, the Bush administration in the US initially adopted a stance of non-intervention in the conflict. Along with the European

---

[5] International Committee of the Red Cross, 'Croatia: safe playgrounds in danger zones', viewed 7 October 2012, from http://www.icrc.org/eng/resources/documents/misc/croatia-mines-300905.htm.

capitals, and in great part influenced by newspaper reports and the official position of Milosevic, the US supported the thesis that the war was a product of 'ancient ethnic disputes' that were to be contained within the sovereignty of the Yugoslav state. The German government adopted a different stance and recognised both Slovenian and Croatian independence in December 1991. This forced the rest of the European states to recognise the two breakaway republics in January 1992. After 1992, the international community adopted a more proactive posture. It was with Bill Clinton's intervention that the UN Security Council and NATO fully played a role in the resolution of the conflict, by changing the balance of power militarily and coercing the parties into the Dayton Peace accords.

4. *The War in Bosnia-Herzegovina (1992–1995)*

Bosnia-Herzegovina (BiH) is a miniature Yugoslavia. In 1991, its population breakdown was 44% Muslims (Bosniaks), 32.5% Serbs, and 17% Croats. The issues and conflicts in the decomposition of Yugoslavia were therefore mirrored in the decomposition of Bosnia: should each of the ethnic groups gain territorial autonomy, or should a multi-ethnic BiH be preserved? At the first multi-party elections, in 1990, nationalists from the three communities won votes. The three main parties were the Party of Democratic Action (PDA, Muslim), led by Alija Izetbegović, the Serbian Democratic Party (SDS), led (among others) by Radovan Karađić and the Croatian Democratic Union in Bosnia and Herzegovina (HDZ-BiH) led (among others) by Mate Boban.

On 15 October 1991, the parliament passed a memorandum to proclaim the independence of BiH from the Yugoslav Federation with the strong opposition of the Serbian SDS, who boycotted the vote. On 29 February and 1 March 1992, a referendum was organised to decide whether BiH should become independent. Following a favourable vote of 92.7%, independence was declared on 5 March 1992. The Serbian parties, who had boycotted the referendum, walked out of parliament and established a new state, the Republika Srpska in August 1992. Earlier, on 18 November 1991, the HDZ BiH, directly connected to Tuđman's HDZ in Croatia, had declared the independence of the Croatian Republic of Herzeg-Bosna, an independent state within Bosnia, with the purpose of uniting it with Croatia (Ramet 2002: 166).

On March 1991, Tuđman and Milošević had secretly agreed to carve out large sections of BiH and unite them with their respective republics in what would be known as the Karađorđevo agreement. When BiH declared its independence, the Bosnian Serb army (VRS), with the support of the JNA launched a widespread offensive against the central government, with the aim of conquering Serbian-populated lands, and 'cleansing' the non-Serbs enclaves by forcibly removing, or killing the people that lived there. Croatian paramilitary organisations such as the Croatian Defence Council (HVO) operated with the same goal with covert support from Zagreb. The central government in Sarajevo deployed a multiethnic army (ARBiH) composed of Muslims, Croats and Serbs, that had occasional support from international Muslim organisations.

Thanks to heavy weaponry supplied by the JNA, Serbs rapidly took over around half of the territory and used indiscriminate violence to reach their objectives. The policy of 'ethnic cleansing', with its deportations, rapes and murders took root in most parts of BiH. By 1992, Bosnian Serb authorities opened concentration camps—the most important were in Keraterm, Trnopolje and Omarska—in which Bosnian Muslims and Bosnian Croats were detained in conditions reminiscent of the Holocaust (Ramet 2002: 218). The siege of Sarajevo, which lasted for four years, became the symbol of the war.

After responding to the first push from the Serbian forces in which the Croats and the multi-ethnic ARBiH fought side by side, the HVO turned its guns against the Bosnian Army in order to pursue the plans of division set up in Karađorđevo in 1991. The HVO's decision was not shared by other nationalist organisations that did not withdraw their support for the ARBiH, and entered in conflict with the HVO. In October 1992, after the massacres of Muslims committed by the HVO in the towns of Prozor (1992), Gornji Vakuf (1993) and in the Lašva Valley (1993) it became clear that the Croatian forces were behaving very similarly to the Serbian forces. Under pressure from Zagreb and the international community, the Croat-Bosniak war ended with the Washington Agreement of March 1994, through which Croatian and Bosnian sides founded the Federation of Bosnia and Herzegovina. But the conflict with the Serbian forces did not cease.

On 5 February 1994, Serbian forces bombarded the Markale market located in the heart of Sarajevo. The brutal death of sixty eight people in a single attack shook international public opinion and provoked a swift international reaction after years of dormancy. Three days later, on 9 February, following the demand of the UN Security Council, NATO began an air strike campaign against Serbian positions around Sarajevo, that was to be extended to other missions in the rest of the country.

The international community had tried to intervene unsuccessfully on several occasions. The first peace negotiation, the Carrington-Cutileiro plan was proposed by the EC in March 1992, but failed when Izetbegovic refused an ethnic partition of the country. The Vance-Owen plan, which proposed to divide the country in three ethnically homogeneous parts in 1993 was another failure. It was rejected by the Serbian side and had an additionally perverse effect: as David Campbell (1988) acutely describes it in *National deconstruction*, the plan reinforced the will of the armies to 'fit' the map, in particular from the Croatian side, therefore accentuating the ethnic cleansing effort.

In June 1992, the UNPROFOR, initially deployed in Croatia was deployed in BiH. It secured the Sarajevo airport, and assisted humanitarian efforts without any mandate to stop the hostilities. In 1993 with resolutions 824 and 836, the UN established 'safe havens'; demilitarised zones to be protected by the UNPROFOR in Goražde, Srebrenica, Tuzla, Žepa and Bihać. The UNPROFOR deployment was complemented by the enforcement of a no-fly zone over Bosnia (UN resolution 816), which started in April 1993 with NATO's Operation 'Deny Flight'. In the worst episode of ethnic cleansing, the 'safe area' of Srebrenica was captured by the Serbian forces led by Ratko Mladić in July 1995. With the Dutch battalion (Dutchbat) unable to counter the attack, eight thousand men were massacred. The war came to a close with the renewal of the Muslim-Croat alliance, and in particular the operations Flash and Storm in Croatia, which added to the intensification of NATO and UNPROFOR actions under the label of Operation Deliberate Force. On 1 November 1995 a peace treaty was finally signed in Dayton, USA. The war displaced 4.3 million citizens, killed about two hundred and fifty thousand and left the country economically destroyed (Ramet 2005: 186).

While many still ponder the exact mechanisms that led to the war, arguing over the importance of economic, cultural and political factors, many authors also question the sustainability of the Dayton Peace accords. For European and US heads of state, it was the best possible agreement that could have been struck at the time. However, David Campbell (1999) argues that the Dayton agreement institutionalises an 'apartheid cartography', promoting ethnic separation and preventing reconciliation (Campbell 1999). On the other hand, David Chandler (2000) argues that with the powers conferred to the High Representative in Bosnia-Herzegovina by the Dayton accords (such as revoking elected officials from office if they promote nationalism) and what the international community set up in Bosnia-Herzegovina are more like imperial protectorates than democratic institutions (Chandler 2000). The current situation of Bosnia-Herzegovina, in which ethnic tensions still persist fifteen years after the end of the war, gives these hypotheses some validity.

5. *Kosovo*

The short-term origins of the tensions in Kosovo can be traced back to 1981. In March 1981, Kosovar Albanians led a series of protests motivated by a mix of economic reasons—the region had among the highest levels of unemployment of Yugoslavia—and political reasons, namely greater autonomy for a mostly Albanian-speaking autonomous province. Some even asked for the status of a Republic. Tensions between pro-Albanian and pro-Serbian groups rose, and several incidents of discrimination against Serbs were reported. It is in this context that Slobodan Milošević made his famous visit in 1987, arguing to the Serbian crowd that 'no one should dare to beat you'.

Under the new constitution of 1989, and as a consequence of Milošević's new grip on power, the autonomy of the province of Kosovo was revoked, and a decade of oppression began for Albanian Kosovars. The use of the Albanian language was suppressed in the official media; ethnic Albanians were purged from public administration and institutions. The Albanian curriculum was revoked at school. To oppose this, Kosovar Albanians organised a peaceful response. In unofficial elections held in 1992, Ibrahim Rugova's Democratic League of Kosovo (LDK) won the majority of votes, running on a non-violent platform. Under the LDK leadership, parallel Kosovo Albanian institutions were created, such as government offices or schools. However, many in Kosovo felt that this strategy did not yield significant results. With the Dayton accord of 1995, many felt that while other nationalities of Yugoslavia had obtained recognition, Kosovar Albanians were left behind. In 1996, the Kosovo Liberation Army (UÇK) took over the political scene, determined to use violence.

The UÇK began a guerrilla-style war with the JNA, using ambushes and bomb attacks. By 1998, the confrontation escalated to a low-intensity conflict. The Kosovo Police and JNA carried out heavy-handed operations and used indiscriminate force against the Albanian population, with the aim of rooting out the UÇK. On the other hand, the UÇK was accused of carrying out 'ethnic cleansing' and war crimes. Wary of its experience with the Croatian and Bosnian conflict, the international community was determined to intervene quickly. In March 1999, under the threat of a military intervention, the Serbian government was invited to peace negotiations in Rambouillet, France. On 18 March, the Belgrade authorities withdrew from an agreement they deemed too unfavourable. The response was immediate: on 24 March 1999, operation 'Allied Force', an air campaign targeting JNA objectives, begun. It lasted until 21 June 1999. The Serbian troops left Kosovo, and the province, while still under Serbian control in international law, passed under the administration of the United Nations Mission in Kosovo (UNMIK) and the protection of the KFOR (Kosovo Force, manned by NATO). Kosovo's independence was proclaimed almost ten years later, on 17 February 2008. The country is still divided between Serbs and Albanians, and is under UN and NATO protection.

The NATO military campaign in Kosovo is still controversial. Many commentators focus on the purported illegality of the war, since it did not have UN Security Council approval. In addition, some argue that the intervention was based on false premises: the Kosovo Verification Mission, sent by the Organization for the Security and Cooperation in Europe (OSCE) prior to the intervention was biased against the Serbs, and the Rambouillet peace talks were a smokescreen to justify the intervention. Bellamy (2002: ix–x) offers a well-argued rebuttal to these allegations, arguing that the main reasons for the intervention lay in the moral outrage of the international community, and the more pragmatic necessity to avoid undoing the stability obtained in the region through the Dayton peace accords. Furthermore, many authors argue that while the war may not have been legal, it was legitimate, as it helped a morally just cause: it prevented a bloodshed similar to what had happened in Bosnia (Weymouth & Henig 2001).

6. *Macedonia*

With the end of the conflict in Kosovo and fall of Milošević in 2000, it seemed that the conflicts in the region were over. But in February 2001, an armed conflict erupted in the Republic of Macedonia, opposing the ethnic-Albanian National Liberation Army (UÇK) to the government of Macedonia.

When it declared its independence on 8 September 1991, ethnic Albanian-Macedonians comprised more than 20% of its population. Ethnic Albanians were represented by several Albanian parties who had always participated in government coalitions since the fall of communism. Throughout the years, some fringes of the Albanian political sphere have claimed more linguistic and cultural rights, polarising the debates and fuelling nationalist rhetoric on the Slav-Macedonian side.

When the Kosovo conflict erupted in 1999, Macedonia hosted about three hundred thousand refugees from the neighbouring province. The Kosovo UÇK established links with groups in Macedonia, and with the easy availability of weapons, a Macedonian UÇK (the National Liberation Army) was set up, led by Ali Ahmeti. It launched its first operations in January 2001, attacking a police station at the border with Kosovo. The conflict expanded to other Albanian-majority cities in and around Tetovo and Kumanovo, escalating to a full-fledged conflict by May 2001. After four months of heavy fighting, closely monitored by the international community and NATO, both sides agreed to stop hostilities (Brunnbauer 2002).

The Ohrid Framework Agreement, signed on 13 August 2001, offered increased linguistic and cultural rights for the Albanian minority (Albanian became one of the official languages in some municipalities) and increased Albanian participation in public institutions including the security forces. As part of the agreement, NATO deployed troops to disarm the UÇK and destroy their weapons. It is estimated that no more than one hundred people died during the war, while about one hundred and fifty thousand to two hundred thousand were displaced because of the conflict (Brunnbauer 2002).

7. War Crimes

The conflict in Macedonia is the last episode of large-scale violence in the former Yugoslav territories since 1991 (at least until the publication of this book in 2013). The entire Yugoslav conflict has killed over a quarter of million people, and among those who survived, it has created a generation of young men and women affected by post-traumatic stress disorder (PTSD). It has left countries such as Bosnia-Herzegovina and Kosovo with extremely tense ethnic relations. It has presented occasions for international organisations to deploy, fail and learn from peacekeeping operations as well as 'peacebuilding' and 'nation-building' projects. But it has also been an occasion for the extraordinary development of international justice. In May 1993, the ICTY was set up by the UN Security Council Resolution 827. It is a key instrument in prosecuting war crimes and crimes against humanity linked to the war in Yugoslavia, established in the city of The Hague, in the Netherlands. To date, the tribunal has indicted one hundred and sixty one persons, of which thirty five are in on-going proceedings, sixty four have been sentenced, thirteen acquitted, thirteen referred to a national court, and thirty six had their indictment withdrawn or died before the end of the trial. Here are some of the most representative cases.[6]

With regard to the war crimes in Croatia, the two sides of the conflict have been accused of committing war crimes, and leaders from both the Croatian and the Serbian side have been indicted by the ICTY. JNA officials General Pavle Struggar and General Miodrag Jokić have been condemned for war crimes related to the shelling of Dubrovnik. Similarly JNA officials Veselin Šljivančanin and Mile Mrkšić have been condemned to ten and twenty years of prison for the atrocities in Vukovar. There, the JNA collaborated with irregular forces, which massacred injured men, women and elderly people indiscriminately. Such massacres took place with the JNA often turning a blind eye, and many of the trials in the Hague have concerned the activities of paramilitary sections of the Serbian parties. The JNA also created prison camps in Sremska Mitrovica or Stajićevo, where prisoners were abused. The Croatian paramilitary forces and the Croatian army also committed war crimes. The massacres of innocent Serbian civilians in the towns of Gospić, Pakrac, Sisak and Osijek in 1991–2 are now well documented, and perpetrators have been tried in the Hague and in Croatian courts. Renowned officials of the Croatian regular army, heralded as heroes by many supporters of the HDZ, Janko Bobetko, Rahim Ademi and Mirko Norac have been also put to trial for their role in war crimes in 1993. Finally, Ante Gotovina, one of the key figures of Operation Storm was sentenced by the ICTY to twenty four years in prison for the death of at least one hundred and fifty civilians in 1995.

The war in Bosnia was the most atrocious in terms of war crimes and crimes against humanity. Individuals from all sides of the conflict (Serb, Croat, Bosniak) have been put on trial, although a large majority was from the Serbian side. On the Serbian side, Biljana Plavšić, Momčilo Krajišnik, Radoslav Brđanin, Duško Tadić—most of the Bosnian-Serb leaders were indicted and judged guilty for war crimes and crime against humanity. Slobodan Milošević died before he could be tried in relation to the crimes in Bosnia. Radovan Karadžić and Ratko Mladić are currently under trial. Mladić will have to answer to charges of genocide in relation to the massacre of Srebrenica and the siege of Sarajevo. On the Croatian side, Dario

---

[6] This is not an exhaustive list. For more information, please visit the website of the ICTY: http://www.icty.org/.

Kordić and other Croatian leaders has been condemned for war crimes. Members of the ARBiH such as Rasim Delić or Enver Hadzihasanović have been sentenced to short prison terms, while Hazim Delić, the commander of a prison camp who was found guilty of rape and torture is serving an eighteen year term.

With respect to the war in Kosovo, both JNA officials and UÇK fighters have committed war crimes in Kosovo. Slobodan Milošević was only one of the many Yugoslav commanders charged by the ICTY of crimes against humanity, along with, among others, Šainović (Yugoslav Deputy Prime Minister, twenty two years), Ojdanić (Chief of General Staff, fifteen years) and Pavković (Commander of Third Army, twenty two years). On the Albanian side, the court indicted several members of the UÇK, including former Kosovo Prime Minister Ramush Haradinaj. While Haradinaj has been acquitted, other members of UÇK are currently being detained, such as Haradin Bala (thirteen years).

Conclusion

So, to conclude, why did the Yugoslav wars erupt, what are the remote and immediate causes of the conflict? Serious scholarship agrees on the list of possible factors that have led to the tragic decade of 1991–2001: a dysfunctional economic system, a weak institutional system based on ethnic identities, changes in the international balance of power and the role of specific 'ethnic entrepreneurs'. Yet authors disagree as to the weight of these factors. The debate on the blame for the conflict is not settled either. While scholars like James Gow (1997) and James Sadkovich (1998) represent a great number of western scholars who attribute the responsibility mainly to the Serbian side (Milošević, Jović, Karadžić), others such as Susan Woodward (1995) and Warren Zimmerman disagree and emphasise the role of the Slovenian and Croatian governments, and in particular their decision to leave the federation (Ramet 2005: 306). Despite more than two decades of scholarship on the issue, there is still no agreement on responsibility for the war, nor on the importance that each factor carries, nor who is immediately responsible for the conflict.

The reasons for the resolution of the wars, on the other hand, can be more easily traced to the acts of specific actors both involved in the conflict and outside the conflict: the military balance of power between authorities in Croatian, Bosnia, Serbia and Kosovo, the role of the US, the European heads of State and international organisations such as the

UN and NATO. Yet here again, important questions such as the role of Germany and the early recognition of Slovenia and Croatia, the role of countries such as Turkey, Iran and Saudi Arabia, and the importance of diasporic communities in causing and solving the conflict are still open for discussion.

Finally, the debate surrounding the characterisation of the war is still open. Was the war an 'ethnic war'? Not a single scholar agrees with the thesis of the 'ancient hatreds', yet those scholars who want to emphasise the ethnic mobilisation that occurred during the war have decided to use the term. Those who are afraid that this might give credit to the 'ancient hatreds' theory decide to avoid it (Ramet 2005: 308). This chapter should however provide enough material to form your own opinions, and provide enough direction as to how to pursue further research when considering these questions.

Further Reading

Banac, I., 1984, *The national question in Yugoslavia: Origins, history, politics*, Cornell University Press, Ithaca.

Campbell, D., 1998, *National deconstruction: Violence, identity, and justice in Bosnia*, University of Minnesota Press, Minneapolis.

Chandler, D., 2000, *Bosnia: Faking democracy after Dayton*, Pluto Press, London.

Denitch, B.D., 1996, *Ethnic nationalism: The tragic death of Yugoslavia*, University of Minnesota Press, Minneapolis.

Gagnon, V.P., 2004, *The Myth of ethnic war: Serbia and Croatia in the 1990s*, Cornell University Press, Ithaca and London.

Glenny, M., 1996, *The fall of Yugoslavia*, Penguin Group USA, New York.

Gow, J., 1997, *Triumph of the Lack of Will*, C. Hurst & Co. Publishers, London.

Judah, T., 2009, *The Serbs: History, myth and the destruction of Yugoslavia*, Yale University Press, New Haven.

Lampe, J.R., 2000, *Yugoslavia as history: Twice there was a country*, 2nd edn., Cambridge University Press, Cambridge.

MacDonald, D.B., 2002, *Balkan Holocausts? Serbian and Croatian victim centred propaganda and the war in Yugoslavia*, Manchester University Press, Manchester.

Malcolm, N., 2002, *Bosnia: A short history*, Pan, London.

Ramet, S.P., 2002, *Balkan babel: The disintegration of Yugoslavia from the death of Tito to the fall of Milošević*, Westview Press, Boulder.

Silber, L. & Little, A., 1997, *Yugoslavia: Death of a nation*, Penguin Group USA, New York.

Wachtel, A., 1998, *Making a nation, breaking a nation: Literature and cultural politics in Yugoslavia*, Stanford University Press, Stanford.

Woodward, S., 1995, *Balkan tragedy*, Brookings Institution, Washington.

References

Allcock, J.B., 2000, *Explaining Yugoslavia*, Hurst, London.

Banac, I., 1984, *The national question in Yugoslavia: Origins, history, politics*, Cornell University Press, Ithaca.

Bellamy, A.J., 2002, *Kosovo and international society*, Palgrave Macmillan, Basingstoke, UK.

Brunnbauer, U., 2002, 'The implementation of the Ohrid Agreement: Ethnic Macedonian resentments', *Journal on Ethnopolitics and Minority Issues in Europe* 1.

Campbell, D., 1998, *National deconstruction: Violence, identity, and justice in Bosnia*, University of Minnesota Press, Minneapolis.

——, 1999, 'Apartheid cartography: The political anthropology and spatial effects of international diplomacy in Bosnia', *Political Geography* 18, 395–435.

Chandler, D., 2000, *Bosnia: Faking democracy after Dayton*, Pluto Press, London.

Denitch, B.D., 1996, *Ethnic nationalism: The tragic death of Yugoslavia*, University of Minnesota Press, Minneapolis.

Gagnon, V.P., 2004, *The Myth of ethnic war: Serbia and Croatia in the 1990s*, Cornell University Press, Ithaca and London.

Glenny, M., 1996, *The fall of Yugoslavia*, Penguin Group USA, New York.

Gow, J., 1997, *Triumph of the Lack of Will*, C. Hurst & Co. Publishers, London.

Judah, T., 2009, *The Serbs: History, myth and the destruction of Yugoslavia*, Yale University Press, New Haven.

Lampe, J.R., 2000, *Yugoslavia as history: Twice there was a country*, 2nd edn., Cambridge University Press, Cambridge.

MacDonald, D.B., 2002, *Balkan Holocausts? Serbian and Croatian victim centred propaganda and the war in Yugoslavia*, Manchester University Press, Manchester.

Magaš, B., 1993, *The destruction of Yugoslavia: Tracking the break-up 1980–92*, Verso, New York and London.

Malcolm, N., 2002, *Bosnia, a short history*, Pan, London.

Ragazzi, F., 2009, 'The Croatian "diaspora politics" of the 1990s: Nationalism unbound?', in U. Brunnbauer (ed.), *Transnational societies, transterritorial politics: Migrations in the (post-) Yugoslav region, 19th–21st century*, pp. 143–166, Oldenbourg, Verlag.

Rajak, S., 2009, *Yugoslavia and the Soviet Union in the early Cold War*, Routledge, London.

Ramet, S.P., 2002, *Balkan babel: The disintegration of Yugoslavia from the death of Tito to the fall of Milošević*, Westview Press, Boulder.

——, 2005, *Thinking about Yugoslavia: Scholarly debates about the Yugoslav breakup and the wars in Bosnia and Kosovo*, Cambridge University Press, Cambridge.

Sadkovich, J., 1998, *The U.S. Media and Yugoslavia*, Praeger Publishers, USA.

Silber, L. & Little, A., 1997, *Yugoslavia, death of a nation*, Penguin Group USA, New York.

Wachtel, A., 1998, *Making a nation, breaking a nation: Literature and cultural politics in Yugoslavia*, Stanford University Press, Stanford.

Weymouth, T. & Henig, S., 2001, *The Kosovo crisis*, Pearson Education, London.

Woodward, S., 1995, *Balkan tragedy*, Brookings Institution, Washington.

CHAPTER TEN

THE IRAQ WAR

Edmund Frettingham

Introduction

Few recent wars have been as controversial as the US-led invasion of Iraq in 2003. It aroused passionate public dispute around the world about what was happening, why it was happening, and whether it should be happening. Although the causes and ethics of the war remain contentious a decade after the invasion, the basic war-plot can be set out briefly and with less controversy. The Iraq War was a project of the United States (US), for which it sought to enlist international support by making the case that the Iraqi leader Saddam Hussein supported terrorists, had aggressive designs on his neighbours, and was covertly developing weapons of mass destruction (WMDs) in breach of Security Council resolutions. Although some states were receptive to the US case, many others were not persuaded. French and Russian opposition made it impossible for the US to gain explicit authorisation for war from the Security Council, but the US was determined to overthrow Saddam's regime. Coalition forces led by the US invaded on 20 March 2003, reaching Baghdad in less than three weeks but failing to find any evidence of WMDs. The Coalition's efforts to construct a stable Iraqi state were soon undermined by an anti-occupation insurgency and rising levels of sectarian and inter-communal violence. The conflict, which took a heavy toll on Iraqis and US forces, peaked in 2006 before subsiding to levels at which withdrawal could be contemplated. The US ended combat operations in 2010, before finally withdrawing all its forces at the end of 2011.

This chapter narrates the most important events of the war, focusing the discussion on two major questions: how did the Iraq War become possible? And why did the Coalition occupation of Iraq descend into sectarian civil war? The first section examines what lay behind the US decision to remove Saddam Hussein, how the case for war could successfully be made domestically, and why the Bush administration's claims over Iraq received a mixed reception internationally. After describing the brief ground war and the fall of the regime, the chapter moves on to examine the dynamics of the insurgency and the Coalition response against the background of efforts to stabilise and consolidate the Iraqi state. It concludes with a discussion of the costs and long term implications of the war.

1. *The Road to War*

The 2003 Iraq War was, in many respects, the continuation of a crisis initiated by Iraq's invasion of Kuwait thirteen years earlier. The US responded to that attack by assembling a multinational military coalition that ejected Iraqi forces from Kuwait in January 1991 (Freedman & Karsh 1995). Iraq was easily defeated in the end, but had shown itself capable of threatening two major US strategic priorities in the Middle East. Firstly, Saddam threatened the security of Israel and regional stability when he fired missiles at several Israeli cities during the Gulf War. Israel was persuaded to stay out of the war, but the attacks aroused the ire of its powerful domestic supporters in the US who became convinced Israeli security depended on Saddam's removal (Little 2004: 77–116; Mearsheimer & Walt 2007).

Secondly, and even more significantly, Saddam gained a degree of power over Persian Gulf oil that was unacceptable to the US. The Persian Gulf region contains more than half of the world's proven reserves; US control of this oil not only ensures its continuous flow to American industry and world markets but gives the US a hegemonic position in the global economy (Harvey 2003: 18–25; Stokes 2007). Hegemony in the Persian Gulf has therefore been a key US policy objective in the Middle East since the Second World War (Little 2004: 43–76; Klare 2012). The fear that Persian Gulf oil could come under the control of unpredictable or hostile forces was behind a steadily increasing US military presence in the region from the late 1970s onwards, and it seemed borne out by Saddam's invasion of Kuwait. Iraq already controlled ten percent of the world's proven reserves; in occupying Kuwait, Saddam added a further ten percent, and his army also now sat within several hundred miles of another twenty five percent located in Saudi oilfields close to the Kuwaiti border. The power this gave Saddam over oil production and prices allowed him to threaten serious economic disruption and use this power to gain leverage over the US (Ritchie & Rogers 2007: 7–19).

After the Gulf War, the US pursued a policy of containment intended to control Saddam, if not force him from power (Mazaheri 2010). The US stationed troops in Kuwait, established a safe area in the north to protect the Kurdish population, and declared 'no fly zones' patrolled by British and American aircraft in the north and south of the country. The heart of the containment policy was a punitive sanctions regime and a disarmament programme imposed as part of the 1991 ceasefire. The terms of this ceasefire were set out in Security Council Resolution 687, which required Iraq to destroy all of its WMDs along with any missile with a range greater than one hundred and fifty kilometres. Only when Iraq had produced evidence of compliance would the sanctions and oil embargo be lifted.

The containment policy succeeded in eroding Saddam's ability to threaten his neighbours. By the late 1990s, Iraq's WMD programmes had largely been dismantled and economic collapse had forced radical reductions in his conventional forces (Zunes 2005: 23). Yet, the containment policy appeared to be failing. Far from being overthrown after the Gulf War, Saddam had strengthened his hold on power (Tripp 2007: 244–276; Mazaheri 2010). He had succeeded in obstructing the United Nations (UN) inspection process and he was beginning to circumvent the sanctions regime. Critics in the US began to denounce containment as the appeasement of a dangerous dictator who sought to rearm and dominate the Persian Gulf. The most vocal and persistent of these critics were associated with the neoconservative movement, who believed that regimes like that in Iraq could not be controlled through international law or multilateral diplomacy, but must be confronted with unilateral military action (Ehrenberg *et al.* 2010: 1–50; Fukuyama 2006: 12–65; Kagan & Kristol 1996; 2000).

It was not until after the terrorist attacks of 11 September 2001 (9/11) that US policy on Iraq became more confrontational. There was no evidence that Iraq had assisted the hijackers, but some in George W. Bush's new administration, such as Secretary of Defense Donald Rumsfeld and his deputy Paul Wolfowitz, were nevertheless convinced that al Qaida was in league with Saddam, and viewed 9/11 as an opportunity to deal with him. It soon became apparent that the War on Terror, declared by Bush in response to the attacks, would be a military action that made no distinction between terrorists and the states accused of harbouring them. Afghanistan was the first objective, but the administration's rhetoric made clear that this was merely the first phase in a more expansive campaign in which Iraq, named by the State Department as a sponsor of terrorism, was highly likely to be targeted. The intention to include Iraq was signalled even more strongly in January 2002, when Bush described Iraq, Iran and North Korea as an 'axis of evil' united by their willingness to use WMDs and pass them on to terrorists (Ritchie & Rogers 2007: 71–83).

Not everyone in the Bush administration was convinced that military intervention was necessary. Secretary of State Colin Powell favoured a tougher policy of containment aimed at longer term regime change, and Bush supported his efforts in early 2002 to breathe new life into the sanctions regime. Yet Vice President Dick Cheney, Wolfowitz and other administration officials were pushing hard for war, and Bush himself was leaning towards a more aggressive stance on Iraq, even as he supported Powell. A number of factors made regime change seem an attractive option (Callinicos 2005). Replacing Saddam with a friendly regime in Baghdad would remove a persistent opponent of US hegemony in the Middle East and demonstrate the consequences of opposing US power. It would give the US control over the country with the second largest oil reserves in the world, giving it greater leverage over other oil producers and consumers. It would allow withdrawal from Saudi Arabia, whose ruling family now faced growing opposition from domestic Islamists opposed to US military presence in the Kingdom, and remove a potential threat to Israel. Neoconservative elements in the administration hoped that a democratic Iraq with a free market economy would be a catalyst for liberalising change in other Middle Eastern states. And finally, regime change seemed feasible: the rapid defeat of the Taliban in Afghanistan, with few US casualties, had encouraged the belief that a quick and easy victory could be won in Iraq as well.

These reasons can be extrapolated from longer term continuities in US foreign policy in the Middle East, but they did not generally feature in the Bush administration's public justifications of the war. The case they began making during 2002 presented Saddam as a threat to international peace and stability who must be confronted. This was supported with a series of claims: Saddam possessed chemical and biological agents and was close to acquiring a nuclear device; he had taken advantage of the departure of UN weapons inspectors to increase his stockpiles; his refusal to allow weapons inspectors to return proved that he had something to hide; he had used such weapons in the past and was looking for opportunities to use them against the US and its allies; he actively sponsored terrorist groups, including al Qaida, who shared his enmity towards the US and its values; and finally, he aspired to control the Persian Gulf and dominate the Middle East.

Regime change in Iraq was framed as an extension of the War on Terror, necessary for defending the US homeland as well as regional peace in the Middle East. There was no evidence that Saddam had immediate plans to attack the US, but Bush made it clear that the US would act unilaterally and pre-emptively to eliminate a potential threat from Iraq before the danger became imminent. An important lesson of 9/11, he claimed, was that strategies of containment and deterrence were redundant when mass casualties could be inflicted through terrorist-style attacks with little or no warning. The fight against terrorism and rogue states must therefore be waged proactively, eliminating potential threats before they acquired the capability to damage the US and its allies, irrespective of whether they had any specific plans to attack. Saddam must inevitably be confronted, Bush argued, and it was better that this should happen sooner rather than later, before he became even stronger and developed more powerful weapons.

The case against Saddam centred on allegations about secret activities and intentions rather than any recent acts of aggression. For this reason, the Bush administration relied to an unprecedented extent on intelligence in building support for the conflict (Freedman 2004). However, the available intelligence did not support the claims the administration was making about Iraqi capability and intentions. Although the US intelligence agencies agreed that Saddam probably had an active WMD programme and a small stockpile of chemical and biological weapons, many in the intelligence community insisted that there was no reliable evidence indicating an alliance between Iraq and al Qaida, and that cooperation between them was extremely unlikely. Written reports from the intelligence agencies were often highly speculative and hedged with qualifications emphasising the uncertainty in their estimates. This element of doubt frustrated Cheney, Rumsfeld and other senior figures in the Bush administration who wanted intelligence to provide firm evidence of an Iraqi threat. In policy discussions and public speeches, they cherry-picked intelligence supporting the case for war, exaggerated its certainty, and ignored or downplayed evidence contradicting it (Isikoff & Corn 2007: 100–14; Jervis 2010; Ritchie & Rogers 2007: 125–33).

The flawed and distorted use of intelligence was not generally recognised until after the invasion, when it became clear that the Bush administration's major claims had been false. Before the invasion, these claims were readily accepted by leading opinion-formers and the US public. Iraqi defectors and expatriate opposition activists had been lobbying for a policy of regime change since the 1990s, and they stepped up their efforts after 9/11, exaggerating the threat from Saddam and the welcome that US intervention would receive (Vanderbush 2009). There was ample support from the media, most obviously from the battery of neoconservative pundits maintaining the pressure for military action, but also from the mainstream news media who accepted many of the administration's claims with little critical scrutiny (Dobbins 2007: 63). The US public was also very receptive to the Bush administration's claims about Iraq. Bush's rhetoric, which consistently linked Iraq with terrorism and al Qaida, resonated strongly in a nation still traumatised by 9/11 (Gershkoff & Kushner 2005; Jacobson 2010). Congress, whose members were eager to reflect the weight of public opinion and appear patriotic, was equally supportive of the war (Dumbrell 2005: 41–5; Ritchie & Rogers 2007: 114–24).

The strongest international support came from the British government under the leadership of Prime Minister Tony Blair, who made an early commitment to support military action despite facing serious opposition from the general public and from within his own party (Kennedy-Pipe & Vickers 2007; Keohane 2005; Sharp 2012). Few foreign leaders shared Bush and Blair's conviction that military action was necessary (Ehrenberg *et al.* 2010: 116–62). Bilateral diplomacy by Powell and Cheney during the spring and summer of 2002 revealed considerable ambivalence about the prospect of war. Governments in the Middle East would not openly support regime change, in part because their domestic publics were resolutely suspicious of US intentions in the region. The most significant international opposition came from France and Russia, both of which are permanent and veto-wielding members of the Security Council, together with Germany, a traditionally staunch ally of the US. Anti-militarism and opposition to military involvement abroad were still strong in Germany, whose government announced that it would not involve itself in any military action against Iraq, even under a UN mandate (Timmins 2005). France and Russia agreed that Saddam was a problem, but were concerned about damage to their considerable economic interests in Iraq as well as the precedent that would be set by a policy of regime change (Golan 2004; Howorth 2005; White 2005).

International opposition was not an overriding consideration for Bush, who was willing to proceed unilaterally if necessary. The US claimed that this would be justified by the inherent right to self-defence that states enjoy under international law and also because military action was already authorised under the terms of existing UN resolutions (Murphy 2003; Thornberry 2005; Sandholtz 2009). The latter case rested on a series of interrelated arguments: Security Council Resolution 678 (1990) had authorised the use of force to reverse the Iraqi invasion of Kuwait and restore peace and security to the region; Resolution 687 (1991), which ended the Gulf War and imposed disarmament obligations, merely suspended 678 rather than superseding it; and Iraq's persistent breach of 687 nullified the ceasefire established under it, reactivating the authority to use force under 678.

Military action against Iraq would therefore be part of an on-going attempt to enforce existing resolutions. Yet the international legitimacy of military action depended on the US being seen to exhaust all diplomatic options, and would be enhanced further if it was backed by a coalition and explicitly sanctioned by the UN. Bush was accordingly prevailed upon by Powell and Blair to seek a new Security Council resolution authorising the use of force if Iraq should remain in breach of existing resolutions.

Throughout the autumn of 2002, Bush presented the administration's case against Iraq with increasingly confident assessments of the Iraqi threat, while the British government published a dossier containing allegations about Iraq's WMD capabilities. These diplomatic efforts bore fruit on 8 November, when UNSC Resolution 1441 was passed unanimously. It required Iraq to readmit UN inspectors and supply documentary evidence to the Security Council concerning its past and present WMD programmes. The resolution threatened 'serious consequences' if Iraq remained intransigent. Iraq cooperated, allowing unhindered access to suspect sites to inspectors from the International Atomic Energy Agency (IAEA) and the UN, as well as submitting twelve thousand pages of evidence concerning its WMD programmes to the Security Council. Despite this apparent openness, the inspectors delivered a mixed report when they returned to the UN in late January 2003: nothing had been found, but the information Iraq had provided was incomplete (Fawn 2005: 3–4). The US and United Kingdom (UK) seized on these assessments to claim that Iraq was in 'material breach' of Resolution 1441, and there was support for this interpretation from some European states. But opposition among other states hardened as it became apparent that the US was determined to go to war whether or not the inspectors uncovered evidence of Iraqi duplicity. The French and German governments announced that they would support the peaceful disarmament of Iraq through inspections and oppose any resort to force before the inspection efforts were exhausted. Russia was less direct in its resistance, but made it clear that it would not support the use of force without further, explicit authorisation from the UN.

The US denied that any further authorisation was necessary, because a mandate to use force had been in place since Resolution 678 in 1990. Resolution 1441 had given Iraq a final opportunity to comply with the disarmament obligations imposed at the end of the Gulf War; Saddam's refusal to comply was sufficient in itself to void the ceasefire and authorise force. Nothing in Resolution 1441 required another resolution; the 'serious consequences' it threatened included war. Yet Blair needed a second resolution to satisfy domestic critics and Bush agreed to assist him in seeking one, sending Colin Powell to the Security Council on 5 February to set out the US case against Iraq. But the likelihood of a second resolution receded during February, in spite of Powell's efforts and a concerted Anglo-American diplomatic offensive. The inspectors continued their work, finding nothing to verify Powell's claims; France and Germany continued to rally international opposition with a proposal to reinforce the inspection regime; and anti-war protests around the world registered popular disquiet over military action. By mid-March, it had become apparent that the non-permanent members of the Security Council would not support a second resolution, and on 17 March it was withdrawn by the US, who blamed the French threat to veto it. Bush issued an ultimatum to Saddam that evening, before announcing two days later that military operations in Iraq by a US-led coalition had begun.

2. *The Military Campaign*

When the war began on 19 March, Coalition commanders had more than two hundred thousand American and forty thousand British troops at their disposal, a force less than half the size of that which had fought the Gulf War. Rumsfeld believed that the development of precision weapons and high-tech reconnaissance and communications systems had made it possible to replace large armies with smaller, more mobile forces. With his direction, US planners had developed a strategy built around speed and surprise: the ground invasion from Kuwait would not follow a lengthy air campaign, but begin almost simultaneously. British forces would take Basra, while US troops would push rapidly towards Baghdad, bypassing Iraqi forces where possible in order to speed the advance. The capture of Baghdad, Iraq's 'centre of gravity' with its ministries and regime commanders, was expected to force any remaining Iraqi units outside the capital to surrender. Coalition commanders also hoped that victory would be hastened by rebellion in the south, where Saddam's persecution of Iraq's Shi'a majority had been especially harsh, and perhaps even by a coup within the regime itself (Gordon & Trainor 2006: 3–157).

In the end, there was no coup. As British and American forces moved into southern Iraq, they encountered more resistance than expected as nationalist opposition to the invasion among Shi'as outweighed their antipathy towards Saddam. But US forces advancing towards Baghdad proved too powerful for Iraqi conventional forces, and even the armoured formations of the Republican Guard—the best-equipped and most loyal of Saddam's troops—could mount little serious resistance. The chemical and biological weapon attacks never came. The most effective opposition came from the Fida'iyin, a paramilitary force of thirty thousand committed Ba'athists that had stockpiles of weapons hidden in villages and towns all over southern Iraq. Regular troops who did not simply give up and go home often joined up with the Fida'iyin, who dressed in civilian clothes and operated in small units, harrying US forces with hit-and-run tactics, ambushes and roadside bombs. Their weapon caches, together with a decentralised command structure that gave power to numerous local commanders, allowed them to continue the fight even when cut off from Baghdad by the US advance (Dodge 2005: 213).

This advance was extremely swift at the beginning. By the 23 March, the oilfields of the south had been secured and US forces had moved to within one hundred and sixty kilometres of the capital. Fida'iyin resistance in towns bypassed by the main advance continued to tie down US troops and threaten the lengthy supply and communication lines behind the frontline. These problems, together with the onset of bad weather, slowed the advance but did not stop it completely. Baghdad International Airport was captured on 3 April, and US troops were already beginning to move into the capital as Basra fell to British forces three days later. The symbolic end of the regime came on 9 April, when US Marines assisted a group of Iraqis in pulling down a statue of Saddam, who fled Baghdad the next day. Fighting continued elsewhere: Mosul and the major northern oil region of Kirkuk were taken by US troops and forces from the autonomous Kurdish region, before US units fought their way into the last major objective of the campaign on 14 April: Saddam's hometown of Tikrit. On 1 May, Bush declared triumphantly that major combat operations in Iraq were over. This period of the war had cost the lives of twenty two British and one hundred and thirty nine American service personnel and at least seven thousand five hundred Iraqi civilians (Iraq Body Count 2012). There are no reliable figures for Iraqi military deaths, but the figure is likely to exceed seven thousand (DeFronzo 2010: 158–9; Tripp 2007: 275). Despite Bush's confidence, the overthrow of the regime proved to be merely the conventional phase of the war. Iraq was by no means stable, and within a few months the US was faced with a serious and widespread insurgency, made worse by a disastrous mishandling of the security and reconstruction efforts.

3. *Occupation and Insurgency*

The Bush administration initially hoped to avoid an extended stay in Iraq. The intention was to remove Saddam and his leadership group while preserving the institutions of the Iraqi state. Coalition forces would withdraw within months, with power being handed to a new Iraqi government under US influence. If a transition to democracy could be encouraged, so much the better, but the priority was the swift installation of an effective and authoritative government sympathetic to US interests: internal and regional stability, a stable flow of oil, and a capitalist restructuring of the Iraqi economy (Tripp 2004).

After the fall of Baghdad, it soon became apparent that the withdrawal from Iraq would be much more difficult than the optimists in Washington had expected. Firstly, institutions of the Iraqi state were on the brink of collapse. They had been severely dilapidated even before the war, having been neglected during the general economic collapse under the sanctions regime (Dodge 2005: 211–212). The state then lost control of almost all its remaining human and material resources during three weeks of uncontrolled looting that followed the fall of Baghdad. The looters targeted government ministries, police stations and even military sites, stripping them of anything that could be reused or sold. Numerous army and Fida'iyin arms dumps discovered by US forces during the conflict had been left unprotected; their contents were now stolen, and arms became available at very low prices. Criminal gangs were looting for material gain, but others sought political authority: militias seized government buildings and fought each other for the control of Iraqi towns and suburbs. The state lost its monopoly on violence to numerous sub-state criminal, political and tribal groups, many of which had more support and legitimacy among local people than the central government (Dodge 2007; Herring & Rangwala 2006: 48–55).

The second problem was a lack of suitable Iraqi leaders. The US had intended to install a group of Iraqi exiles at the head of a post-invasion government; they would draft a constitution and oversee democratic elections for a new government in a sovereign Iraq. It soon became apparent that the exiles had overstated the extent of their influence inside Iraq, and were too divided amongst themselves to form a coherent administration. They had little support among the Iraqi people, many of whom were glad Saddam had been removed but deeply suspicious of US influence and intentions. With the exception of the Kurds in the north, a majority of Iraqis regarded Coalition forces as occupiers and opposed their continuing presence, with many also expressing support for attacks on US forces (Herring & Rangwala 2006: 201–2). Within weeks of the invasion, Iraqi hostility to the US presence was voiced, organised and exploited by indigenous political movements—often linked to armed militias—that commanded high levels of support. In this context, early elections risked national power falling into the hands of leaders such as Shi'a cleric Muqtada al-Sadr, who would be difficult to co-opt and was actively hostile to US priorities in Iraq.

In response to these problems, US policy shifted away from early withdrawal towards a more active state-building project, involving a much longer US presence in Iraq. The handover of power was delayed and the Coalition Provisional Authority (CPA) was established to govern directly, reconstructing Iraq while bolstering the position of leaders amenable to US interests and preventing the emergence of potential challengers to Coalition authority (Herring & Rangwala 2006: 12–18). Internationally, there was concern that the Coalition's intentions violated the international law of occupation, which allowed occupying powers to preserve but not transform the institutions of the occupied state, but the US and UK secured a Security Council resolution (1483) sanctioning it (Sandholtz 2009: 229–33; Yordan 2007). Domestically, the decision to postpone elections and rule Iraq directly served to reinforce the suspicion that the US was more interested in controlling Iraq than liberating it.

Further resentment was generated by CPA's state-building strategy. The establishment of the CPA had provided an opportunity for the neoconservatives within the Bush administration who favoured a far more radical reorganisation of the Iraqi state. They wanted to break the power of the security services and significantly reduce the role of the state in society and the economy, transforming Iraq into a liberal, capitalist and democratic state that would be a model for the region (Dodge 2010: 1278; Tripp 2004). Paul Bremer, the neoconservative career diplomat appointed to lead the CPA, began with two policies that were intended to signify a break with the past and prevent members of the old regime from disrupting the state-building project, but alienated large sections of the Iraqi population. The first was a programme of 'de-Ba'athification', in which all Ba'ath party members above a certain rank were banned from holding any position in government service. The second policy was the disbanding of the Iraqi army and the security services of the old regime. These two edicts made around 300,000 soldiers unemployed and discarded 30,000 of the government's most experienced senior staff, generating deep resentment that would fuel the insurgency (Tripp 2007: 282).

The legitimacy of the occupation was further undermined by the chronic lack of security in Iraq. US troops had been unprepared to take responsibility for law and order when they arrived; having expected that Iraqis would take care of their own affairs once they were liberated, they did nothing to stop the looting in April. Disbanding the police and army undermined the CPA's ability to impose order, for it would be months before a replacement police force was installed and several years before a new Iraqi army could be recruited and trained (Gordon & Trainor 2006: 534–5; 553–7). Having invaded with a small force, the Coalition now lacked sufficient troops to fill the security vacuum (Herring & Rangwala 2006: 52). In the summer of 2003, it was unable to seal borders, guard military sites and arms caches, or prevent the takeover of Iraqi towns by the militias, let alone tackle the surge in criminal violence after the invasion.

The perception that the Coalition was unwilling or unable to impose order encouraged a growing insurgency aimed at undermining its state-building efforts (Dodge 2005: 214–8; Hashim 2009; Herring & Rangwala 2006: 164–72). Armed opposition to the occupation began to grow from May 2003; it was supported especially strongly by Sunni Arabs and was most intense in the central provinces of Iraq where the majority of this group lived. The insurgency was not a single movement, but involved as many as eleven major organisations with diverse motives, tactics and ideologies and no unified national leadership or agenda (DeFronzo 2010: 212). Some were Ba'ath party loyalists, remnants of the Fida'iyin and Saddam's security services, and people who had benefited from his patronage networks. Others were motivated by an ideology that fused Iraqi nationalism with Sunni and Shi'a versions of Islam, framing opposition to the foreign and Christian presence as a patriotic and Islamic duty. A third type was the Salafists: less nationalist but more radical in their Islamism, they rejected democracy and sought universal application of shari'a law in the state. A large majority of insurgents were Iraqi, but a small proportion (between four and ten percent) were foreign Islamist fighters drawn to Iraq by the opportunity to fight US forces. Some of these belonged to groups that affiliated themselves with al Qaida to form al Qaida in Mesopotamia (AQM) (Hashim 2009: 13–24; Herring and Rangwala 2006: 166–8).

Resistance was spontaneous and localised at first, involving hit-and-run attacks directed at US forces, primarily in Sunni areas such as Tikrit and Fallujah. But within a few months the insurgency had spread and the insurgents' tactics and organisational networks were becoming more sophisticated. They operated in small groups, making effective use of guerrilla tactics, roadside improvised explosive devices (IEDs), car bombs and attacks with machine guns, mortars and rocket-propelled grenades. US convoys were vulnerable to ambush from the outset, but as insurgents became better armed and trained they mounted increasingly complex attacks against US bases and government buildings. From September 2003, insurgents began targeting those supporting the occupation as well. Foreign workers and their private security guards became targets, as did Iraqis who worked for the CPA and the Iraqi state. The UN, the Red Cross and foreign embassies were also attacked to deter international and multi-lateral assistance (Hashim 2009: 43–51).

The insurgency was exacerbated by the US' response, which initially involved killing rather than isolating the insurgents, and coercing the Iraqi population into compliance instead of protecting them and building support for the Coalition authorities. The US attacked insurgent strongholds to kill or capture fighters and deny them secure areas from which they could organise and plan attacks, while taking as few risks as possible to keep US casualties low. The result was often large numbers of civilian casualties but few long term gains against the insurgents. Fallujah was largely destroyed in an assault by US marines in 2004, but it soon reverted to control by nationalist and Islamist militias because the US did not have sufficient troops to maintain control. This pattern was repeated in similar and equally ineffective operations throughout 2005 and 2006: coalition forces would make short term gains in one place only to see insurgent activity rise in others, while popular resentment about the ongoing violence was directed at the US (Herring & Rangwala 2006: 179–85).

By this time, mounting US casualties and Iraqi demands for greater participation in government had forced the Coalition to rethink its state-building effort. In the autumn of 2003, it decided to bring forward the handover of power. Iraqi sovereignty was restored in June 2004 when an appointed transitional government took over from the CPA; this appointed government then organised elections in 2005 for a new constitution and national assembly. Even after sovereignty had passed to the Iraqi government, the Coalition retained responsibility for security because Iraqi forces were still incapable of providing it on their own. In joint operations with US forces they were highly unreliable, often failing to turn up, remaining neutral or even fighting with the insurgents. It also proved difficult to spread the burden among international allies. The Bush administration's unilateral foreign policy had alienated allies who might otherwise have contributed troops to assist with post-war stabilisation efforts. The few troops that were sent by coalition partners other than Britain were ill-equipped for the role, or else bound by restrictive rules of engagement that prevented their involvement in offensive action against the insurgents. The US was forced to commit steadily increasing numbers of troops throughout 2004 and 2005 and co-opt Shi'a militia as 'irregular brigades'—a tacit acceptance that they could not be disarmed (Herring & Rangwala 2006: 195–201).

These alliances proved counterproductive when the paramilitary forces pursued a sectarian agenda or were accused of human rights abuses. The image of the Coalition was further tarnished by evidence that the US was unwilling to investigate human rights abuses by its own personnel. Coercive interrogation techniques, secret detention, rendition to countries practicing torture, and systematic mistreatment of prisoners were all documented in US-run prisons—most notoriously at the Abu Ghraib detention centre near Baghdad. Yet it was difficult for Iraqis to gain redress for injuries suffered at the hands of Coalition forces and private security contractors, of whom there were large numbers in Iraq, because both groups were declared immune from prosecution under Iraqi law and subject only to the domestic law of their own country. These practices reinforced the impression that the Coalition had little interest in obedience to the rule of law (Ehrenberg *et al.* 2010: 403–55; Herring & Rangwala 2006: 186–203).

The CPA's efforts to prosecute those accused of war crimes, genocide and crimes against humanity under Ba'athist rule were also flawed. Saddam Hussein was captured in December 2003, joining nearly forty other senior figures from his regime in Coalition custody. To try them, the CPA created the Iraqi High Tribunal in Baghdad. The court was modelled on existing UN war crimes tribunals and assisted by international experts, but with Iraqi leadership and significant elements of Iraqi legal procedure and tradition. Internationally, the court was dismissed by many countries and NGOs as an attempt to legitimise an invasion they considered unlawful. This limited the international assistance it received, while its creation by the CPA harmed its domestic legitimacy. The proceedings were affected by the security situation in Iraq; witness protection efforts often hindered adequate preparation by the defence lawyers, three of whom were murdered. Saddam was convicted in November 2006 and sentenced to death for his role in a massacre of Shi'a villagers in 1982. His conviction made little contribution to peace and reconciliation in Iraq in the short term: many Iraqis doubted that he had received a fair trial, a perception that was reinforced when Saddam's execution by Shi'a militiamen in December resembled a sectarian revenge-lynching (Scharf 2007; Sissons 2006).

The shambolic enactment of Saddam's death sentence reflected and fuelled a violent fragmentation of the state along sectarian lines that had begun in late 2003 (Herring & Rangwala 2006: 147–59). The Sunni minority feared the consequences of a Shi'a dominated state and resented their marginalisation under the CPA, which viewed them as tainted by connection with the old regime. Sunni extremists, often linked to AQM, began to bomb Shi'a neighbourhoods and mosques, provoking reprisals by Shi'a militia. A vicious circle of atrocities hastened the militarisation of Iraqi society as neighbourhoods organised armed vigilante groups to protect themselves (Hashim 2009: 55–9; Tripp 2007: 287–8). Sectarian violence steadily increased through 2004 and 2005, reaching a peak in February 2006 when insurgents destroyed the al-Askariyya mosque—one of Shi'a Islam's most important shrines. Sunni mosques throughout the country were attacked in retaliation by Shi'a militia groups: the fighting grew so intense in Baghdad that twelve thousand US and Iraqi troops had to be deployed (Hughes 2010: 167).

The sectarian conflict threatened to derail state-building efforts in Iraq and contributed to discontent over the war in the United States. The violence in Iraq did not begin to subside until 2007. The reduction came about through an alliance between US forces and Sunni groups formerly involved in the insurgency (Hashim 2009: 58–65; Karsh & Wilbank 2010; Sky 2011). A number of factors contributed to this alliance. Firstly, Sunnis involved in the nationalist insurgency had come to the conclusion by late 2006 that the Iranians and the Shi'a-led government in Baghdad were a greater threat to their interests than the US, who would leave eventually. Secondly, the decision to 'surge' troops into Iraq in early 2007 convinced the Sunnis that the US could not be defeated militarily. Finally, there was also a growing split within the Sunni insurgency between the mainstream nationalist groups and those affiliated with al Qaida. AQM had become deeply unpopular with other Sunni groups on account of their extreme violence and interference with traditional power structures and sources of revenue. When Sunni tribal sheikhs in Anbar and Ba'athists in Baghdad and other provinces began organising militias to suppress AQM in 2007, they accepted arms and money from the US, calculating that it would help them to bolster their own position relative to the Shi'a community as well as deal with al Qaida. As AQM was responsible for most of the sectarian attacks on the Shi'a community, its suppression reduced the sectarian violence and prompted Shi'a action against their own militia, whose primary justification had been protecting the community from Sunni violence (Sky 2011: 119–20).

The competition between communities for power and resources that underpinned the sectarian tension had not been addressed. Nevertheless, the reduction in bombings and shootings made it possible to discuss US withdrawal. In 2008, the US agreed with the Iraqi government that it would withdraw from Iraqi cities by June 2009, and from the country completely by the end of 2011. This agreement also placed US soldiers accused of serious crimes under Iraqi jurisdiction, signalling a willingness to operate under the rule of law. President Barack Obama announced the end of combat operations in Iraq on 31 August 2010, marking the end of Operation Iraqi Freedom and the handover of security responsibilities to the Iraqi government, although fifty thousand troops remained in the country to train and support the Iraqi military. When the last of these troops left on 31 December 2011, the US military presence in Iraq finally ended.

Conclusion

The US mission in Iraq succeeded in removing a hostile regime that threatened Israeli and US access to Persian Gulf oil, giving it a new ally in a region increasingly suspicious of US influence. Yet in other respects the US failed in its objectives. Iraq is outwardly more calm than at the height of the sectarian conflict in 2006, but the country is far from stable (Parker 2012). Criminal and political violence remain high, tensions between religious and ethnic groups persist, democratic institutions are fragile, and it now ranks among the world's worst places to do business (World Bank 2012). Neither did the war appreciably increase US security. There were no WMDs to be found, regime documents recovered after the invasion indicated that almost all had been destroyed soon after the Gulf War. Iraq was framed as an important front in the War on Terror, but it has been a factor in the radicalisation of Muslims and provided would-be jihadists with an arena in which to attack US forces.

Any gains that were made have come at a considerable cost to the people of Iraq as well as the US and its allies. Even the most conservative estimates suggest that around thirty thousand Iraqi soldiers and insurgents were killed during the US presence, with more than one hundred and ten thousand civilian deaths from violence (Iraq Body Count 2012). More than two million people were displaced and two decades of sanctions and war have had a serious impact on health, sanitation, and education systems (DeFronzo 2010: 256; Parker 2012). The cost to the US and its allies was relatively slight in comparison, but it still exceeded the optimistic expectations of those who pushed for war. By the end of August 2010, four thousand four hundred and forty nine US military personnel had been killed in Iraq, while British forces had lost one hundred and seventy-nine (United States Department of Defense 2012; Ministry of Defence 2012). Many more were wounded. The US had expected that invasion and reconstruction would largely pay for itself with Iraqi oil revenues. By March 2008, however, 500 billion US dollars had been spent directly on the invasion and occupation—more than ten times the original estimate (DeFronzo 2010: 256).

It is the less tangible effects of the conflict that are likely to prove most costly over the long term. With the invasion, the US demonstrated its willingness to act unilaterally, without UN consent and in defiance of international opinion; during the occupation, it showed a preference for US control over indigenous democracy, a reluctance to prioritise civilian protection, and a readiness to suspend basic rights in pursuit of security. These attitudes have damaged the US' standing in the world and will undermine any future claims it may make to moral leadership on international issues. It remains to be seen whether others will follow the precedent the US has set.

Further Reading

Danchev, A., & MacMillan, J. (eds), 2005, *The Iraq war and democratic politics*, Routledge, Abdington.

DeFronzo, J., 2010, *The Iraq war: Origins and consequences*, Westview Press, Boulder, CO.

Ehrenberg, J., *et al.* (eds), 2010, *The Iraq papers*, Oxford University Press, Oxford.

Fawn, R., & Hinnebusch, R. (eds), 2005, *The Iraq war: Causes and consequences*, Lynne Rienner, London.

Gordon, M., & Trainor, B., 2006, *Cobra II: The inside story of the invasion and occupation of Iraq*, Atlantic Books, London.

Hashim, A.S., 2009, *Iraq's Sunni insurgency*, International Institute for Strategic Studies, London.

Herring, E. & Rangwala, G., 2006, *Iraq in fragments: The occupation and its legacy*, Hurst & Company, London.

Hughes, G., 2010, 'The insurgencies in Iraq, 2003–2009: Origins, developments and prospects', *Defence Studies* 10(1), 152–76.

Little, D., 2004, *American orientalism: The United States and the Middle East since 1945*, The University of North Carolina Press, Chapel Hill.

Ritchie, N., & Rogers, P., 2007, *The political road to war with Iraq: Bush, 9/11 and the drive to overthrow Saddam*, Routledge, Abingdon.

Tripp, C., 2007, *A history of Iraq*, 3rd edn., Cambridge University Press, Cambridge.

References

Callinicos, A., 2005, 'Iraq: Fulcrum of world politics', *Third World Quarterly* 26(4), 593–608.

DeFronzo, J., 2010, *The Iraq war: Origins and consequences*, Westview Press, Boulder, CO.

Dobbins, J., 2007, 'Who lost Iraq? Lessons from the debacle', *Foreign Affairs* 86(5), 61–74.

Dodge, T., 2005, 'War and resistance in Iraq: From regime change to collapsed state', in R. Fawn & R. Hinnebusch (eds), *The Iraq war: Causes and consequences*, pp. 211–24, Lynne Rienner, London.

Dodge, T., 2007, 'The causes of US failure in Iraq', *Survival* 49(1), 85–106.

———, 2010, 'The ideological roots of failure: The application of kinetic neo-liberalism to Iraq', *International Affairs* 86(6), 1269–86.

Dumbrell, J., 2005, 'Bush's war: The Iraq conflict and American democracy', in A. Danchev & J. Macmillan (eds), *The Iraq war and democratic politics*, pp. 35–46, Routledge, Abingdon.

Ehrenberg, J., *et al.* (eds), 2010, *The Iraq papers*, Oxford University Press, Oxford.

Fawn, R., 2005, 'The Iraq war: Unfolding and unfinished', in R. Fawn & R. Hinnebusch (eds), *The Iraq war: Causes and consequences*, pp. 1–18, Lynne Rienner, London.

Freedman, L., 2004, 'War in Iraq: Selling the threat', *Survival* 46(2), 7–50.

Freedman, L. & Karsh, E., 1995, *The Gulf conflict, 1990–1991: Diplomacy and war in the New World Order*, Princeton University Press, Princeton, NJ.

Fukuyama, F., 2006, *America at the crossroads: Democracy, power, and the neoconservative legacy*, Yale University Press, New Haven.

Gershkoff, A. & Kushner, S., 2005, 'Shaping public opinion: The 9/11-Iraq connection in the Bush administration's rhetoric', *Perspectives on Politics* 3(3), 525–37.

Golan, G., 2004, 'Russia and the Iraq war: was Putin's policy a failure?', *Communist and Post-Communist Studies* 37, 429–59.

Gordon, M. & Trainor, B., 2006, *Cobra II: The inside story of the invasion and occupation of Iraq*, Atlantic Books, London.

Harvey, D., 2003, *The new imperialism*, Oxford University Press, Oxford.

Hashim, A.S., 2009, *Iraq's Sunni insurgency*, International Institute for Strategic Studies, London.

Herring, E. & Rangwala, G., 2006, *Iraq in fragments: The occupation and its legacy*, Hurst & Company, London.

Howorth, J., 2005, 'France: Defender of international legitimacy', in R. Fawn & R. Hinnebusch (eds.), *The Iraq war: Causes and consequences*, pp. 49–59, Lynne Rienner, London.

Hughes, G., 2010, 'The insurgencies in Iraq, 2003–2009: Origins, developments and prospects', *Defence Studies* 10(1), 152–76.

Iraq Body Count, 2012, Documented civilian deaths from violence, viewed 10 June 2012, from http://www.iraqbodycount.org/database/.

Isikoff, M. & Corn, D., 2007, *Hubris: The inside story of spin, scandal and the selling of the Iraq war*, Random House, New York.

Jacobson, G.C., 2010, 'A tale of two wars: public opinion on the U.S. military interventions in Afghanistan and Iraq', *Presidential Studies Quarterly* 40(4), 585–610.

Jervis, R., 2010, *Why intelligence fails: lessons from the Iranian revolution and the Iraq war*, Cornell University Press, Ithaca.

Kagan, R. & Kristol, W., 1996, 'Toward a neo-Reaganite foreign policy', *Foreign Affairs* 75(4), 18–32.

—— (eds), 2000, *Present dangers: Crisis and opportunity in American foreign and defence policy*, Encounter, San Francisco.

Karsh, E. & Wilbank, M., 2010, 'How the "sons of Iraq" stabilised Iraq', *Middle East Quarterly* 17(4), 57–70.

Kennedy-Pipe, C. & Vickers, R., 2007, 'Blowback' for Britain?: Blair, Bush and the war in Iraq, *Review of International Studies* 33, 205–21.

Keohane, D., 2005, 'The United Kingdom', in A. Danchev & J. Macmillan (eds), *The Iraq war and democratic politics*, pp. 59–78, Routledge, Abingdon.

Klare, M.T., 2012, 'Blood for oil, in Iraq and elsewhere', in J.K. Cramer & T.A. Thrall (eds), *Why did the United States invade Iraq?*, pp. 129–44, Routledge, Abingdon.

Little, D., 2004, *American orientalism: The United States and the Middle East since 1945*, University of North Carolina Press, Chapel Hill.

Mazaheri, N., 2010, 'Iraq and the domestic political effects of economic sanctions', *The Middle East Journal* 64(2), 253–68.

Mearsheimer, J.J. & Walt, S.M., 2007, *The Israel lobby and US foreign policy*, Farrar, Strauss and Giroux, New York.

Ministry of Defence, 2012, Operations in Iraq: British fatalities, viewed 20 September 2012, from http://www.mod.uk/DefenceInternet/FactSheets/OperationsFactsheets/Operations InIraqBritishFatalities.htm.

Murphy, S., 2003, 'Use of military force to disarm Iraq', *The American Journal of International Law* 97(2), 419–32.

Parker, N., 2012, 'The Iraq we left behind: welcome to the world's next failed state', *Foreign Affairs* 91(2), 94–110.

Ritchie, N. & Rogers, P., 2007, *The political road to war with Iraq: Bush, 9/11 and the drive to overthrow Saddam*, Routledge, Abingdon.

Sandholtz, W., 2009, 'The Iraq war and international law', in D. Armstrong (ed.), *The Routledge handbook of international law*, pp. 222–38, Routledge, Abingdon.

Scharf, M.P., 2007, 'The Iraqi high tribunal: A viable experiment in international justice', *Journal of International Criminal Justice* 5(2), 258–63.

Sharp, J.M.O., 2012, 'Tony Blair nurtures the special relationship', in J.K. Cramer & T.A. Thrall (eds), *Why did the United States invade Iraq?*, pp. 167–200, Routledge, Abingdon.

Sissons, M., 2006, 'And now from the green zone ... reflections on the Iraq tribunal's Dujail trial', *Ethics and International Affairs* 20(4), 505–15.

Sky, E., 2011, 'Iraq: From surge to sovereignty', *Foreign Affairs* 90(2), 117–27.

Stokes, D., 2007, 'Blood for oil? Global capital, counter-insurgency and the dual logic of American energy security', *Review of International Studies* 33, 245–64.

Thornberry, P., 2005, 'The legal case for invading Iraq', in A. Danchev & J. MacMillian (eds), *The Iraq war and democratic politics*, pp. 115–33, Routledge, Abingdon.

Timmins, G., 2005, 'Germany: Solidarity without adventures', in R. Fawn & R. Hinnebusch, *The Iraq war: Causes and consequences*, pp. 61–70, Lynne Rienner, London.

Tripp, C., 2004, 'The United States and state-building in Iraq', *Review of International Studies* 30, 545–58.

——, 2007, *A History of Iraq*, 3rd edn., Cambridge University Press, Cambridge.

United States Department of Defense, 2012, Operation Iraqi Freedom (OIF) US casualty status, viewed 20 September 2012, from http://www.defense.gov/news/casualty.pdf.

Vanderbush, W., 2009, 'Exiles and the marketing of US policy toward Cuba and Iraq', *Foreign Policy Analysis* 5, 287–306.

White, S., 2005, 'Russia: Diminished power', in R. Fawn & R. Hinnebusch (eds), *The Iraq war: Causes and consequences*, pp. 71–81, Lynne Rienner, London.

World Bank, 2012, 'Ease of doing business in Iraq', viewed on 20 September 2012, from http://www.doingbusiness.org/data/exploreeconomies/iraq/.

Yordan, C.L., 2007, 'Why Did the UN Security Council support the Anglo-American proj-ect to transform postwar Iraq? The evolution of international law in the shadow of the American hegemon', *Journal of International Law and International Relations* 3(1), 65–94.

Zunes, S., 2005, 'The United States: belligerent hegemon', in R. Fawn & R. Hinnevbusch (eds), *The Iraq War: Causes and consequences*, pp. 21–36, Lynne Rinner, London.

CHAPTER ELEVEN

THE PACIFIC WAR

Maja Vodopivec[1]

Introduction

The inclusion of a chapter on 'The Pacific War' in a textbook on the global challenges and peace might give the reader a certain feeling of being 'out of place'. The word 'global' is associated with the age in which we live today, and the Pacific War is the only case study among six selected in this book that is not, relatively speaking, a contemporary issue. The case, of course, is not included simply to cover the area of East Asia as 'equally' as other regions. And it does not mean that it would not be possible to historicise some contemporary conflicts through the trajectory of events from World War II or even before it. Nevertheless, reasons for including this case are much more complex in the age of global economic and political hegemonies to which we are witness today.

The Pacific War (Taiheiyō sensō) is a term used for the war fought in East Asia, and signifies only fighting between the United States (US) and Japan that started after the Japanese Imperial Army attacked Pearl Harbor in December 1941. The US occupation forces deployed the term in 1945 in order to replace 'the Greater East Asian War' (Daitōa sensō)—a term that the Japanese government used to emphasise its 'liberating mission' in Asia, and the final goal of the war—the creation of the Co-Prosperity Sphere. However, by December 1941 the conflict in East Asia had already lasted for a decade. It had started with the Japanese occupation of Manchuria and the formation of its puppet government, Manchukuo, in September 1931 and was transformed to a total war with the Marco Polo Bridge Incident and the start of the full-scale Japanese invasion of China in 1937, known as The Second Sino-Japanese War. In this context, names such as 'The Asia Pacific War' (used in the late 1980s) or 'The Fifteen-Year War' (Jūgonen sensō, a term used first by philosopher Tsurumi Shunsuke in the 1950s)

[1] This chapter has been written during postdoctoral research at Leiden University, supported by the 'Japan Society for the Promotion of Science (JSPS) Institutional Program for Young Researcher Overseas Visit'.

are considered to emphasise better that Japan was not only involved in the war with the US, but with China, Korea, Southeast Asia, the Pacific Islands and other places in Asia and the Pacific. Both terms suggest more sensitivity to the issue of the war, and assign more responsibility to Imperial Japan that postwar Japan has never properly addressed, all being a result of specific domestic and international circumstances under the US occupation policy (1945–52), as well as the later course of events.

The unresolved issues from the Asia Pacific War such as war responsibility, war reparations, individual compensation and 'the problem of the recognition of history' (*sensō ninshiki mondai*) burst to the surface in the 1990s when right-wing tendencies to revise history in Japan became amplified. This was concurrent with requests on the side of the progressive intellectuals to redress the victims, most famously those of the sexual slavery practice of the Japanese military in the occupied regions, popularly labelled the 'comfort women' issue, but there were many other war-related issues that were raised as well.

The chapter's main concerns are to reveal the circumstances in which Japan failed to recognise its colonial and war responsibility in regard to its Asian neighbours. In the official war narrative in which both sides—the US and Japan—emphasised the war as their mutual conflict, Japan's colonial past in Asia was mostly concealed. While Japan's defeat was mostly understood as a defeat by the US and has been inextricable from Japan's postwar pacifism, Japan's colonial past has been rapidly forgotten. This fact is considered to be crucial in creating a certain space for the continuity of the prewar and war state with the present state (Dower 1979; Igarashi 2000: 13; Katō 2000: 94). In this context, the chapter will discuss issues of Hiroshima's peace politics and debates on Japan's pacifist constitution, particularly Article 9, which is becoming more and more controversial in an increasingly 'globalised world' in which concepts of the nation-state's sovereignty are losing their meaning in light of the contested human security agenda and 'responsibility to protect' discourse.

Therefore, the main question in the chapter is how did post-war Japan's oblivion of its inconvenient past in Asia happen, and what were the circumstances that caused this 'nearly total amnesia of empire?' (Katō 2000: 5).

1. Setting the Stage

Since Tokugawa Japan opened its doors to the outside world under the pressure of Commodore Perry's 'black ships' in 1853, Japan realised that the most burning issue for the country was whether or not to modernise in order to defend itself from the imperialist tendencies of the great powers in a time which had already brought China into a semi-colonised status. The Dutch trading port's chief in his letter from 1844 to Shōgun (military commander) quoted the Opium War (1840–42) as a warning for Japan, and recommended the opening of the country to trade with foreign powers (Katō & Maruyama 1991). The Tokugawa Shogunate was overthrown, the institution of the Emperor was restored and in 1868 the Meiji era of Japan's history started, famous for including one of the quickest modernisations in the world. A tremendous amount of books were translated into Japanese, new technologies were imported and numerous Japanese missions and students were sent abroad to improve its negotiation position in unequal treaties and to collect information from all fields of human development. From this period, there is a telling slogan of the Meiji government; 'Fukoku kyōhei' ('rich country, strong military').

The result of this effort came very quickly—in the First Sino-Japanese War (1894–5), modern Japanese steam ships defeated the Chinese navy, and the Japanese, for the first time in their more than one thousand year long history of exchange with China, felt that they were superior. By the Treaty of Shimonoseki, Japan acquired its first colonies: Taiwan, Pescadores/Penghu islands and Liaodong peninsula, along with a huge indemnity (as large as five times the Japanese annual GDP) and the right to control Korea. The second war won by the Imperial Japanese Army after 'opening its doors' was the Russo-Japanese War (1904–5) in which the Japanese military was backed up by the British with whom they had already made an alliance (The First Anglo-Japanese Alliance) two years earlier in 1902. The alliance after its two renewals officially ended in 1923. The Russian defeat was the first case in history that a European power was defeated by an Asian nation.

The war with Russia acquired for Japan the southern part of Sakhalin and the strategically important twenty five year long lease for use of The Port Arthur (Liaodong Peninsula), as well as the removal of Russian troops from Manchuria. Russians had settled there during the Boxer Rebellion when the Eight Nations Alliance, including Russia and Japan, sent their troops to help to liberate foreign diplomats kept under siege for fifty five days by the Boxers and Imperial Army of China. Japan had free range to exploit Manchurian and Korean raw materials. In 1905 under pressure and intimidation, The Protectorate Treaty was signed with Korea, and in 1910 Japan annexed Korea. The Western powers were not in favour of this act—nevertheless, they chose not to react because of their own colonial preoccupations. The US, too, did not react in exchange for Japan's non-interference in the Philippines. This is due to the fact that many Western powers were becoming increasingly involved in their own conflicts that would soon escalate into World War I.

Japan declared war on Germany in 1914 upon the request of the British government. In a short time, Japan occupied Shandong province and Tsingtao, territories leased to Germany. It also seized the German island colonies in the Pacific—Mariana, Caroline and Marshall islands.

According to the Versailles Treaty in 1919, Japan was awarded Chinese territories controlled by Germany prior to the war. China expected to get them back in return for its fight on the side of the Allied powers, and the disappointment stemming from this loss triggered the May Fourth Movement and strong anti-Japanese sentiment that persists to the present day.

Internationally, there was no doubt that Japan, with its industrial and military power, was equal to other great powers. On the international scene, it acquired a permanent seat in the Council of the League of Nations, while inside the country it had a short period of liberal democracy called 'The Taisho' democracy under the reign of the emperor Taisho (1912–1926).[2] That period did not last long and was not without controversies. The impact of the October Revolution in Russia on the workers movements was huge in Japan. Japanese workers organised politically around the Socialist and Communist parties that were seen as a threat to the government and ruling elites. Anti-Japanese sentiment in China and Korea was growing because of oppressive Japanese measures that treated conquered nations as inferior races to the Japanese 'kokutai' or 'national polity'. The Japanese race was believed to be unique and superior by its national characteristic symbolised primarily in the figure of the Emperor.[3]

The Great Kanto Earthquake of 1923 destroyed the whole of Tokyo, and it remained infamous because of the subsequent atrocities against Korean immigrants and socialists, who were accused of arson and poisoning the wells. As a consequence of these social changes and racial discrimination,

---

[2] The Japanese era name is based on the reign of current emperor. The longest and the most contested was the Showa era (1925–1989). The occupation forces abolished use of eras named by emperors' reign in official documents. In 1979 the Diet legalized the custom of 'gengō hōseika' again. According to some, it was a reversion to the emperor-centred nationalism of the past times.

[3] For Japanese colonial policy in its first formal colony, Taiwan, see Ching 2001.

The Peace Preservation Law was enacted in Japan in 1925 in order to legally purge the growing left wing in Japan. Additionally, it was a sort of counter-law to oppose the US Immigration Act of 1917 that discriminated against Asian immigrants in the US. Special attention was given to development of police methods to 'convince' the arrested leftists to change their beliefs and publicly announce their ideological conversion (tenkō). The Taisho era, as well as the liberal social climate ended in 1926. Hirohito, the Showa emperor, came to the throne and stayed there until his death in 1989. This was the longest era in Japan's history and it remains the most contested one.

At the end of the 1920s, Japan together with the rest of industrialised world, was heavily affected by the Great Depression and found its coping mechanism in political totalitarianism, ultra-nationalism and industrialisation which rapidly transformed into militarisation. In 1931 the Japanese army fabricated an attack on Japanese posts close to the railway in Manchuria. The army used it as an excuse to invade Manchuria and establish its puppet government Manchukuo under its hand-picked ruler, Pu-yi, the last Qing emperor. In 1933 Japan dramatically withdrew from the League of Nations, after the commission sent by the League to Manchuria produced a compromising report for Japan in 1932, and the League passed a remonstration bill against Japan at its General Assembly in 1933. Matsuoka Yōsuke, the Japanese representative at the Assembly, walked out of its session. His act was domestically presented as resulting from unjust pressure on Japan and Matsuoka himself was called the hero of Geneva.[4] In 1936 in Berlin, Japan signed the Anti-Comintern Pact, together with Germany, and in 1937 without declaring war, invaded the rest of China.

Some of the worst atrocities the world had ever seen had now begun: biological and chemical experiments conducted in Manchuria by the monstrous Unit 731, the military sexual slavery (the so-called 'comfort women' issue), forced mobilisation and labour, brutal treatment of prisoners of war (POWs), and the most notorious, The Nanjing/Nanking massacre or the Nanjing rape, wherein tens of thousands of Chinese citizens including women and children had been massacred in the name of 'eternal peace in the Orient' and 'friendship with neighbours' in Nanking. In the majority of

---

[4] In the period 1935–39, Matsuoka became the president of the South Manchurian Railway. In 1940, as foreign minister he signed The Tripartite Pact with Germany and Italy, and The Japan-Soviet Neutrality Pact in 1941.

these crimes, the actors were never prosecuted and the individual victims were never compensated. Neither was the command responsibility of the Shōwa Emperor Hirohito (r. 1926–1989) addressed.

The war was domestically justified by the concept of Greater Asian Co-Prosperity Sphere, or slogans such as 'hakkō-ichiu' ('the whole world under one roof') or 'the spirit of universal brotherhood'. The concept itself is inextricably related to another concept that was used as a tool for spiritual mobilisation, the concept of the 'overcoming modernity', also the name of the symposium organised in summer 1942 at Kyoto Imperial University (Calichman 2008). The idea of the 'overcoming modernity' originally appeared in Europe after World War I in the book written by Oswald Spengler (1918), *The decline of the West*. Spengler criticised the Eurocentric view and Western model as the only way to modernise. According to him, Europe was not capable of offering an exclusive model for modernisation for Asia. Furthermore, according to some Japanese intellectuals, it was now Japan, as the most developed Asian nation-state, to become the leader, first in liberating the colonised Asian nations, and, then, to lead them towards progress. Many Japanese intellectuals of that time, most notably the Kyoto School of Philosophy (Goto-Jones 2005), supported the idea and in that way took part in the process of 'spiritual mobilisation' for the war.

The war on European territory started in 1939. When Germany attacked the Soviet Union in the summer of 1941, the Japanese were tempted to join the attack, in spite of the Neutrality Pact signed with the Soviets in April of the same year. However, the memory of severe losses to the Soviet troops over the control of Outer Mongolia bordering with Manchukuo (The Nomonhan incident) from May to September 1939 instead turned Japan towards the south east Asian Pacific-Rim British and Dutch colonies. The US government that officially kept neutral because of their public's strong resentment towards entering the war and imposed a series of economic embargoes against Japan in order to stop Japan's plans for expansion in Southeast Asia. In 1939 the US terminated the commercial treaty with Japan from 1911, and in July 1940 F.D. Roosevelt brought up the Export Control Act that authorised him to prohibit the export of 'essential defense materials', in turn enabling him to restrict exports of aviation motor fuels, iron and steel. On 16 October 1940, Roosevelt completely embargoed the export of steel to all countries other than Britain and some others in the Western hemisphere. In October 1941, Roosevelt froze all Japanese assets in the US. The British and the Dutch followed the American steps in economically sanctioning Japan. All Japanese diplomatic attempts to remove some of these sanctions ended in failure. Foreign Minister Teijiro Toyoda had communicated to Ambassador Kichisaburo Nomura on 31 July 1941:

> Commercial and economic relations between Japan and third countries, led by England and the United States, are gradually becoming so horribly strained that we cannot endure it much longer. Consequently, our Empire, to save its very life, must take measures to secure the raw materials of the South Seas. (Barnes 1953: 329)

Japan attacked Pearl Harbor on 8 December, 1941. The US public was shocked and made no objection to entering the war that would eventually lead to the collapse of the Great Japanese Empire: complete devastation of Japan's cities in the air-raids, the atomic bombing of Hiroshima and Nagasaki on 6 August and 9 August respectively,[5] and the postwar occupation by the Allied Powers—General Headquarters (GHQ) and Supreme Commander of Allied Powers (SCAP), Douglas MacArthur.

Until today historians are not unified in their understanding of the decisive reasons that made Japan surrender on 15 August 1945. According to official justification for the use of two atomic bombs, it caused Japan to surrender three to four months earlier, without land battles in which human losses would be even greater. However today many historians on both sides question this justification, and wonder what would have happened if the Soviet Union did not break the Soviet-Japanese Neutrality Pact in April 1945 and, consequently declared war on Japan. According to the agreement made in Yalta, the Soviet Union obliged itself to enter the war in Asia three months after the defeat of Germany. On 9 August, the Soviet troops invaded Manchuria, inner Mongolia, northern Korea, southern Sakhalin and the Kuril Islands. According to some historians (Alperovitz 1965, 1995; Bernstein 1976; Lifton & Mitchell 1995; Sherwin 1975), the use of atomic bombs was not a decisive factor for Japan to surrender and accept the Potsdam Declaration on 15 August. It was rather the Soviet troops' entry into the war that made them capitulate. However, it cannot be argued that the two atomic bombs that were used for the first time in

---

[5] In total, US Forces dropped one hundred and sixty eight thousand tons of bombs, including napalm bombs, on more than one hundred cities throughout Japan. Ninety percent of these were dropped by B-29 bombers in the last five months of the Asia-Pacific War. According to statistical data compiled by the Centre of the Tokyo Raid and War Damages, the estimated casualties of these bombings, including those of the two atomic bombings, come to one million and twenty thousand, including five hundred and sixty thousand deaths.

the history of humankind signalled an unprecedented nuclear arms race in the post-war era.

2. *Post-War Japan and the Failure of the 'Historical Recognition'*

The Japanese system changed considerably after the defeat. The US occupation army was well aware of the persistent mentality of Japanese society and made disarming and making Japan defenseless its first goal. They set democratisation as the second goal. Those two goals, of course, were not unrelated, and they were the expression of a myth that a democratic nation will never commit aggression against other nations. Both of these goals, were considerably distorted, a fact that was already clear during the Tokyo War Crimes Tribunal (officially called The International Military Tribunal for the Far East, or IMTFE). The Tribunal differentiated three grades of war criminals and was not as rigorous as the Nuremberg Tribunal. The justice was selective—the Emperor, although by the constitution commander-in-chief of the army, and besides the fact that the Japanese army put strong emphasis on the moral of soldiers to whom it was told that all orders from their commanders should be considered to be from the Emperor himself,[6] was not prosecuted. The notorious Unit 731 that used live human beings for experimentation was never brought to justice.

Military sexual slavery victims (by some estimates there were one hundred thousand of them) who survived had to wait for more than half of a century to be given a public voice, and yet, The Women's International War Crimes Tribunal on Japan's Military Sexual Slavery held in Tokyo on 8–12 December 2000 had no power to sanction the accused or pursue execution of justice. The organisers were several NGOs and Asian women's and human rights organisations.[7] The judges found both the Japanese state and the Emperor Hirohito guilty of war crimes and crimes against humanity, and requested that the Japanese government apologise and compensate the surviving victims. The information on the tribunal was

---

[6] The Emperor in Japan is considered to be a semi-deity until the "gyoku-on hōsō" (the radio broadcast of the Emperor's announcement of Japan's surrender on 15 August, 1945 when for the first time in history a Japanese emperor addressed the common people).

[7] VAWW-NET (Violence against Women in War Network). For details on the Tribunal see www.iccwomen.org/tokyo/, www.jca.apc.org/, and www.vaww-net-japan.

poorly reported in Japanese media, if not completely omitted or excused with banal explanations.[8]

The judge and the chief prosecutor at the tribunal were Gabrielle McDonald (former President of the International War Crimes Tribunal on the Former Yugoslavia) and Patricia Viseur-Sellers (Legal Adviser for Gender-Related Crimes in the Office of the Prosecutor for the International Tribunal for the Former Yugoslavia, and the Rwanda Tribunal).[9]

The ignoring of non-Japanese victims in the Hiroshima bombing also displays a lack of Japanese responsibility in colonial conflict and war. Hiroshima and Nagasaki, two symbols of the most terrifying and solely Japanese human catastrophe that the twentieth century has seen presented conflicting and controversial stories of their respective unfolding. A Japanese writer and activist Oda Makoto,[10] questioned the official story according to which atomic bombing was the turning point in Japan's surrender, and a more 'humane' solution than the ground battles. The two atomic bombs were also events that turned attention away from, by the immediate number of civilian victims, similar catastrophe such as the US indiscriminate air raids against dozens of Japanese cities. For seven years of the occupation, Hiroshima and Nagasaki were topics to be avoided. Even today the topic of air raids remains largely unaddressed.[11] Moreover,

---

[8] See *Bangumi wa naze kaizen sareta ka: NHK ETV jiken no shinsō*, 2006, Media no kiki wo uttaeru shimin network (Mekichinetto), Tokyo, Ichiyōsha.

[9] The systematic rape in situations of armed conflict was enlisted for the first time as a separate war crime in any international proceedings, at the ICTY (The International Criminal Tribunal for the Former Yugoslavia), in 1996 and it is no wonder that the judges were those who participated in that historical process. Moreover, both of them were women. Before, sexual slavery or rape in the armed conflict was considered to be a part of crimes against humanity of enslavement, or ill-treatment of POWs, but it was never defined separately, as a crime of systematic enforcement to prostitution and rape. The Batavia Military Tribunal in the Netherlands, in 1948 tried the Japanese for forcing thirty five Dutch women POWs to prostitution, but according to Carol Gluck, that case 'had violated Western racial boundaries, and it was racial transgression that counted more than the sexual exploitation' (Gluck 2007: 67). The Asian 'comfort women', Gluck continues, were 'doubly excluded, once by sex and once more by the oblivion drawn over race and empire' (Gluck 2007: 67).

[10] Oda Makoto (1932–2007) was writer and activist, most famous as founder of the anti-Vietnam War movement in Japan—Beheiren, Peace-for-Vietnam Citizen's Alliance. In 2004, he was a co-founder of the Association for preservation of Article 9 of the Japanese constitution.

[11] At the Tokyo War Crimes Tribunal, the issue of the indiscriminate bombing of many Chinese cities by Japanese Imperial Forces during the Asia Pacific War was never raised, despite repeated wartime condemnation by the US government of Japan's aerial attacks on Chinese civilians. It is obvious that the reason for not bringing this matter before the court lay in America's own conduct against Japanese civilians, which took the form of the

the survivors of the atomic bombing (hibakusha) waited a long time before they could receive limited assistance from the state to cover medical costs.

Alternately, Hiroshima as a symbol of peace was industriously developed since the Hiroshima Peace Memorial was established in August 1955. It became a symbol for those aspiring for world peace while at the same time became an inspiration for collective victimisation and nationalist sentiments (Dower 1995; Yoneyama 1999). With such unique tragedy caused by the atomic bombs and its long-lasting effects, collective war experience in Japan was transformed from being an aggressor in Asia to being a victim, and arguably, its sense of guilt for war misdeeds was obfuscated. While remembering its victims and pledging for world peace in their name (Yoneyama 1999: 16),[12] Hiroshima authorities for decades did not recognise the Korean, Chinese and other non-Japanese victims of the bombs who were doubly victimised—firstly by Japanese colonial rule since the majority of them were brought to the Japanese war factories and mines as forced labour, and secondly as victims of radiation. The post-war universal plea for world peace in Hiroshima in its many aspects confirmed 'the complementary and mutually reinforcing relationship between universalism and particularism' (Yoneyama 1999: 231). As Sakai Naoki argued, 'the claim to universality frequently serves to promote the demands of nationalism' (Harootunian & Miyoshi 1988: 480), and that universalism serves as a legitimating discourse for one society's domination over another (Yoneyama 1999: 227).

There are two insightful details about the Memorial itself that are not so well known and might illustrate the depth of its ongoing contestations—firstly, the history of its design that was made by the famous Japanese architect Kenzō Tange (Yoneyama 1999: 24). According to Yoneyama (1999: 219) who quotes Inoue Shōichi's original discussion of the similarities between Tange's two designs (Inoue 1987: 192–297), the design of the memorial resembles Kenzō's design that was made in the midst of the

---

most extensive aerial campaign against civilians, destroying sixty four Japanese cities with incendiary bombs and two with atomic bombs. The fact that the Nazis' indiscriminate bombing of various cities in Europe and England was never a topic of criminal investigation at Nuremberg was probably due to the same reason.

[12] The inscription on the Peace Memorial Park's central cenotaph says: Please rest in peace (yasuraka ni nemutte kudasai, / For we shall not repeat the mistake (ayamachi wa kurikaeshimasen kara). However, the 'we' does not exist in the Japanese original, and this absence of the grammatical subject (characteristic of Japanese language), has generated numerous debates about 'whose' and 'which' mistake the sentence refers to.

war, for the 1942 competition for a grandiose Shintoist memorial zone to be built at the foot of Mount Fuji to envision the concept of the Greater East Asia Co-Prosperity. It appears that Kenzō's design was revived in 1949 to be realised in 1954 with the completion of Hiroshima's Peace Memorial Park (Yoneyama 1999: 1–2). The second contentious story is one about the memorial for the (South) Korean atomic bomb victims (although at that time there was no division of Korea and its people). Many of them were forced labourers brought from colonised Korea to work in Japanese war factories or mines under severe conditions. South Korean descendants in Hiroshima erected their own memorial to the victims of the bombing in 1970. However, in spite of their continuous requests to relocate it inside the Peace Park, they were not allowed to do it until 1999. The Korean victims were recognised and given equal status in Japan, but it happened forty four years after the Peace Park was made. And then, again it was relocated to the contentious location—inside the Park, but away from the visitors' path and the main monuments along it. If a visitor does not purposely go to see the Korean memorial, it will, almost certainly be missed.

Whatever the contestations related to Hiroshima, its victims and their representation or the lack of it (like it is the case with the American POWs who also lost their lives in the air-raids and atomic bombing), the fact remains that it was not an 'ordinary' part of war. It was a large-scale catastrophe with the continuous effect of radiation, and a tragedy from which major postwar issues were born; such as the Japanese so-called nuclear-allergy,[13] the crime of science and the necessity for consideration of the moral aspect of its development, the Non-Proliferation Treaty and its essential inequality in the heritage of the Cold War. The abolition of nuclear power is considered by many in Japan to be humanity's final 'goal', similar to the renouncement of war methods in resolving disputes.

One more unique 'feature' of Japan's pacifism is its postwar Constitution and Article 9. The origin of Article 9 itself is contested; its purpose is sometimes said to be an abrupt forgetting of the inconvenient past and war responsibility. There is strong evidence that it was designed according to the proposals of Prime Minister Kijūrō Shidehara, a pre-war diplomat

---

[13] The Japanese nuclear allergy was an obstacle to realisation of the 'Atoms for Peace' plan of economic development based on nuclear energy, designed by Dwight D. Eisenhower. A Japanese daily, Yomiuri Shimbun on 1 January 1955 started a media campaign in order to persuade Japanese people that nuclear power plants are necessary, safe and cheap source of energy. On the campaign see documentary (Japanese) 'Genpatsu dōnyū shinario—resien shita no tai nichi genshiryoku senryaku' [An introducing nuclear energy scenario—nuclear strategy vs. Japan under the Cold War structure], NHK, 1994.

and pacifist. Japan is obliged not to maintain an army, navy or air-force, and rejected the right of belligerency, and it is said in some memoirs that Douglas MacArthur could not be more satisfied after a two and a half hour long meeting with Shidehara. Shidehara's motivation was not only to limit some future Japanese government to militarise or develop police terror, but to raise an awareness that Japan had no chance to recover economically if they would have military expenditures. Since the formation of the Police Reserve and its eventual transformation to the Japanese Self-Defense Forces (JSDF), Article 9 is unambiguously breached without any space for varying interpretations of it. However, the issue of Article 9 intensified in 2003 with the Iraq War. For the first time since 1945 the Japanese government sent its JSDF troops on an overseas mission. The next mission came soon after the Iraqi one—in the 'War on Terror' in Afghanistan where Japan was one of five powers being tasked with the responsibility to coordinate the disarmament process. When Japan sent its defense forces to Iraq in 2004, there was a debate among the soldiers whether any of their deaths should be commemorated at the Yasukuni shrine (Takahashi 2007: 18–19).

Regardless of the contestations related to Article 9, its preservation, according to progressive Japanese intellectuals who publicly appealed for it in 2004,[14] became an especially important issue in the post-Cold War era. According to influential postwar intellectual Katō Shūichi, if Article 9 would be changed there would be no more legal obstacle to the JSDF troops participating in war in any place of the world where the US is fighting. For him, it was a question of the utmost importance for the security of Japan and inseparable from the stability of East Asia as a whole.

Article 9 today is an intriguing issue among many non-Japanese intellectuals, as well. According to Galtung, the father of peace studies, peace, just like conflict and violence, is a relation. Negative peace examines how to reduce/eliminate negative/disharmonious relations, while positive peace examines how to build positive relations. From this point of view Article 9 is a 'negative peace' (Galtung 2008: 99–103), while the Preamble of the Japanese constitution that mentions a 'joint project' is more promising from the aspect of building peace. According to Galtung (2008:

---

[14] One of the first nuclear power plants to be built was the Fukushima power plant that on 11 March 2011 caused the biggest environmental crisis since Chernobyl. In June 2012, the Parliament commission officially confirmed that the disaster was 'man-made' and should not have happened as a consequence of the earthquake and tsunami on 11 March if it was properly maintained and if the disaster when happened was competently dealt with.

99–103) the general understanding of building a positive peace is still at a low level.

3. SCAP's Politics of Democratising Japan

The favourable climate for the shared values of humanism and liberal democracy, although it existed in the prewar Japanese political thought (Koschmann 1996: 11), was created by the Allied Powers of World War II.

The Atlantic Charter of August 1941 represented the basis of democratic discourse for the postwar era. A great number of Japanese intellectuals of postwar enlightenment thought (sengo keimō) experienced the defeat and the newly acquired freedom of thought and speech as a liberation. SCAP and General Douglas MacArthur released the political prisoners (mostly pre-war leftists who did not convert under pressure, and who survived), and started with demilitarisation of Japan according to July 1945 Potsdam Declaration that envisaged the total demilitarisation of Japan. They also brought up with the democratic self-government the legislation for land, judicial and police reform, dissolution of zaibatsu (industrial and financial business conglomerates) and the establishment of free market competition, freedoms of religion, assembly, speech and the press and a democratic multi-party system. The early guiding principles of SCAP were said to be 'negative' since the democratisation was primarily seen as 'removing obstacles' (Koschmann 1996: 15). The workers movements or the farmers' unions at the beginning were supported as legitimate political groups in the liberal democracy.

However, the democratisation policy of the Occupation forces entered the zone of conflicting interests only two years after the defeat—the ideological war with the Soviet Union was heating up and the Cold War was on the horizon. 'The tolerance of SCAP' for workers' requests soon reached its limits, during the general strike on 1 February 1947 when Japanese workers announced a strike and their request to overthrow the PM Yoshida Shigeru. SCAP frustrated the strike and completely changed the course of its politics. This change is known as *reverse course* (gyaku kōsu). SCAP moved from the original goals set up in the framework of liberal democracy towards neo-conservatism and the economic rehabilitation of the country. Japan was supposed to become a success story to show the world the superiority of capitalism. It is important to note that the first impetus for Japan's postwar economy arrived thanks to war—Japan supplied the US forces involved in the Korean War (1950–53) with special procurements. In this context, the San Francisco Peace Treaty by which the almost seven-year-long occupation of Japan ended made Japan wholly unaccountable for its past actions. The stipulation in Article 14 of the Treaty was apologetic:

> It is recognized that Japan should pay reparations to the Allied Powers for the damage and suffering caused by it during the war. Nevertheless it is also recognized that the resources of Japan are not presently sufficient, if it is to maintain a viable economy, to make complete reparation for all such damage and suffering and at the same time meet its other obligations. (Chiba 2008: 179)

The single reason for this favourable treatment was 'America's intent to co-opt Japan as its ally against the Soviet bloc in the already started Cold War' (Chiba 2008: 179). The Soviet Union and the People's Republic of China (its civil war and communist revolution ended in 1949) were not even invited to the peace conference. All Asian nations who were victims of Japanese imperialism, were (quite understandably) deeply disappointed with the Treaty. In 1952, soon after the San Francisco Peace Treaty was signed, the Japanese workers protested against the First US-Japan Security Treaty (which was a part of peace settlement) in an event commonly called 'Bloody May Day'. The police suppressed the protests and in those clashes many workers were killed and injured. It was the culmination of the so-called 'red-purge' by SCAP and GHQ that had started in June 1950. The purges quickly spread from the Prime Ministers' cabinet to the public and private sectors. Incidentally, June 1950 marked the beginning of the Korean War.

Before the beginning of the Korean War, in his annual New Year's statement in January 1950, General MacArthur suggested that Japan had the right to self-defense (Maruyama 1969: 291). Only two months later, in August 1950, postwar Japan established the Police Reserve (*keisatsu yobitai*). The Police Reserve was changed to the Security Force (Hoantai) in 1952 (the same year in which the First US-Japan Security Treaty came into effect as a part of the San-Francisco Treaty), to be finally transformed into 'Jieitai' or JSDF in 1954. There is no doubt, and no ambiguity in an interpretation that could justify this act as constitutional. Namely, the Japanese postwar constitution and its pacifist clause, Article 9, that was imposed by the US and in accordance with the goals of Potsdam declaration, states as follows:

> Renunciation of war: Aspiring sincerely to an international peace based on justice and order, the Japanese people forever renounce war as a sovereign

right of the nation and the threat or use of force as means of settling international disputes.

In order to accomplish the aim of the preceding paragraph, land, sea, and air forces, as well as other war potential, will never be maintained. The right of belligerency of the state will not be recognized. (Maruyama 1969: 320)

This pacifist clause was first contested by US Vice-President Richard Nixon during his visit to Japan in 1953, only five years after the constitution was enacted. He made the famous remark that it was a mistake for America to insert Article 9 into the Japanese constitution. The domestic requests for constitutional revision appeared at the beginning of the 1950s and continue to exist to the present day. With changes on the international scene in the mid 1990s, the revisionist voices became much louder.

Alternately, Japan has had several important moments of resistance to the ruling neo-conservatives in Japan, significant ones being the protests against the renewal of the US-Japan Security Treaty in 1960 (Anpo-tōsō) under the Prime Minister Kishi Nobusuke (once imprisoned but never accused as the 'Class A' war criminal by SCAP: in 1979 he was awarded the United Nations Peace Medal), the Japan Peace-for-Vietnam Citizen's Alliance (Beheiren) social movement that emerged in 1965 (protests against US war planes that were taking off from Japanese airports), and the protests against the military-industrial-academic complex (gun-san-gaku fukugōtai) in 1968. All those events marked the end of the 'postwar' era in Japan. Japan was already emerging as an economic giant, obviously so when the Olympic Games were hosted in Tokyo in 1964 (Igarashi 2000: 131–63).

4. Historical Revisionism in the 1990s

The term 'revisionism' was first used in the 1960s in relation to a debate by A.J.P. Taylor and Fritz Fischer on the role of Nazi Germany in the outbreak of World War II and the consequences of the Versailles Treaty (Iwasaki & Richter 2008: 509). The whole spectrum of contestations and interpretations of the events and the denial of historical liability for past events by right-wing groups is defined as 'historical revisionism'. In Germany it went so far as to completely deny that the Holocaust ever happened. A similar tendency arose in Japan in the 1990s, but it can be traced as far back as the mid 1950s.

1955 was the year in which several important events occurred: two conservative parties, the Democratic Party of Japan and the Liberal Party merged into the Liberal Democratic Party (LDP). The political system was named 'The 1955 System' and it dominated the Japanese political scene for almost 50 years (it was interrupted for a short time in the period 1993–94, when it regained and maintained power until 2009). The first public controversies concerning the historical interpretation of the events of the Asia Pacific War arose with the book Shōwa-shi ('Shōwa history') by the Marxist historian, Tōyama Shigeki. It was a history of the first thirty years of the current Shōwa era. This was one of the first postwar attempts to write a compact contemporary national history. The author was influenced by the Marxist socio-economic explanation (class-struggle) of historical events. Therefore, the book was grounded in historical materialism, scientific inquiry, and objectivity that aimed at 'historical truth' as its basic principle and motivation. It denied imperial-centred historiography and explained Japan's defeat as the logical consequence of the fascist and military oppression of democracy since the end of the Taishō era. The book became an immediate bestseller, but also has raised a heated debate between the author Tōyama and the literary critic Kamei Katsuichirō, who famously participated in the 'overcoming modernity' war-time symposium. Kamei characterised Tōyama's history as a 'national history without people', 'poor-in-individual-experience' and as one that cannot reflect the voices of the dead (Chūo Kōron 1956). Kamei wrote (Chūo Kōron 1956) 'There must be many voices of those who did believe in the holy war, and who died while calling banzai (Long live the emperor)'. There must be, he claimed, 'earnest soldiers who loved Japan from the bottom of their heart and died for it' (Chūo Kōron 1956). The neo-conservatives considered such history books to be anti-Japanese and a masochistic view of history.

In 1965, the history textbook by historian Ieanaga Saburo resulted with his lawsuit against the Ministry of Education, Culture, Sports, Science and Technology (MEXT). Ienaga did not approve of the Ministry's screening process, with its admonishment that it contains too many dark pictures of the war, including the pictures of devastated Hiroshima and other cities in the air raids (it is important to note that Hiroshima, as well as the air-raids, were taboo subjects for a long time within Japanese public discourse). Ieanaga's lawsuits continued for almost thirty years, but they culminated in 1982 with a first-class diplomatic scandal: the Ministry requested Ieanaga to change the word 'aggression' (shin-ryaku), in reference to the Japanese military in China, to the word 'advance' (shin-shutsu). Additionally, Ienaga was asked to write about the 'uprising of Korean people' instead of the 'March First Independence Movement'. The reactions of China and Korea were so strong that the Ministry withdrew its comments, and added a new criterion in the textbook screening process that it should be in international harmony with neighbouring countries. The interpretations of history became much more 'democratised' in the early 1990s when the 'Study Group for the Liberal View of History' (Jiyūshugi shikan kenkyūkai) was formed with the aim to correct the 'historically negative view of the Japanese past'.

In 2005, the group arrived to Okinawa to 'discover the truth about mass-suicides' (Iwasaki & Richter 2008: 507) that took place during the Battle of Okinawa. The battle of Okinawa happened at the end of the war, lasted for almost three months and was the only land battle in Japan. It caused a tremendous loss of life and suffering among Okinawans, who even today do not consider themselves to be Japanese. It was common that the witnesses of the orders of the Imperial army's commanders were pressured in different ways to change their statements about the events in Okinawa. Much publicity surrounded the 'Ōe-Iwanami' case where the Nobel Prize winner Ōe Kenzaburo and his publisher, Iwanami Shoten, were sued because of Ōe's (1970) *Notes on Okinawa* (Okinawa nōto), which discussed the role of Captain Akamatsu in the Tokashiki island's mass suicides. After visiting Okinawa in 2005 the 'Study Group for the Liberal View of History' persuaded captain Akamatsu's relatives to sue Ōe for defamation of character (Iwasaki & Richter 2008: 507–8). Ōe wrote that the Japanese Imperial army commanders during the US invasion of Okinawa in 1945 forced the local population to commit mass suicides by giving them hand grenades to kill themselves, in order to be saved from the rape and brutal tortures allegedly perpetrated by the advancing American troops. The court in Osaka dismissed the charges against Ōe and his publisher and concluded that the Japanese military was indeed deeply involved in the incident.

In addition, the Study group published a series of books beginning with 'The history that textbooks don't teach', and in the same way, they all explained the events—a small, heroic nation of Asia fought to preserve their independence against Western colonial domination and racial discrimination which all dragged them to the Asia Pacific War. All events, from the first Sino-Japanese War to the Tokyo War Crimes Tribunal (IMTFE) became part of the same narrative of the 'East Asian Hundred Year War'. Iwasaki and Richter emphasise that much of this narrative was already present in Hayashi Fusao's 1964 *Affirmation of the Greater East Asian War*. Hayashi (1964) wrote, 'it is natural for the warriors of the Hundred Year War to rest and heal their wounds . . . someday history will call

forth the sons of these warriors to the forefront of the stage of history'
(Iwasaki & Richter 2008: 522–3). The historical revisionism of the 1990s,
Iwasaki and Richter (2008: 524) conclude, 'must be seen as the unfortu-
nate realisation of Hayashi's prediction'.

The case of Yasukuni, the symbol of Japanese militarism and the shrine
of war, reached its culmination when Japanese Prime Minister Koizumi
Junichiro paid five visits to Yasukuni on 15 August (the anniversary of
Japan's defeat) in the period between 2001 and 2006. The history of this
controversial shintō shrine goes back to the early Meiji period (1868–1912)
and the year 1869. It honoured the dead souls of about two million four
hundred and sixty thousand Japanese soldiers (including soldiers from the
colonies) killed in foreign wars starting with The Boshin War and Taiwan
Expedition and up to the Pacific War (1941–45). This number includes
fourteen A-class war criminals sentenced at the IMTFE. Before the Meiji
Restoration, the Japanese Emperor never had the political power that it
acquired in 1868. Previously the Emperor had solely a ceremonial role,
associated more with religious (Shinto) power than he was a sovereign.
With being 'restored' and moved from Kyoto to the Shogunate's capital
Edo (today's Tokyo), the Meiji emperor built several Shinto shrines, either
to show his imperial power (such as Meiji-jingu shrine), or to enshrine
the heroes who gave their lives in the fight to achieve it. After the defeat,
under the new secular constitution, the Yasukuni shrine was put out of
the state's control and registered as a private religious association. There
were a significant number of proposals to 'remove' the A-class criminals
from the shrine since any tribute to Yasukuni clearly meant denial of
war responsibility. Nevertheless, this argument hid a certain cover up,
according to Takahashi Tetsuya (Takahashi 2007). First, Takahashi argues,
Japan's war responsibility did not start with the Pacific War, but much
earlier, with the start of Japan's colonialism. This fact alludes to the Japanese denial of colonial responsibility. Secondly, those enshrined are not
all Japanese (although the shrine officials stated that they were 'Japanese'
at the moment of their death). For the majority of Taiwanese, Korean and
even Okinawans, the enshrinement of their fellow citizens is a source of
irritation that has been manifested in a series of protests and requests
for the removal of their names from the shrine. And thirdly, Takahashi
continues, various visits of PMs were a reminder that the most responsible one, the commander-in-chief of Japanese military and the highest
religious authority, Emperor Hirohito, was spared his war responsibility
by the US; afraid of Japan falling to communism, the US kept him in place
as a 'symbol of Japan and the unity of people' (Takahashi 2007).

The voices of the state officials to 'nationalise' the shrine are, naturally, the calls for revision of the constitution itself. The most famous article of Japanese postwar constitution, Article 9, lies at the heart of these debates.

Conclusion

The chapter's intention to introduce a war that has ended almost seven decades ago inevitably focuses on analysing the present state of affairs in East Asia. The reason for Japan's collective forgetting of its war past (and responsibility) is found in the US-Japan relationship in the postwar period and the 'bipolar' world. The course Japan had already clearly taken in the end of the 1950s—a security and economic alliance with the US often showed to be more in agreement with the pre-war nationalist aspirations than with the ideals of a liberal democratic society. However, the turning point for the rise of Japan's historical revisionism is the period of the 1990s that was the period of 'democratisation' in its history. The politics of interpreting the war in East Asia was determined by political circumstances that have radically changed with the end of the Cold War. In other words, international, domestic and ideological transformations have caused the emergence of a variety of identity politics of suppressed groups inside the grand narrative of the Cold War. On the one hand, this trend has caused a sense of historical relativism and calls for revisionism while on the other it turned attention toward human rights discourses and transitional justice (Levy 2011: 482–492). Important for the study of these multiple narratives on the Pacific War are its frequent contestations, more than factuality itself. It is within the current and future relationships in East Asia that the narratives of events from the Pacific War matter.

The effects of the recent changes in Japanese society triggered by the '3.11 triple catastrophe' (earthquake-tsunami-nuclear disaster) on these narratives, is still unclear. Without any doubt, 3.11 is the most important event that has occurred in modern Japanese history after its defeat in World War II. It has caused an unprecedented rise of patriotism and nationalism, alongside large scale anti-nuclear (and anti-governmental) protests of the Japanese citizens. These protests fundamentally reassess the whole socio-political structure of Japanese postwar economic development. While the government of Japan is losing its domestic legitimacy while confronted with the rising anti-nuclear movement, there is a perilous possibility to try to cover it up with the (currently intensifying) territorial dispute with China or the North Korean nuclear threat.

Further Reading

Ching, T.S.L., 2001, *Becoming 'Japanese': Colonial Taiwan and the politics of identity formation*, University of California Press, Berkeley and Los Angeles, California.

Calichman, R.F. (transl. & ed.), 2008, *Overcoming modernity: Cultural identity in wartime Japan*, Columbia University Press, New York.

Goto-Jones, C., 2005, *Political philosophy in Japan: Nishida, the Kyoto School and co-prosperity*, Routledge, London.

Iwasaki, M. & Richter, S., 2008, 'The topology of post-1990s historical revisionism', transl. R.F. Calichman, *East Asia Critique* 16(3), 507–38.

Koschmann, J.V., 1996, *Revolution and subjectivity in postwar Japan*, University of Chicago Press, Chicago.

Lifton, J.R. & Mitchell, G., 1995, *Hiroshima in America: Fifty years of denial*, Grosset/Putnam, New York.

Maruyama, M. & Morris, M. (eds), 1969, *Thought and behaviour in modern Japanese politics*, Oxford University Press, Oxford.

Miyoshi, J. & Mitter, R., 2007, *Ruptured histories: War, memory and the post-Cold War in Asia*, Harvard University Press, Cambridge.

Molasky, M.S., 1999, *The American occupation of Japan and Okinawa*, Routledge, London.

Murakami, Y. & Schoenbaum, T.J. (eds), 2008, *A grand design for peace and reconciliation: Achieving kyosei in East Asia*, Edward Elgar Publishing Ltd., Northampton, MA.

Sakai, N., de Bary, B., Iyotani, T., 2005, *Deconstructing nationality*, East Asia Program, Cornell University, Ithaca, New York.

Yamanouchi, Y., Koschmann, J.V., & Narita, R., 1998, *Total war and 'modernization'*, East Asia Program, Cornell University, Ithaca, New York.

Yoneyama, L., 1999, *Hiroshima traces: Time, space, and the dialectics of memory*, University of California Press, Berkeley, Los Angeles and London.

References

Alperovitz, G., 1965, *Atomic diplomacy: Hiroshima and Potsdam*, Simon and Schuster, New York.

Alperovitz, G., 1995, *The decision to use the atomic bomb and the architecture of an American myth*, Alfred A. Knopf, New York.

Barnes, H.E., 1953, *Perpetual war for perpetual peace*, Caxton Press, viewed 8 July 2012, from http://mises.org/document/3204/Perpetual-War-for-Perpetual-Peace.

Bernstein, B., 1976, 'Atomic diplomacy and the Cold War', in B. Bernstein (ed.), *The atomic bomb: The critical issues*, Little Brown, Boston.

Calichman, R.F. (transl. & ed.), 2008, *Overcoming modernity: Cultural identity in wartime Japan*, Columbia University Press, New York.

Chiba, S., 2008, 'For realizing wa and kyosei in East Asia', in Y. Murakami & T.J. Schoenbaum (eds), *A grand design for peace and reconciliation, achieving kyosei in East Asia*, pp. 176–98, Edward Elgar Publishing Ltd., Northampton, MA.

Ching, L.T.S., 2001, *Becoming 'Japanese': Colonial Taiwan and the politics of identity formation*, University of California Press, Berkeley, Los Angeles and London.

Dower, J.W., 1995, 'The bombed: Hiroshima and Nagasaki in Japanese memory', *Diplomatic History* 19(2), 275–95.

Galtung, J., 2008, 'Toward a grand theory of positive and negative peace and reconciliation: Peace, security and conviviality', in Y. Murakami & T.J. Schoenbaum (eds), *A grand design for peace and reconciliation: Achieving kyosei in East Asia*, pp. 90–107, Edward Elgar Publishing Ltd., Northampton, MA.

Gluck, C., 2007, 'Operations of memory, "comfort women" and the world', in J. Miyoshi & R. Mitter (eds), *Ruptured histories: War, memory and the post-Cold war in Asia*, pp. 47–77, Harvard University Press, Cambridge.

Goto-Jones, C., 2005, *Political philosophy in Japan: Nishida, the Kyoto School and co-prosperity*, Routledge, London.

Harootunian, H. & Miyoshi, M. (eds), 1988, 'Postmodernism and Japan', in *South Atlantic Quarterly* 87(3), 387–99.

Inoue, S., 1987, *Ato, kicchu, japanesuku: Daitoa no posutomodan*, Seidosha, Tokyo.

Iwasaki, M. & Richter, S., 2008, 'The topology of post-1990s historical revisionism', transl. R.F. Calichman, *East Asia Critique* 16(3), 507–38.

Katō, S., 2000, *Watashi ni totte nijū seiki*, Iwanami shoten, Tokyo.

Katō, S. & Maruyama, M., 1991, *Nihon no shisō, Nihon kindai shisō taikei 15*, Iwanami shoten, Tokyo.

Koschmann, J.V., 1996, *Revolution and subjectivity in postwar Japan*, University of Chicago Press, Chicago.

Levy, D., 2008, 'Memory practices and theory in global age', in G. Delanty & S.P. Turner (eds), *International handbook of contemporary social and political theory*, pp. 482–92, Routledge, New York.

Lifton, J.R. & Mitchell, G., 1995, *Hiroshima in America: Fifty years of denial*, Grosset/Putnam, New York.

Maruyama, M. & Morris, M. (eds), 1969, *Thought and behaviour in modern Japanese politics*, Oxford University Press, Oxford.

Miyoshi, J. & Mitter, R., 2007, *Ruptured histories: War, memory and the post-Cold War in Asia*, Harvard University Press, Cambridge.

Molasky, M.S., 1999, *The American occupation of Japan and Okinawa*, Routledge, London.

Morgenstern, G., 1953, 'The actual road to Pearl Harbor', in H.E. Barnes (ed.) *Perpetual war for perpetual peace: A critical examination of the foreign policy of Franklin Delano Roosevelt and its aftermath*, pp. 315–406, Caxton Printers Ltd., Caldwell, IDA.

Nakaya, K., et al., 1956, 'Gendai-shi no kakikata wo megutte (zadankai)' [On writing modern history (symposium)], *Chūō Kōron*, December 1956, pp. 74–85, Chūō Kōron-sha, Tokyo.

Sakai, N., 2011, 'Museki-nin no taikei, san-tabi', *Gendai shisō*, 5-gatsu, vol. 39–7, 26–33.

Sherwin, M.J., 1975, *A world destroyed: The atomic bomb and the Grand Alliance*, Alfred A. Knopf, New York.

Takahashi, T., 2007, 'Yasukuni shrine at the heart of Japanese national debate: History, memory, denial', viewed 8 July 2012, from http://www.japanfocus.org/-Takahashi-Tetsuya/2401.

Yoneyama, L., 1999, *Hiroshima traces: Time, space, and the dialectics of memory*, University of California Press, Berkeley, Los Angeles and London.

CHAPTER TWELVE

WAR AND PEACE IN COLOMBIA

Håvar Solheim and Eric Storm

Introduction

The violent conflict in Colombia is quite typical for the second half of the twentieth century. It began with communist inspired uprisings against a weak, but nominally democratic state in the 1960s, and rapidly developed into a prolonged asymmetric armed conflict between the security forces of the Republic of Colombia and four left-wing guerrilla movements, of which the *Fuerzas Armadas Revolucionarias de Colombia* (FARC; Revolutionary Armed Forces of Colombia) is the best known. Although the guerrillas do not possess the weapons, the manpower or the financial means of the state, they still succeed in continuing their struggle by largely unconventional means, such as terrorist attacks and hit and run tactics. The FARC even became one of the strongest guerrilla movements of Latin America. Partly because of the failure of the state to protect its citizens and their properties, right-wing groups began to organise paramilitary groups to take matters in their own hands. The chaotic reality on the ground with security forces, paramilitaries and guerrillas using propaganda, intimidation, extortion, drug trafficking and violence to get their way has often been interpreted from the outside in the contexts of the Cold War, the War on Drugs and the War on Terror. In this chapter we will briefly review the historical background, the conflict in its different phases, the international context and the various attempts to negotiate peace.

1. Historical Background

Colombia is a vast country covered with mountains, savannahs and jungle. It has its fair share of natural resources (oil, gas, coal and other minerals), a considerable amount of industry and a large agricultural sector. Dire poverty is not a major problem in Colombia, and its economic development is more advanced than in most Latin American countries. Nonetheless, the division of wealth and income is very unequal even for the standards in the region. Almost half of the population lives under the poverty line and about fifteen per cent of the inhabitants have to survive with less than two dollars a day. Although the population has more than tripled over the last fifty years, reaching approximately forty three million people in 2005, large stretches of the country are virtually uninhabited. While more than two thirds of the inhabitants live in urban areas, rapid population growth has strained living conditions in the countryside. Peasants, large landowners and agricultural enterprises—among which many were multinational companies—struggled over the scarcely available resources, or tried to develop uncultivated parts of the country. In these remote areas conflicts over land quickly escalated. The widespread social misery and injustice provided a fertile breeding ground for the guerrilla movements, and the sparsely populated agricultural zones and the jungle enabled them to find cover. In the end, the guerrilla forces were not strong enough to gain power, but they could easily escape persecution from the state's security forces.

Colombia inherited a weak centralised state from the Spanish colonial period, which ended in the early decades of the nineteenth century. Although nominally a constitutional democracy, Colombian politics has been characterised by instability and recurring violence. Several authors, such as Kline (1999), argue that the fear of a strong state by the Colombian elites impeded the formation of a well-functioning military and police organisations in Colombia. Like elsewhere during the nineteenth century, the economic elites preferred a low tax burden and even tried to avoid taxation; at a local level power remained mostly in the hands of large landowners. In many cases, these local power holders also became the informal law enforcers. The lack of a well-functioning state apparatus thus paved the way for violence, impunity and private justice practices, which still affect the country today.

Until the 1960s, Colombia's history was largely shaped by severe political rivalry. Although both the dominant Liberal and Conservative parties accepted constitutional democracy and the market economy, they fiercely competed with each other by trying to monopolise political power at the expense of their rivals. Since personal bonds were often more important than ideological issues, both political parties consisted of various rivalling factions that sometimes caused severe internal crises. Thus, although the Liberals dominated the government since the early 1930s, internal divisions split the party and as a result the Conservatives were able to win the presidential elections of 1946.

While the political rivalry between Conservatives and Liberals had been relatively peaceful since the last civil war that ended in 1902, the assassination in 1948 of the left-wing populist Jorge Eliécer Gaitán introduced a new period of turmoil. The charismatic Gaitán had become the new leader of the Liberals and would probably have won the next presidential elections. The news of his death accordingly provoked a violent reaction in his followers. Large-scale riots in the capital Bogotá caused the death of thousands of people and destroyed large parts of the city centre. This so-called *Bogotazo* was the beginning of more than a decade of chaos and widespread sectarian violence, a period generally known as *La Violencia*.[1] Throughout the country Liberals and Conservatives started to harass or murder political opponents, Conservative landowners tried to expel Liberal farmers and vice versa, whereas members of the Liberal and the rather marginal Communist Party, which had close links with the Soviet Union, started to organise self-defence groups. Particularly in the countryside the already weak authority of the state collapsed and a great number of armed groups and factions tried to control their own piece of territory. In the end, *La Violencia* is estimated to have cost approximately three hundred thousand victims, most of them being poor inhabitants of rural areas (Palacios 2003).

A short-lived military dictatorship between 1953 and 1957 somewhat improved the situation by offering a wide-ranging amnesty in order to calm down the political turmoil. However, authority would only be restored after the most influential leaders of the Conservatives and Liberals decided to form a National Front. They agreed to present a common candidate for the 1958 presidential elections and strictly alternate the presidency for the coming sixteen years between themselves. They concurred that the Liberals and Conservatives would each get fifty percent of the seats in all representative bodies—from the national parliament down to municipal councils—and that major decisions could only be made by a majority of two thirds. The National Front began to function and slowly political violence faded away, while the army liquidated most of the remaining armed bands. Nevertheless, the budget for the security forces did not increase

---

[1] Please note that scholars often disagree about the precise initiation of the period known as *La Violencia*. However, the murder of Gaitán and the subsequent escalation of violence is commonly regarded as the beginning of this period.

and the structural weakness of the state remained unchanged (Palacios 2003: 170–90).

The National Front agreement between the Liberals and Conservatives depolarised the elections, as with the seats already divided evenly between the two political parties, only the rivalry between the various factions within each of the traditional governing parties made any sense. The National Front also practically excluded outsiders, such as the Communist Party, from participating in the elections. Over the years, this political compromise faced increased criticism from those who were formally or informally excluded from political participation. The National Front officially ended in 1974 and for the first time since 1946 free presidential elections were held. The Liberal candidate Alfonso López Michelsen (1974–78) became president of the Colombian republic.

2. *The Conflict*

As we have seen, *La Violencia* had a grave impact on the state's governing ability in large parts of the country. Thus, at the end of the 1940s, several armed groups or guerrilla movements emerged; since the government was dominated by the Conservatives, most of them had strong ties to the Liberals, while others were linked to the still relatively small Communist Party. In areas where Communism dominated, the armed conflicts were not only caused by political rivalries, but perhaps even more so by socioeconomic disputes. These disputes were the result of a long-lasting rivalry for land control, where deep-rooted conflicts were ongoing between large landowners and poor peasants, as well as the fact that many farmers were deprived of their land by local insurgent groups of different origins. As police and military were largely concentrated in urban territories, in many parts of the country the possession of land (which often was not officially registered) was easily usurped with irregular means, as state authorities were unable to provide justice. According to Oquist (1980), this lack of a well-functioning and impartial state supervision only increased the confrontations over land control.

As a consequence, the Communist Party gained its principal political and armed support in the countryside. The Communist guerrilla groups (with its support base among those local peasants that were in favour of land reform) and the Liberals (who generally enjoyed support from large landowners) rapidly fell into political disagreement. Meanwhile, the Conservative government compensated for the absence of state authorities by organising counterinsurgency raids in rural areas. By this time, an armed dispute had also begun between the Liberal and the Communist guerrillas. On top of that, armed factions of outlaws contributed to a total collapse of political stability, especially in the regions where the Communists were active. Following the military coup of 1953, several Liberal guerrillas were demobilised. Others joined the Communists, who effectively began to control various parts of the country where land plots had fallen under control of the local peasants.

After Fidel Castro and his Communist guerrilla forces took over power in nearby Cuba, the Colombian government—aided by the United States— stepped up its counter insurgency measures. In 1964 and 1965 the Communist dominated areas, such as those of Marquetalia and Riochiquito came under heavy attack by the state military forces. The Conservative government claimed to reinstate order, while the attacks were also meant to prevent parts of the country from coming under effective Communist control (Osterling 1989: 96–103). After repeated military attacks, the Communist guerrillas were forced to abandon these areas. The guerrillas' military strength and their political ideology however remained largely intact (Oquist 1980). As a consequence armed peasants summoned a meeting in July 1964 and merged their different guerrilla groups into the Southern Bloc, which two years later was transformed into the FARC. During the following years, the rebel movement succeeded to expand its operational basis in rural areas, where they received the support of many peasants who hoped to advance their own interests. In these areas, local guerrilla groups, peasant movements and the Communist Party created, according to Pizarro, a 'regional power to be reckoned with' (Pizarro in Bergquist et al. 1992: 180–2). In the subsequent decades, the FARC would become one of the best organised guerrilla movements in Latin America.

During the 1960s, three other guerrilla movements were founded in different parts of Colombia. Like in the case of the FARC, the creation of these armed groups was closely linked with the dynamics of *La Violencia*. They were all inspired by various types of Communism, and especially by the example of Fidel Castro. The first, the *Ejército de Liberación Nacional* (ELN; National Liberation Army) was created in 1964, mostly by university students, as a revolutionary Marxist liberation movement. The ELN received active support from Castro's regime in Cuba. In 1967, dissident Communists, following the ideas of the Chinese leader Mao Zedong, would found the *Ejército Popular de Liberación* (EPL; People's Liberation Army), which also had its power base in rural areas. A few years later, in 1970, the quite different urban guerrilla movement *Movimiento 19 de Abril* (M-19;

19th of April Movement) became operational. This insurgent group was founded as a reaction to the allegedly fraudulent presidential elections of 19 April 1970, the date from which the group was named. The movement only started to draw attention a few years later with spectacular terrorist actions, mostly in the Colombian capital, such as the 1980 storming of a cocktail party at the embassy of the Dominican Republic. Only after two months the *guerrilleros* released the fifty seven diplomats they had held hostage. Five years later a siege of the Palace of Justice in the city centre of Bogotá ended in a bloodbath with over one hundred casualties (Carrigan 1993).

The internal conflict in Colombia was not limited to a violent struggle between four (more or less) Marxist guerrilla movements and the Colombian state and its security forces: it included many paramilitary groups that originated from the period of *La Violencia* as well. As the armed forces of the state were not able to protect the inhabitants of the more remote parts of the country, citizens started to defend themselves and often took justice into their own hands. During the 1970s and the 1980s, civilians again took the initiative to defend their own interests as they were tired of the constant demands and harassment from the guerrillas. Landlords, employers and army officers also created their own, often right-wing paramilitary groups, while others received arms from major drug traffickers. As a consequence, the use of violence became endemic, especially after the 1970s. On top of that, as a part of its counterinsurgency policy, in 1968 the government passed Decree 48, which provided the legal foundation for the flourishing of paramilitary groups in Colombia. Indeed, as Hristov (2009) asserts, many paramilitary groups came into existence due to the state's need for military aid. The expansion of paramilitary groups was largely facilitated by US assistance and by the active Colombian economic elites' role and interest in fighting the guerrillas.

Among other academic works, Hristov (2009: 63) points to the weak state apparatus as a reason for this '(unofficial) policy toward the partial privatization of coercion' by the Colombian state. Cubides (in Bergquist et al. 2001: 130) argues that the principal objective of the paramilitary groups was to combat the guerrilla threat throughout the Colombian territory. The paramilitaries adopted guerrilla warfare tactics and combat strategies in order to defeat their enemy. The author further details that the paramilitaries took 'as their preferred targets the support networks, the sympathisers or auxiliaries of the guerrillas, in regions where the guerrillas have recently installed themselves, beginning with regions where the abruptness of guerrilla installation has produced a growing reaction'. As a consequence, paramilitarism produced even more conflict, while human rights violations and terrorism reached alarmingly high numbers during the 1980s.

In addition to the guerrilla movements and the paramilitaries, new major players were added: the drug barons. After a major drive against drugs trafficking in Mexico had been quite successful in 1975, Colombian drug entrepreneurs took over the all-important North American drugs market. Within a few years the United States was flooded with large quantities of marijuana and cocaine from Colombia. During the 1980s, Colombian drug cartels were allegedly responsible for about eighty percent of the cocaine smuggled into the United States, while drug dollars probably equalled that of almost a third of the foreign income of Colombia. In 1981 a secret national convention of the Colombian illicit drug industry, represented by two hundred and twenty three drug traffickers, decided to create a death squad, called *Muerte a Secuestradores* (MAS; Death to Kidnappers), to violently end the guerrilla practice of abducting people for ransom, which included 'honest, hard-working drug gang bosses' (Kline 2003: 169). This was a measure in order to increase their own security as well as a means to protect their economic interests (Hristov 2009: 64–5). Death squads and paid assassins have since killed a great number of guerrilla fighters, rival drug dealers, state officials, and ordinary citizens.

In the meantime, of the four guerrilla movements, the FARC especially enjoyed further expansion, particularly in military terms, by decentralising its combating fronts that were dispersed throughout the national territory, which nevertheless were directed by one sole commanding body. By the late 1970s, the FARC also became part of the coca cultivation boom, as this provided an important alternative source of income. The guerrillas came to rule many coca-producing areas, by claiming 'protection money' from local drug producers. For several years, agreements between the guerrillas and drug lords maintained a relatively tranquil situation. Given the military strength of the former, the drug producers had no option but to comply by paying the imposed taxes. However, this status quo ended by increased pressure from the Colombian security forces and the paramilitaries and by the decision of the drug trafficking organisations to create their own armed groups to combat the guerrillas (Molano in Bergquist et al. 1992: 195–216).

The FARC's final objective was to overthrow the government and impose its Marxist-Leninist ideals. The guerrilla movement's anti-imperialist discourse and the fight for land reform were thus central issues in its politics. At the beginning, the FARC, the ELN, the M-19 and EPL received sympathy and active support from many Colombians, especially from the poor inhabitants of the countryside. Although their ideology, particularly in the case of the FARC, is still expressed in the form of demands for social and political equality and justice, for many years their ideals are being overshadowed by their human rights violations and organised crime activities, especially by their financial interest in drug trafficking.

The Colombian conflict intensified considerably in the 1980s. The main victims of the violence were the inhabitants of the countryside. The proliferation of armed members of guerrilla movements, drug trafficking organisations and paramilitary groups, as well as the Colombian armed forces' combat against the irregular armed groups contributed to one of the world's highest homicide rate at the time. In particular, by the end of the decade the drug trade had become the principal reason of murder. Narcoterrorism against the Colombian state continued until the death of Pablo Escobar, the most powerful drug baron, and the dismantling of the Medellín drug cartel towards the end of 1993.

The government took some measures to improve the situation. In April 1989 Decree 48, which had created a legal basis for the existence of Colombian paramilitarism, was nullified and followed by Decree 1194 that prohibited paramilitary activities. Even so, without any legal protection the paramilitary groups continued to expand at the beginning of the 1990s and gained much territorial control in the country.[2] Despite considering themselves as guardians of law and order in the Colombian countryside, a method commonly used has been that of acquiring land by purchasing low priced properties in areas infested by guerrillas. Once the lands were bought, they privately used force in order to drive out the insurgents before gaining full control of the territory (Cubides in Bergquist et al. 2001: 132–3). By the end of the 1990s, most of the paramilitary groups had become part of a paramilitary confederation named the *Autodefensas Unidas de Colombia* (AUC: United Self-Defence Forces of Colombia). The AUC was officially demobilised in 2006 after three years of peace talks between the organisation and the government of president Álvaro Uribe Vélez (2002–10).

---

[2] The paramilitary expansion during the 1990s coincides with FARC's expansion of military presence in new areas, an ongoing process since the early 1980s. FARC's advancement seems to have been financed by an increase of protection money from drug traffickers, landowners, large-scale farmers and multinational corporations. In response, these FARC victims contracted paramilitary groups and private security entities for protection purposes. This led to a large-scale expansion of the paramilitary phenomenon (Richani 2002: 78).

Although many scholars, such as Hough (2011), point out the fact that the FARC enjoyed at least some popular support during the movement's first years of existence, this appears to have dwindled substantially during recent decades. While at the start the guerrillas mainly depended on the more or less voluntary support of the local population, later on the FARC became more independent, since its income was increasingly provided by extortion, ransoms from kidnappings (such as the notorious abduction in 2002 of presidential candidate Ingrid Betancourt by the FARC, which lasted until her liberation by the armed forces in 2008) protection money and drug trafficking. According to Hough (2011: 380), the FARC has lost most of its legitimacy because the rebel movement increasingly used 'violence against the very social groups and classes—the peasantry and working class—who were theorized to be their natural political allies'. Over the years, the guerrilla movement's popular appeal has diminished considerably. Nonetheless, still in 2002 it was able to recruit Tanja Nijmeijer, a young Dutch idealist, who as a student of Spanish did an internship in Colombia. In the following years she would rise in the ranks of the FARC, making international propaganda for the FARC.

Ever since they began, guerrilla movements have been considered the main internal threat by the various Colombian governments. During recent years, the FARC has lost many of their key ideological and military leaders in combat against the Colombian security forces. Despite the movement's military strengthening after disrespecting a truce assigned with Andrés Pastrana's government (1998–2002) in 1998, the FARC has weakened and lost much of its popular support. A particularly heavy loss for the guerrillas has been the death of its sole and indisputable leader and founder Manuel Marulanda, alias Tirofijo ('Sure shot'), in 2008. During the same period, Marulanda's second-in-command, Raúl Reyes was killed by the Colombian armed forces, along with FARC's military leader alias Mono Jojoy, who was killed in 2010. Nonetheless, of all four guerrilla movements, the FARC is the only one that currently maintains the military capacity to seriously threaten public order in Colombia. The ELN also remains active, although on a much smaller scale than the FARC.

3. *International Context and Human Rights*

The endemic violence in Colombia has been a constant concern to international human rights organisations such as Amnesty International and Human Rights Watch. Additionally, various countries also took a large interest in what happened in Colombia. Besides some minor diplomatic incidents with neighbouring countries such as Venezuela and Ecuador, and the limited support of some communist countries to the various guerrilla movements, the main international actor on the Colombian scene has been the United States (US).

All the American presidents since Lyndon Johnson (1963–69) have given active support to the Colombian state in order to combat the various guerrilla movements. However, US policies have clearly changed over time as the focus was determined first by the Cold War, then by the War on Drugs and, since 2001, by the War on Terror. Thus, whereas from the 1960s US officials were primarily worried about a communist take-over in Colombia, since 1989 the struggle against drug trafficking has taken precedence. After the Al Qaeda attacks of 11 September 2001 in New York and Washington, the FARC and the ELN were labelled as terrorist organisations. As a result, especially since the late 1990s, Colombia has become the main recipient of US military and police assistance in the Latin American region.

The human rights situation in Colombia has been largely shaped by the complex, interconnected problems that arose from the multiplicity of violent actors and their dangerous behaviour. The decrease in violence that took place after the National Front was established did not last. The human rights situation worsened considerably as a result of the military strengthening of the FARC, the expansion of the paramilitary groups, the boom in drug production and trafficking activities, and the military operations of the Colombian armed forces (Welna & Gallón 2007).

Human right violations are regularly committed by all parties involved—although to varying degrees—and include unlawful killings, the mistreatment of captured enemy forces, the use of illegal weapons such as land mines, the recruitment of child soldiers, the forced displacements of the civilian population, kidnappings, civilian murders, rape, arbitrary detentions and harassment. In many instances, those who try to improve this situation, such as human rights defenders, trade unionists and other social activists have been intimidated, prosecuted or even killed. In addition to this socio-political violence, Gallón (in Welna & Gallón 2007: 353–411) argues that the human rights crisis was further complicated by crime, social inequity and impunity. During the 1980s and 1990s, the situation has worsened considerably; although statistics are often lacking or are incomplete, Tate (2007: 33) reports that during the beginning of the 1990s, there was an estimated yearly homicide rate of eighty six per one hundred thousand in Colombia. By 2002, this number had decreased to sixty six per one hundred thousand.

Despite the many risks involved, the first local human rights organisations were founded in Colombia during the 1970s. These organisations directed their attention principally to the families and relatives of persons affected by forced disappearances and of individuals imprisoned due to political reasons. During the tenure of Liberal president Julio César Turbay Ayala (1978–82), human rights organisations raised considerable awareness about violations happening in the country. However, once the Conservative Belisario Betancur (1982–86) came to power, the national government prioritised another route to achieve peace: engaging in dialogue with various guerrilla movements. After the breakdown of the peace talks between Betancur's administration and the guerrilla movements, the violation of human rights again became a primary issue during Virgilio Barco's Liberal presidency (1986–90) when a Human Rights Advisory Council was established. Although this council's prime objective consisted of raising awareness of human rights within the armed forces and the Colombian people, Restrepo (in Bergquist et al. 2001) maintains that the newly formed entity also served as a tool to protect the government against national and international critics by blaming the drug traffickers and guerrillas for carrying out human rights violations, and not the state authorities themselves. A similar strategy was also implemented during Turbay Ayala's presidency, when paramilitary groups were blamed for the human rights violations perpetrated by the armed forces. Despite the fact that the Human Rights Advisory Council was expanded in subsequent years, the human rights situation did not always receive the highest priority, frequently it was overshadowed by the effort to fight insurgent groups and strive for a military solution to the conflict (Restrepo in Bergquist et al. 2001: 95–126).

By the 1990s, the international pressure regarding human rights forced various Colombian governments to assume a more active role in this domain.[3] This pressure was principally generated by the United Nations,

---

[3] This pressure coincided with the Colombian state's war against narcoterrorism, which increased in intensity between 1989 and 1993. During this period, the extreme levels of violence and terror affecting Colombian society reached the nation's main cities. According to Restrepo (in Bergquist et al. 2001: 105) 'a consciousness began to awaken in Colombians... of the necessity of creating certain guidelines or living together so that we would not all be destroyed'.

the European Union, and the Inter American Commission for Human Rights. A country office of the United Nations High Commissioner for Human Rights was created in Bogotá during Ernesto Samper's presidency (1994–98). Through this office human rights again occupied centre stage, although a political crisis of the Liberal government soon overshadowed most of the advances made in maintaining human rights in Colombia. A further escalation of the armed conflict in the late 1990s seriously hindered the government's attempts to improve the human rights situation in the country. With the expansion of paramilitary groups and their military operations under the banner of the AUC, international pressure was put on the paramilitaries and their operations. In addition, the fluctuating intensity and dynamics of the armed conflict appear to have considerably influenced the Colombian governments' activities: at times human rights concerns have been overshadowed by the necessity to defeat the guerrilla insurgency. Bergquist (in Bergquist et al. 2001: 207) indicates in his conclusive remarks that it is precisely the absence of peace that obstructs the creation of an 'environment that favours the development of organizations and parties that can sustain and advance the democratization of Colombian society in the future'.

4. *Peace*

The Colombian conflict increased in complexity during the late 1970s and early 1980s. As already discussed above, besides the leftist guerrilla movements, drug dealers and paramilitary groups contributed greatly to the violence and instability of the country. The Colombian government's counterinsurgency strategy [4] against the guerrilla movements only worsened the situation. During the 1980s, great international concern for the human rights situation stimulated the Colombian government to change its policies in order to resolve the crisis, which from the official side was defined as an insurgency and never as a civil war. As a result, peace efforts have been made by various Colombian presidents ever since the end of the National Front.

However, there is an important difference between the guerrilla movements and other armed groups, such as the paramilitaries. Whereas the guerrillas seek to legitimise their cause by being accepted in society,

---

[4] These counterinsurgency strategies were aided militarily and financially by the US government's assistance programmes, which consisted of anti-guerrilla operations and new intelligence techniques (Kline 1999: 15).

paramilitaries and drug traffickers mostly use violent means in order to serve their own interests (Restrepo in Bergquist et al. 2001: 116). Despite the use of criminal acts and severe human rights violations for financial reasons, their political convictions and clearly delineated ideologies set the guerrilla groups (especially the FARC) apart from paramilitaries and drug traffickers: the state is obliged to deal with them differently, as has been illustrated by the several peace negotiation attempts since the late 1970s.

It has to be admitted that most presidents have made sincere efforts to improve the situation, although their strategies varied considerably. Some, like Uribe, stepped up their military efforts in order to weaken the guerrilla movements, while others preferred negotiations over military solutions. However, all peace attempts were seriously hindered by opposition from hardliners. Most presidents were obstructed by people from within the armed forces, right-wing groups and the paramilitaries. On the other hand, radical elements within the guerrilla movements often opposed compromises that were needed to end the conflict. Nonetheless, a few important steps were made, especially when the international situation changed considerably with the fall of communism in the Soviet Union and Eastern Europe.

The Liberal Alfonso López Michelsen was the first president who, in the late 1970s, initiated peace talks with the guerrillas, although he was soon confronted with strong opposition from within his own armed forces. His successor Turbay Ayala also intended to peacefully terminate the conflict by decreeing an amnesty law for insurgent groups in exchange for a peace accord, but this attempt also ended without any result. As the Conservative Belisario Betancur took office yet again a Colombian president invited the guerrillas to the negotiation table. This time prospects seemed more promising. The new president believed that the lack of political participation of the rural masses as well as widespread poverty and injustice constituted a fertile breeding ground for the guerrilla movements and he was prepared to offer major concessions. Thus, in May 1984 he implemented a ceasefire as a part of an agreement with the FARC, EPL and M-19 guerrilla movements. Accordingly the FARC was allowed to create a political movement called *Unión Patriótica* (UP; Patriotic Union) to voice their political demands in the public arena and Betancur even travelled to Spain to talk directly with the leadership of M-19. However, the killing of hundreds of UP-activists and several leaders of M-19 by right-wing paramilitaries as well as terrorist actions by M-19, such as the already mentioned storming of the Palace of Justice, ended any prospects for peace.

In the following years, with communism crumbling in the Soviet Union and Eastern Europe, M-19 and EPL decided to lay down their weapons and negotiate a peace agreement with the new Liberal government of president Barco. In 1991, a new constitution was proclaimed, which aimed at broadening political participation and contained a large section on human, political, indigenous and gender rights. However, even though M-19 and EPL abandoned the armed struggle, the level of violence only seemed to increase. In 1998 the Conservative president Andrés Pastrana made a new effort to reach a peace-agreement with the remaining guerrilla movements. He even awarded a considerable demilitarised zone in the south of the country to the FARC. The guerrillas took control of the area and some of its most radical leaders profited from the situation to strengthen themselves militarily, politically and financially.

With these actions, they violated several agreements signed with the Colombian government. The FARC also continued with their kidnapping and drug related practices, and intensified the armed attacks against the state and its infrastructure. In 2002, the peace process was terminated and the Colombian armed forces immediately increased their military operations against the insurgent group yet again. After the failure of president Pastrana to make peace with the leaders of the remaining guerrilla movements, his successor Uribe embarked upon a different strategy. He significantly increased the state's security budget and by combating the guerrilla movement with renewed resources, he 'postponed' any hope of future peace talks. Moreover, during his eight year mandate the increased presence of the state in rural areas considerably reduced the extremely high levels of violence and crime since the early years of the twenty-first century. He also succeeded in weakening the fighting power of the FARC. In addition to the apparent loss of the social recognition of the guerrilla movement, this may have been the reason that, in September 2012, the Colombian government under president Juan Manuel Santos (in office since August 2010) and the FARC announced to open yet another round of peace talks which were initiated in Oslo, Norway, in October 2012. If an agreement is reached, Colombia will take a major step towards ending the fighting after almost fifty years of severe armed conflict, which is estimated to have cost approximately two hundred and fifty thousand lives.

Conclusion

It must be admitted that the prospects for a peace agreement now are better than they were before. Much has changed since the 1960s; communism has lost its appeal and the FARC ultimately failed to convince the general population of its intentions. Since 2001, the use of terror for political goals has become more suspect than ever before. On the other hand, especially since the end of the National Front, the democratic system seems to function more efficiently and has opened up to growing popular participation and free national elections. The new constitution of 1991 guarantees all kind of rights, while mechanisms to combat human right violations have been set up. Under president Uribe, the presence of police and the armed forces have extended considerably and this had a positive effect upon the security situation in the country.

However, there are also many things that remain the same. Widespread poverty and an enormous gap between the rich and poor continue to exist. The state still struggles with exercising an adequate presence in the more remote parts of the country, and it has difficulties with providing justice to a significant amount of its citizens. On top of that, since the late 1970s the grand scale production and trafficking of drugs have created a large clandestine economic sector and a considerable increase in criminal activities and related violence. Thus, even if peace negotiations are to be successful, it is doubtful whether security in the countryside will improve quickly. Violence is likely to remain endemic in many parts of the country and only a consistent policy that combines socio-economic development with a firm stand on maintaining public order could, in the long run, improve the situation.

Further Reading

Bergquist, C.W., Ricardo, P. & Gonzalo, S.G. (eds), 2001, *Violence in Colombia, 1990–2000: Waging war and negotiating peace*, SR Books, Wilmington.

———, 1992, *Violence in Colombia: The contemporary crisis in historical perspective*, SR Books, Wilmington.

Bouvier, V.M., 2009, *Colombia: Building peace in a time of war*, US Institute for Peace, Washington.

Camacho, G.A., 2004, *Colombia from the inside: Perspectives on drugs, war and peace*, CEDLA, Amsterdam.

Hough, P.A., 2011, 'Guerrilla insurgency as organized crime: explaining the so-called "political involution" of the revolutionary armed forces of Colombia', *Politics & Society* 39, 379–413.

Kline, H., 1999, *State-building and conflict resolution in Colombia, 1986–1994*, University of Alabama Press, Tuscaloosa.

Livingstone, G., 2004, *Inside Colombia: Drugs, democracy and war*, Rutgers University Press, New Brunswick.

Oquist, P., 1980, *Violence, conflict, and politics in Colombia*, Academic Press, New York.

Palacios, M., 2003, *Between legitimacy and violence: A history of Colombia, 1875–2002*, Duke University Press, Durham.

Payne, J., 1968, *Patterns of conflict in Colombia*, Yale University Press, New Haven.

Pearce, J., 1990, *Colombia: Inside the labyrinth*, Latin America Bureau (Research and Action) Limited, London.

Rojas, C. & Judy, M. (eds), 2005, *Elusive peace: International, national and local dimensions of conflict in Colombia*, Palgrave Macmillan, New York.

Simons, G., 2004, *Colombia: A brutal history*, Saqi, London.

Taylor, S.L., 2009, *Voting amid violence: Electoral democracy in Colombia*, University Press of New England, Hanover.

Welna, C. & Gallon, G. (eds), 2007, *Peace, democracy and human rights in Colombia*, University of Notre Dame Press, Notre Dame.

References

Babbitt, E.F. & Lutz, E.L. (eds), 2009, *Human rights & conflict resolution in context: Colombia, Sierra Leone & Northern Ireland*, Syracuse University Press, New York.

Bergquist, C.W., Ricardo, P. & Gonzalo, S.G. (eds), 2001, *Violence in Colombia, 1990–2000: Waging war and negotiating peace*, SR Books, Wilmington.

——, 1992, *Violence in Colombia: The contemporary crisis in historical perspective*, SR Books, Wilmington.

Carrigan, A., 1993, *The palace of justice: A Colombian tragedy*, Four Walls Eight Windows, New York.

Chernick, M., 1999, 'Negotiating peace amid multiple forms of violence: The protracted search for a settlement to the armed conflicts in Colombia', in C. Arson (ed.), *Comparative peace processes in Latin America*, pp. 159–97, Stanford University Press, Stanford.

Hough, P.A., 2011, 'Guerrilla insurgency as organized crime: Explaining the so-called "political involution" of the revolutionary armed forces of Colombia', *Politics & Society* 39, 379–413.

Hristov, J., 2009, *Blood and capital: The paramilitarization of Colombia*, Ohio University Press, Athens.

Kline, H., 1999, *State-building and conflict resolution in Colombia, 1986–1994*, University of Alabama Press, Tuscaloosa.

——, 2003, 'Colombia: Lawlessness, drug trafficking and the carving up of the state', R.I. Rothberg (ed.), *State failure and state weakness in time of terror*, pp. 161–83, World Peace Foundation, Cambridge.

——, 2007, *Chronicle of a failure foretold: The peace process of Colombian president Andrés Pastrana*, University of Alabama Press, Tuscaloosa.

——, 2009, *Showing teeth to the Dragons: State-building by Colombian President Álvaro Uribe Vélez 2002–2006*, University of Alabama Press, Tuscaloosa.

Oquist, P., 1980, *Violence, conflict, and politics in Colombia*, Academic Press, New York.

Osterling, J., 1989, *Democracy in Colombia: Clientilist politics and guerrilla warfare*, Transaction Publishers, New Brunswick.

Palacios, M., 2003, *Between legitimacy and violence: A history of Colombia, 1875–2002*, Duke University Press, Durham.

Payne, J., 1968, *Patterns of conflict in Colombia*, Yale University Press, New Haven.

Richani, N., 2002, *Systems of violence: The political economy of war and peace in Colombia*, State University of New York Press, New York.

Rochlin, J.F., 2007, *Social forces and the revolution in military affairs: The cases of Colombia and Mexico*, Palgrave Macmillan, New York.

Rojas, C. & Meltzer, J. (eds), 2005, *Elusive peace: International, national and local dimensions of conflict in Colombia*, Palgrave Macmillan, New York.

Simons, G., 2004, *Colombia: A brutal history*, Saqi, London.

Tate, W., 2007, *Counting the dead: The culture and politics of human rights activism in Colombia*, University of California Press, Berkeley.

Taylor, S.L., 2009, *Voting amid violence: Electoral democracy in Colombia*, University Press of New England, Hanover.

Tokatlián, J.G., 1988, 'National security and drugs: Their impact on Colombian-US relations', *Journal of Interamerican Studies and World Affairs* 1, 133–61.

——, 2000, 'Colombia at war: The search for a peace diplomacy', *International Journal of Politics, Culture and Society*, XIV-2, 333–63.

Welna, C. & Gallón, G. (eds), 2007, *Peace, democracy and human rights in Colombia*, University of Notre Dame Press, Notre Dame.

CHAPTER THIRTEEN

GENOCIDE, WAR AND PEACE IN RWANDA

Helen M. Hintjens

The *genocidaires* did not completely unleash the dogs of genocide until after April 21, when they could be certain there would be no international intervention. (Barnett 2002: 157)

Introduction: War and Genocide in Rwanda

The genocide in Rwanda started on 6 April 1994, and intensified on 21 April, when United Nations Assistance Mission to Rwanda (UNAMIR) forces were cut back from two thousand five hundred to just two hundred and fifty. This bizarre decision followed the deliberate torture and brutal murder of Belgian United Nations (UN) peacekeepers, shortly after the murder of the elected Prime Minister, Agathe Uwilingiyimana, whom they had been defending on 7 April. When genocidal forces retreated from Rwanda in July 1994, they had killed almost the entire pre-existing Tutsi population. Military and political 'Hutu Power' extremists had achieved the goal of genocide. Inadvertently, they also brought to power their military enemies: the Rwandan Patriotic Army (RPA).

In 1990, the RPA invaded from Uganda in 1990, and took over the task of reconstructing Rwanda. Genocide hastened the most radical regime change since independence, transforming Rwanda's socio-economic and political landscape. Security problems have persisted since 1994, with cross-border attacks from Zaire by former genocidal forces, assassinations of government critics, and cases of army brutality and torture. However, within Rwanda peace had more or less been restored from 1996–98. The Rwandan Patriotic Front (RPF), the political wing of the RPA, is now the main single party in Rwanda, and is headed by President Paul Kagame. In many ways he seems to personify the country's post-genocide struggles, and the difficulty of reconciling peace and security with justice.

The genocide was not acknowledged by the international community until it was too late. In mid-June, the French, under UN auspices, announced the creation of a 'safe zone' (*Zone Turquoise*) in South-Western

Rwanda. As well as saving some Tutsi lives, French intervention allowed armed killers to flee across the Zairean border. Humanitarian agencies fed almost two million Rwandans stranded in harsh camp conditions in Eastern Zaire. Meanwhile, genocidal ideology dangerously spilled over into Zaire, a country on the brink of collapse.

This chapter discusses Rwanda's civil war from 1990, and the genocide of April to mid-July 1994, in their local, historical and international contexts. The idea of 'Hutu power' which informed plans for genocide is traced back to Belgian colonial administrative practices and European ideas about racial difference. Civil war intensified the multiple crises that started to beset Rwanda from 1986 onwards. Competing explanations of genocide are considered, and the chapter asks why international intervention failed so miserably. Post-genocide reconstruction policies and peace-building efforts are also briefly reflected on.

The main focus is genocide rather than civil war, because of the special nature of genocide, as defined in the Genocide Convention of 1948. Genocide refers to 'acts committed with intent to destroy, in whole or in part, a national, ethnical, racial or religious group'. Unlike civil war, genocide requires other states to intervene to prevent it, and punish the perpetrators. Yet in Rwanda in 1994, most genocide victims were simply abandoned to their killers. Donor funding has paid for prosecutions of genocide organisers at the International Criminal Tribunal for Rwanda (ICTR) in Arusha, created under UN auspices in 1995. The United States (US), United Kingdom (UK) and China have replaced Rwanda's pre-genocide development partners, particularly Belgium and France.

Genocide targeted unarmed Tutsi civilians, for elimination. Any Hutu or Twa thought sympathetic to the Tutsi were also killed during the genocide period. It is estimated that eighty percent of genocide victims were killed within just six weeks of 6 April, a rate of killing roughly five times that of Nazi death camps (Prunier 1995: 174). A large (and still disputed) number of non-Tutsi Rwandans were also killed during the genocide. These victims can also be viewed as casualties of genocide, but this depends on one's definition of: '...a national, ethnical, racial or religious group'. The international community and the UN's failure to act has provoked a great deal of soul-searching since 1994. This chapter briefly considers new forms of humanitarian interventionism elaborated, in part, and at least ostensibly, in response to the evident failure to prevent genocide in Rwanda.

It is beyond the scope of this chapter to cover how civil war and genocide have spilled over from Rwanda into neighbouring Zaire (now the Democratic Republic of Congo), and the killings, warfare, regime changes and violent exploitation that have resulted. However, regional developments such as the decision of diasporic Rwandans from Uganda to invade Rwanda in 1990 are important (Otunnu 2000). Without ignoring the importance of this, this chapter focuses mainly on violent conflict, genocide and peacebuilding *inside* Rwanda.

1. *The Importance of Rwandan History and the Question of 'Race'*

The first kingdoms in what is now Rwanda emerged around the 1350s and expanded until the late nineteenth century. Scholarship based on oral traditions makes up for the lack of archaeological remains.[1] The slave trade did not reach Rwanda; the first Europeans who arrived in 1894 were German soldiers. The centralised kingdom they encountered was described as quasi-feudal, the king and his overlords ruling over minor chiefs, and a majority of peasant subjects. The *mwami*, or king of Rwanda had a court complete with aristocratic mannerisms, entertainers and specially trained royal warriors. The aristocrats' great height and 'Spartan' athleticism became fabled in Europe.[2]

After the Germans were deprived of their colony, Ruanda-Urundi was administered by Belgium from 1921 under a League of Nations Trusteeship. Coffee became the staple export. Belgians introduced sweeping reforms, issuing identity cards labelled with: 'Hutu' 'Tutsi' and 'Twa'. It is from this period that the estimates that Tutsi composed 14% of the population, Hutu 85% and Twa less than 1% are dated. Historically, these social categories were about social class or status. Until such identity markers markers remained on Rwandans' identity papers. They were used to identify victims in the genocide, and only removed after 1994 by the new government.

Classical European race science was also imposed by Belgium, and even after the Holocaust discredited race as 'Man's most dangerous myth',[3] race categories continued to be used by most colonising powers in Africa (Taylor 1999).[4] Labelling Rwandans as Hutu, Tutsi or Twa was inspired by the race categories of men like John Hanning Speke, nineteenth century English scientific explorer. He distinguished 'Bantu' peoples in Africa (with whom Hutu were later equated) from 'Nilotic' or 'Hamitic' peoples

---

[1] One of the most widely cited studies is Vansina (2004).
[2] This is discussed in detail in the book: Bale (2002).
[3] See the classic study: Montagu (1953).
[4] See another thoughtful study: Mosse (1978).

(with whom Tutsis were later equated). Without any evidential basis, Tutsis were said to have been later arrivals in the African Great Lakes region, migrating from North-East Africa or even the Middle East. They were considered a 'natural' elite, dominating Bantu people across the continent (Hintjens 2001: 41–6; Taylor 1999: 55–97). Twa were hunter-gatherers who hardly figured in the racialised mythical narrative. Rwandans learned such stories through mission schools, churches and through the colonial identity categories imposed on them. The 'Hamitic hypothesis' remains a challenge for educators, and such stereotypes still influence how and outsiders see Rwanda, and understand the causes of violent conflict and genocide.

In pre-colonial Rwanda there was war against neighbouring kingdoms, rather than killings between 'groups' of Rwandans. An extremely intricate and hierarchical pre-colonial social order involved granting cattle, land, and taxing 'clients' in kind and in labour, and through men's military service. The Belgians who took over Rwanda and Burundi struggled with this complexity, and decided to simplify governance arrangements. By exaggerating physical differences, they justified a monopoly of public posts for Tutsis, and thus started to 'divide and rule' Rwandans and Burundians alike (Mamdani 2000; Prunier 1995). Rwandans, who had inter-married, who had little spatial separation of housing or land, started to be divided as if they were 'tribes', yet they shared common religious beliefs, common cultural practices, and language. While Tutsi specialised in cattle herding, and Hutu in crop farming, Twa in pottery and hunting, they were all were closely inter-connected through allegiance to kingship, vassalage and clans that cut across 'racial' divisions. Rwandans' social ties had been relatively fluid, although also unequal.

Only in the northwest of the country did the Kingdom not assimilate to European rule. Here, historically independent Hutu kingdoms resisted incorporation until these areas were annexed forcibly under the Belgians in the 1930s. This caused a sense of resentment among Northern Hutu elites. It was this sense of grievance that later helped inform the genocidal extremist ideology of Hutu Power.

After the Second World War, as a Belgian UN Trustee Territory, the Hutu majority started to be viewed as 'victims' by many Belgian colonial administrators and missionaries. In 1959, the aristocratic Tutsi elite who had done the Belgians' dirty work for so long was abandoned to its fate: the emerging educated Hutu viewed the Tutsi political elite as worse than the colonisers, and evoked the 'democratic' right of Hutus to run the country in their own 'majority' interests. The 1957 'Manifesto of the Bahutu', published by Gregoire Kayibanda, who would later become Rwanda's first president, was written in the style of a 'Hutu bill of rights'. When the king, *Mwami* Rudahigwa, died in 1959 in suspicious circumstances, killings of Tutsi elites started across Rwanda. What came to be called the 'Revolution of 1959', marked the start of several years of persecution of Tutsi Rwandans, many of whom fled to Tanzania, Burundi, Zaire and especially to Uganda, where civil wars encouraged Rwandans to take refuge in an 'imagined Rwanda' to which they longed to return.

In 1972, after killings of Tutsi in Rwanda under President Kayibanda, Major Juvenal Habyarimana came to power in a coup. He refused to allow the Rwandan diaspora back into the country, claiming there was no land for them. But in 1988, the Ugandan exiles set up the RPA, and two years later, in October 1990, they decided to invade so as to secure by force the right to return. During 1972–1990, Rwanda was relatively peaceful domestically, with less overt anti-Tutsi violence than during Kayibanda's time. In contrast with neighbouring Burundi, where an estimated one hundred thousand to two hundred thousand Hutu were massacred in 1972, killings of Tutsi in Rwanda were limited after 1972. In 1974, Rwanda became a one-party state and Rwandan Tutsi were oppressed through strict educational quotas, and by being excluded from the army and politics, 'facilitated by the long-instituted practice of identification, right from birth, of all Rwandese nationals by ethnicity on official records and identity documentation' (Goolooba-Mutebi 2008: 13). Tight controls on Rwandans' movements inside Rwanda continued, reinforced by colonial controls.

The relative calm of the Habyarimana years came to an abrupt end in 1986–87, when world coffee prices plummeted. Rwandan peasants even ripped out coffee bushes to plant food crops; such was the desperation. Rwandan refugees in neighbouring countries also started to come under pressure to return to Rwanda. 1990 was a turning point in the path to genocide. It was the year 'structural adjustment' reforms were first imposed by the International Monetary Fund and World Bank, and was the year that President Habyarimana came under donor pressure to allow for multiparty elections. With the Cold War over, one-party regimes like Habyarimana's were becoming an embarrassment for Western allies. The RPA, sensing that Habyarimana's regime was weakening, chose this time to invade in October 1990. They demanded the right to return for three generations of exiles. Habyarimana responded with a massive arms build-up, and French military intervention began at the same time. In contrast, vigilant efforts by Tanzanians and the Organisation for African Unity (OAU) to foster peace were frustrated as the Arusha Accords failed to hold.

2. *1990–94: From Civil War to Genocide*

After 1990, the Rwandan political elite started to respond to the multiple pressures building up by playing the 'race card' more than ever. In 1991, the government faced massive public demonstrations, and Habyarimana was forced to announce elections. His regime took part in Arusha negotiations, but rejected the idea of RPA soldiers being incorporated into the Rwandan army. Senior army officers and 'Hutu power' political elites rallied around the noble-born wife of Habyarimana, and subverted the peace process. New political parties, the Parti Social Démocrate (PSD), and Parti Libéral (PL), at first preached moderation and reform, but soon became split between Hutu Power factions and more 'moderate' factions that supported the Arusha peace process. The extremist Committee for the Defence of the Republic (CDR) organised mass Hutu power rallies in Kigali by 1992, and moderates were identified as traitors to the cause of beating the RPA 'inyenzi' ('cockroaches') in the civil war.

'Hutu power' militias throughout Rwanda started mobilising young men for training in 'self-defence' and football. Elite military officers opposed the Arusha Accords and started to draw up lists of prominent Tutsi 'enemies' within Rwanda. 'Réseau Zero', or the 'Zero Network', disaffected military and Northern Hutu elites, acquired intellectual and media allies and planned for a 'final solution' to the civil war that could prevent regime change. When several thousand Tutsi civilians were massacred in Bugesera in Northern Rwanda in early 1992, a high level UN fact-finding visit concluded that preparations for massacres were underway. The international community, however, felt reassured by a ceasefire that was negotiated under the Arusha Accords in July 1992. Also in 1992, the Rwandan army, trained by French soldiers, had managed to prevent the RPA from reaching Kigali.

In 1993, crop failures resulted in widespread hunger and malaria, the HIV and AIDS resulted in rising mortality, worsening the effects of civil war on civilians and increasingly militarising public expenditure. There were shortages of vital medicines and foodstuffs. When UN forces stationed in Rwanda informed the UN Secretary General in early 1993 of plans to massacre civilians named on lists, the international community appeared to be paralysed. They refused to believe that genocide was being planned and could be executed in Rwanda. As it turned out, 'underdevelopment was [to prove] ... no obstacle to genocide' (Gourevitch 1998: 96). Only one or two non-governmental organisations (NGOs) like Oxfam warned of the dangers ahead. Most 'development community' observers continued to view Rwanda as a model of good practice until the genocide was almost upon them (Uvin 1998; Waller 1993).

In October 1993, the first Hutu President of Burundi, Melchior Ndadaye, was murdered by army officers, just months after being elected. Stories of atrocities from fleeing Burundians destabilised an already volatile situation inside Rwanda. On 6 April 1994, the genocide was triggered when a plane carrying President Habyarimana and the President of Burundi was shot over Kigali into the grounds of the Presidential Palace. Killings started almost at once, including the murder of Prime Minister Agathe Uwilingimana and ten Belgian peacekeepers. The immediate international response was to leave Rwanda as fast as possible: the media showed scenes of white foreigners panicking amidst the dead bodies already lining Kigali's roads. By 10 April, most foreign nationals who could leave had been airlifted out. After 21 April, only a tiny UNAMIR contingent remained, along with some humanitarian agencies like the Red Cross. They were unable to save many Rwandans. By early July, genocide ended, and between five hundred thousand and one million Rwandans were dead. Only around ten percent of those Tutsi who had been living inside Rwanda on 6 April had survived.

Throughout April and May, US and UN Security Council staff repeated the view that what was happening inside Rwanda was not really genocide, but massacres and civil war. Media reports of 'tribal hatreds' reinforced these misperceptions (Prunier 1995). In the face of killings that were astonishingly rapid, the predominant response was indifference and denial. Prunier (1995) estimated that twenty thousand people were killed in Kigali during the first week of the genocide. By the time US authorities admitted that genocide was happening, the genocide inside Rwanda was almost over. The massive scale and speed of the killings appeared to have caught the international community completely off guard (Prunier 1995: 172–5). At the time, Africa correspondents of major media outlets were mostly covering the end of Apartheid in South Africa. The French *Zone Turquoise* in Rwanda's South-West enabled genocidal forces to escape like 'fishes in the sea: almost two million Rwandan civilians ... crossed the Zairean borders' (ibid.). Refugee camps became bases for genocidal militia's whose cross-border raids terrorised Rwandans, and provoked an armed response from the new Rwandan army. Two decades after genocide, the genocidal *interahamwe* militias continue to operate in Eastern DRC.

The RPA has been widely credited with ending genocide and bringing peace to Rwanda. The complete failure of the UN and its powerful member states reinforced the impression that the RPA had ended genocide single-handedly. Belgian and Francophone experts sometimes complained about the 'anglophone' RPA, seeing it as a Trojan Horse of the US, and accusing the new regime of serious war crimes in Rwanda, during the civil war, after the genocide, and later in Eastern Zaire. Inside Rwanda, Tutsi survivors and Hutu who waited to welcome the RPA had to live alongside so-called old caseload refugees returning from Uganda, Tanzania, Burundi and Zaire after decades away. Camps in Eastern Zaire were soon emptied by force, and survivors and old caseload refugees, returning in the hope of recovering houses and land lost, were expected to live alongside 'new caseload refugees'. The changes in both rural and urban communities across Rwanda were to be profound.

In late 1994 Rwanda resembled a graveyard; it was a place of mourning. The 'whole machinery of government that could not be taken out of the country was systematically and deliberately destroyed' by the end of genocide (Government of Rwanda 1995: 13). As Rwanda's new regime gradually started to rebuild the country, they initially received little support, and far more was being spent in the vast refugee camps of Eastern Zaire, which caused considerable bitterness. In 1995, UNAMIR reported on the use of violence by RPA troops to force civilians to leave camps and return home. Some new caseload returnees then spent years in dangerously overcrowded prisons, accused of genocide. Cases of summary justice were documented by the present government. Crimes, its critics would say, still not fully acknowledged.

One researcher, Prunier, confesses that it was easy to support the new regime shortly after a genocide, when feelings of guilt and anger at Western moral cowardice were still very much alive. Yet Rwanda's involvement in Zaire's civil war helped topple President Mobutu, and set off a pattern of violent resource pillage that continues to trouble the entire region. Western donors like the UK, for example, mostly ignored the mounting evidence that unjustified force was used by the new Rwandan army inside Rwanda and in former Zaire.

3. Explanations of the Rwanda Genocide

Some research suggests that genocides occur in the last stages of wars, when one side appears to be losing. Genocide targets unarmed civilians for mass killings; it is a weapon of war used by states and obliterates selected civilians in lieu of militarily defeating an armed enemy.[5] In Rwanda, as in Europe, genocide rested on the prior racial categorisation of the population. Tutsi Rwandans were defined as aliens, the legacy of nineteenth century 'race' theories, which first formed the basis for colonial administration and then for the 'Hutu power' ideology that underpinned the organising of the 1994 genocide.

One of the first studies of the Rwandan genocide, based on detailed oral testimony from survivors and witnesses, was African Rights' report, *Death, despair, defiance* (1995), whose key researcher was Rakiya Omaar. Human Rights Watch later published *Leave none to tell the tale*, also based on oral testimonies, with Alison des Forges as lead researcher.[6] Even before the genocide was over, academic debate started about its underlying and immediate causes. In the face of misleading media reports of 'ancient tribal hatreds', there were efforts to look deeper.

Two early studies by Gerard Prunier (1995) and Philip Gourevitch (1999) proved to be influential. Later Peter Uvin (1998) and Mahmood Mamdani (2001) were also widely cited, in different ways elaborating on the role of the international community. Long-standing Rwandan scholars like Filip Reyntjens and Rene Lemarchand also wrote extensively on the Rwanda Genocide, and were sceptical from the start of the post-genocide regime.[7] The French scholar, Andre Guichaoua elaborated on the unfolding of genocide in Butare, in South Rwanda. His study traced in detail how local officials and others responded to orders coming from Kigali to kill local Tutsis and Hutu sympathisers. In some areas like Butare, there was substantial resistance to such orders (Guichaoua 2005). By contrast with these detailed studies, much economic scholarship on the genocide has

---

[5] On this, see this interesting study that includes Rwanda and the Holocaust: Midlarsky (2005).

[6] The HRW report (but not the African Rights one) is available online at: http://addisvoice.com/Ethiopia%20under%20Meles/Rwanda.pdf, making it a useful research tool. It is still the most widely-cited report on the Rwandan genocide itself and how it unfolded. At around six hundred pages, it is also one of the most exhaustive.

[7] For a full record of Reyntjens' writing, see his profile at the University of Antwerp: http://anet.ua.ac.be/acadbib/ua/00952#1995. Rene Lemarchand's most recent study is *The Dynamics of Violence in Central Africa*, University of Pennsylvania Press, 2011.

been plagued by lack of hard data. A few studies have been more or less successful in using quantitative data to test hypotheses about how the genocide proceeded to try and gain some insight into the dynamics of the killings. Studies have brought out are the differing regional dynamics across the country, for example, by reflecting on the technologies and mechanisms of killings during the genocide.[8]

In particular, one recent study has managed to impress most scholars who study the Rwandan genocide. Combining quantitative and qualitative methodologies, and giving serious attention to the perpetrators of genocide themselves, Scot Straus' book, *The order of genocide* (2006), has become more or less a standard text for teaching about the genocide. Drawing on interviews inside prisons with around a hundred Rwandans prosecuted for genocide crimes, the study draws evidence from those most directly involved. The strength of the study is that different kinds of data are used in addressing different kinds of 'causality'. The study confirms what was already established in the work of Linda Melvern (2004)—that the genocide was planned. However Straus suggests that the transition from civil war to actual genocide was not smooth or inevitable. Instead he proposes that genocide arose in response to the killing of the President, and was only possible because of the powerful capacity of the state to transmit orders. Civil war turned into genocide, not only because plans were drawn up and implemented, but because ordinary Rwandans felt obliged to fight to defend the 'majority' population in the face of their enemies.

Straus' research has helped to discredit some previously popular explanations of genocide—especially the idea of ethnic hatred—as found in many journalists' accounts. The suggestion that civil war and the genocide were both caused by demographic pressures and land hunger was also contested by Straus' findings. Rwanda remains the most densely populated country in Africa, so the neo-Malthusian explanation for conflict and killings still has appeal, even though it is rarely supported with any empirical evidence. Those convicted of genocidal killings did not include property and land as significant factors motivating them at the time of the killings. The main reasons they gave were to avenge the death of the President, to comply with orders by the authorities, and to take part in the 'war effort' (Straus 2006: 122–52). That genocide was closely interconnected with the civil war in the minds of Rwandans is hardly a startling

---

[8] Even this prize-winning article suffered from the problem of a lack of hard data with which to test hypotheses: Verwimp (2006).

proposition, given that the genocide took place in the midst of civil war (Straus 2006: 157, 166). Even so, this confusion and overlapping of categories of genocide and civil war helps to explain both how people complied with orders to kill inside Rwanda during the genocide, and also how the idea that this was civil war was used to justify inaction by the UN.

Ultimately it was the Rwandan state that proved to be the key institution in organising the genocide of one group of the population by the others. Fixed identity markers on ID documents made possible an efficient 'social sorting' process that facilitated rapid genocide. The extremists' Hutu power ideology justified the killings as being Hutu Rwandans' patriotic duty. Political and military elites, with dreams of keeping power for themselves, had come to control the state and the army during the civil war. Some former *genocidaires* remain in exile until today, and they and their foreign supporters in Belgium and elsewhere still deny that the genocide was anything but a phase in a civil war started by the RPA. Protecting themselves from extradition, some genocide suspects in exile support the *interahamwe* militias operating in Eastern DRC, and claim to defend the Hutu majority whilst they only protect themselves. A conspiracy theory has developed, according to which the RPA (having been backed by its Anglophone friends) had shot down Habyarimana's plane on 6 April, and thus deliberately triggered the genocide that brought it to power. At the very least, those who propagate this theory have to admit that the jury is still out on who is responsible for the act that set the genocide in motion.

It is tempting to compare the genocide in Rwanda with the Holocaust of Jews, Gypsies and other groups in World War II. Rwandans sometimes draw such parallels themselves (Eltringham 2004). The actual processes involved were of course very different; the 'low-tech' mass participatory genocide in Rwanda brought a diaspora home, whereas in Europe, the technologically intensive Holocaust, conducted in comparative secrecy, drove most Jewish survivors into exile. Comparative genocide studies can draw rich parallels however, between the Hutu Power ideology that informed genocide in Rwanda and the role that the ideology of Aryan racial superiority played in the Holocaust. In both cases, there is the same hostility to inter-mixing, and the same carefully crafted politics of denial. Both genocides started with a claim to victim status by the perpetrating state, engaging in a form of reverse psychology. Compulsory public killings were perhaps the most unique feature of genocide in Rwanda, resulting in a large number of people being suspected of genocide crimes. These crimes would later have to be dealt with in the name of post-genocide justice.

To sum up this section, several crucial factors have been identified in much of the literature explaining the genocide in Rwanda:

1) The strong Rwandan state with its highly organised and centralised set of structures, was an institution capable of mobilising the entire population. Without the state's capacity to govern, even during wartime, genocide could have been conceived, but not translated into mass civic action through selected killings. This explanation appears central to the studies of both Straus (2006) and Prunier (1995).

2) Multiple crises of 1986–93: By inter-locking and reinforcing one another, the coffee price crisis of 1986, the emergence of new pandemics combined with structural adjustment, enforced 'democratisation', crop failures and hunger all aggravated the impact of the civil war when it began in October 1990. Multi-party elections proved to polarise Rwandans, especially since they took place during a pause in the civil war. Media liberalisation opened up the possibility of newspapers and a radio station promoting extremist Hutu Power ideology.

3) The regional refugee question: Armed refugees wanted the right of return, and land. The Arusha Accords required power-sharing with the RPA in the Rwandan army, and this pushed some senior Rwandan political and military elites to start planning extremist solutions, leading to the actual genocide.

4) International failure to protect: The international community's utter failed to respond to signals and warnings of genocide and mass killings of unarmed civilians is stressed in several accounts (Barnett 1999; Mamdani 2001).

5) Historically inherited genocide ideology: The racial ideology introduced by Europeans, turned into administrative categories of the population, are considered by several researchers and by the Rwandan government itself to have had a lasting influence on the passage from civil war to genocide (Government of Rwanda 1995; Taylor 1999). Colonial rule imported racial categories that took on a life of their own, proving lethal both for Rwandans and for others in the wider African Great Lakes region.

Interestingly, only one area inside Rwanda, the *commune* of Giti, managed to avoid genocide, waiting until the RPA arrived a few days after the start of the genocide (10–11 April). This case was studied by Straus (2006: 85–7) and by Theogene Bangwanubusa (2009: 173–6) in his PhD thesis. Giti, a sleepy, remote place, was fortunate to be relatively close to the RPA front when the genocide started. The local population received orders to kill, but resisted until RPA soldiers arrived. Those who slaughtered Tutsi cattle during the first few days of the genocide were arrested, sending a signal that violence would not be tolerated.

4. Whose Responsibility to Protect?

Unlike many other mass atrocities, there are virtually no records of actual killings during the Rwandan genocide. Obsessive recording did not characterise this genocide as it did the Holocaust, for example. Only radio broadcasts give a contemporary record of what was happening. Filming from her hotel room shortly before fleeing the country, Belgian-Canadian journalist Els de Temmerman recorded the killing of a female genocide victim, in her film The dead are alive.[9] This image was reconstructed in the film Hotel Rwanda, along with other images of the dead at the start of the genocide. For the most part, processes of killing have had to be established, legally and historically, without the benefit of film or direct documentary evidence by perpetrators. Verbal, secondary and 'expert' accounts of events have been a critical source of evidence. Alison des Forges, a Human Rights Watch researcher on Rwanda, and later key expert witness on Rwanda at the ICTR, provided testimony that was instrumental in prosecutions of crimes of genocide, the first of these being Jean-Paul Akayezu, former mayor of Taba.[10]

There is footage as well of the hasty, panicked departure of many foreigners - all those with the privilege of having the 'right' kind of passports. As local Tutsi and moderate Hutu are left behind to face the killers, those who could leave, including 'those who, for years had sown the seeds of ethnic hatred and helped build a vast machinery of death, were lifted to safety in French planes' (Callamard 1999: 176) and other planes, to safety. In Kigali's Ecole Technique, de Temmerman filmed terrified civilians' pleas for protection as French troops played the loud classical broadcast on Rwandan national radio. As the last caucasian stragglers were picked up, armed killers were filmed moving in, and the scene receded out of sight. This case was documented in the ICTR trial which found Georges

---

[9] Unfortunately this film is not generally available, even online. However there is some information on it at the following site: http://www.imdb.com/title/tt0366346/.

[10] For details of the final sentence, see: http://www.unictr.org/tabid/155/Default.aspx?ID=472.

Rutaganda, former leader of Interahamwe militias, guilty of moving into the Ecole Technique and ordering the killing of all Tutsi among those who had sought protection in the grounds. After 21 April, the genocide extended its scope beyond the capital, and included every woman and child with Tutsi origins as a target, moving into schools, municipal offices, churches, sports fields, marshes and banana plantations across the entire country.

One observer noted the mix of 'cynicism, despair, self-deception and wishful thinking' that characterised UN responses to the evidence of planning and execution of a genocide in Rwanda at the time (Barnett 2002: 131). The UN also 'provided a shield behind which member states could hide their individual apathy and indifference' (Barnett 2002: 145). Rwanda was a member of the Security Council at the time, and in mid-May the Foreign Minister of Rwanda's illegal Transitional Government even addressed the Security Council, claiming that the killings were caused by historical traumas of the perpetrators, the Hutus, and their 'collective memory [of]... over four centuries of cruel and ruthless domination...' by the Tutsis (Barnett 200: 146). By blaming the Tutsis for their ruthless crimes, he exonerated their 'traumatised' killers and reinforced the indifference of many inside the UN Security Council. Damning evidence had been presented, but had been ignored. The peace-making efforts of the New Zealand and Czech Ambassadors to the UN, and the calls of Tanzania's Julius Nyerere and the OAU for a stronger UN mandate, were significant exceptions. However, by the time it was acknowledged that genocide was taking place, it was arguably too late to act, or to save the victims.

This spectacular failure to act, followed by aid given to suspected killers in refugee camps in Eastern Zaire, prompted much soul-searching among the international 'humanitarian' community. The UN system appeared morally bankrupt, and seemed unable to help a traumatised, dislocated Rwanda. Meanwhile, donors were accused of abandoning Rwanda and its people to their fate. Within Rwanda, few could see any credible alternative to the RPF regime, whatever its faults—and this largely remains the case today as well—claims of 'never again' sound especially hollow after the Rwandan genocide. Rwanda's genocide tested the limits of international and Western humanitarianism, and found them wanting, prompting a real crisis of confidence. The 1996 report issued by the cumbersomely-named Organisation for Economic Cooperation and Development (OECD) Steering Committee for Joint Evaluation of Emergency Assistance to Rwanda, led by John Eriksson, was to have long-lasting consequences for humanitarian aid. It concluded that: '[by] failing to deal with the festering refugee problem prior to 1990, both the Rwandese and the Ugandan governments set the stage for future conflict' (Eriksson 1996: Chapter 2). On the other hand, the US reluctance to experience 'another Somalia' was accepted as a valid explanation of US failure to acknowledge and intervene in Rwanda's genocide.

The report suggested that indifference to human rights abuses should be avoided in the future, since: '[by] not standing firm on human rights conditionality, donors collectively sent the message that their priorities lay elsewhere. By permitting arms to reach the Rwandese protagonists, the possibilities for demilitarizing the conflict were reduced' (Eriksson 1996: Chapter 2). This helped turn a civil war into a potential genocide. The report is quite diplomatic in its criticisms of Western powers, laying most of the blame on the UN for failing to make use of information available to it so as to formulate a policy in Rwanda. Improved early warning systems are a key recommendation, so that 'complex emergencies', caused by a combination of civil war, genocide and mass flight, can be better anticipated in the future. Cable warnings of the genocide plans and arm caches, militias and death lists, were circulated and sent to UN headquarters and were circulated: 'in a separate Black File, designed to draw attention to its content'.

Yet: 'senior officials in the Secretariat questioned the validity of the information and made no contingency plans for worst-case scenarios' (Eriksson, 1996: Chapter 2). French and Belgian 'intelligence failures' were also blamed in the Synthesis Report.

The Synthesis Report helped redefine how the international community should respond to what were called complex humanitarian emergencies in the future, including the 'R2P', responsibility to protect principles.[11] Humanitarianism, it was suggested, needed reinventing light of the failure to respond to genocide in Rwanda until it was too late. A UN Office for the Coordination of Humanitarian Affairs (OCHA) created in 1998, met one of the Synthesis Report's recommendations, and more 'robust' mandates were accepted for UN forces in DRC (MONUC, or more recently MONUSCO in the French acronym). A more militarised 'humanitarian intervention' was viewed as the key lesson of the international community's failure in

---

[11] See United Nations General Assembly Adoption of the Resolution on the Responsibility to Protect, dated 13 September: http://www.responsibilitytoprotect.org/index.php/component/content/article/35-r2pcs-topics/2626-un-resolution-on-the-responsibility-to-protect.

Rwanda. The results of the new approach have lately been evident, from Kosovo in 1999 to Libya in 2011.

5. Post-Genocide Justice and Reconstruction

After 1994, and especially from 2000, post-genocide governments started to dismantle the hold of racial divisions on Rwandans. The terms Hutu, Tutsi and Twa were removed from all identity documents. Apart from a few official terms like 'Tutsi Genocide', these terms are not to be used in public. By making 'divisionism' and 'genocide ideology' punishable crimes, the government claimed to be undoing the historical damage done by European racial and colonial ideologies. School history syllabi have been rewritten to emphasise common 'Rwandan-ness', which is also taught through *ingando* (official solidarity camps) for former prisoners, school children, military personnel and others.

For the RPF, Rwandans were united and lived peacefully, side by side, until the Germans and especially Belgians divided them along racial lines. Internalised notions of 'race' have to be erased and today, although such racial labels may be used in private, their use is frowned on in many academic circles and on pro-government sites on the internet.

Following the war and genocide of the 1990s, the Rwandan diaspora is even more widespread than it was in the 1960s. The tendency to flee is something the present government—unlike its pre-genocide predecessors—is keen to reverse, as witnessed in its repeated calls for all exiles to return to help rebuild Rwanda.

Meanwhile, the main contribution of the international community to Rwanda has been to prosecute crimes of genocide, rather than preventing conflict or dealing with it. International funding mainly supported the ICTR, based in Arusha, Tanzania, with its appeal chamber in The Hague. By 2012 the ICTR had tried ninety cases, at a total cost of an estimated 1.3 billion Euros. In contrast with this, inside Rwanda, between 2004 and 2012 more than a million genocide crimes (the government talks of 1.9 million crimes) were heard through eleven thousand local people's hearings, known as Gacaca ('the grassy place', pronounced 'gachacha') (Clark 2010), costing an estimated forty million Euros. ICTR and Gacaca trials and hearings were both concluded, at more or less the same time, in 2012. Among those found guilty at the ICTR were former mayors, radio broadcasters (including one Belgian national) and media funders, Ministers in the transitional government and ideologues and leaders of militias, among others.

Notably missing are those who aided and abetted the genocide process from a greater distance, especially non-Rwandans.

The government claims to be working towards an inclusive Rwanda, where political identities no longer divide people. The state seeks to get this message across through various public institutions, including schools, local paid and unpaid officials, churches, *gacaca* post-genocide hearings and the *ingando* solidarity camps that many Rwandans have attended at some time.

We should set aside the stereotypical images of the African state as a chaotic or haphazard institutional set-up with snoozing officials and broken equipment: In Rwanda, many institutions are working with great (sometimes quite unbelievable) efficiency at local and at national levels. The state machinery generally works well in what is a strong state in terms of overall efficiency and its authoritarian, centralising tendencies. At the end of the transitional period Paul Kagame was elected President in 2003 and again in 2010, with a huge majority of the vote. Almost nobody is surprised by this, given the stakes in Rwanda.

Since the genocide, and especially since 2003, the Rwandan economy has boomed, with record growth rates in the African content. The rapidly rising investment in infrastructure, new forms of trade and growth and a growing emphasis on the IT business sector and on cultural and environmental tourism has been backed up by government strategy to ensure that investors experience 'good governance' at the level of the state administration (Golooba-Mutebi 2008). This is the 'Singapore' model of technology and strict political authority, along with economic liberalism. Agricultural innovation has mechanised swathes of land and increased cash crop production for export, and rice in the low-lying marshland areas. There is also oil exploration going on in Lake Kivu, and other possible sources of revenue such as micro-energy and bio-gas are being pioneered. Yet, poverty remains intractable in many parts of the country. Alongside experimentation and innovation, there are growing problems of landlessness, resulting in part from rapid land commercialisation and titling, which, although it can help some women and poor farmers, generally favours those with additional assets, and larger than average plots. More mechanised and high-tech cash crop production is being encouraged, and in some cases imposed, through collaborative efforts with agro-companies whose interests are not always defended against in the public ministries and offices inside Rwanda.

Not surprisingly, widespread poverty and a land-locked location mean that many developmental problems need to be addressed in creative ways in post-war, post-genocide Rwanda. Achievements have been quite astonishing in some respects, with remarkable improvements in major health indicators such as child mortality in relatively short time-periods.[12] HIV-AIDS and infant and maternal mortality rates have improved remarkably since 1994, and infrastructure has also been notably improved, with new buildings and facilities, better trained staff and IT access in most public services.

There is now a mini-boom in information technology, which helps to inform tourists and business partners alike, with free downloadable Rwanda apps available, for instance. Growing tourism accompanies the rising number of investors, donors and aid agencies, that all want to be involved in Rwanda's growing economy. Major airlines are using Kigali as a hub instead of less efficient neighbouring airports. Kigali is rapidly turning into a regional hub, and has become a bustling, high rise city.

Problems are more apparent in rural areas off the main roads, where land titling policies are displacing smaller farmers who are sometimes forced to share their land: This does not always guarantee a family's food security. There is also widespread concern that laws about corruption, divisionism and genocide ideology may be used at times to silence dissents and hound opposition. Both diasporic Rwandans and international human rights NGOs express concerns about human rights abuses by Paul Kagame's regime against its perceived opponents.

Yet, to consider the issue from another perspective, there is little doubt that some of those accused of supporting or perpetrating the killings are guilty, and have been protected by being in exile. Increasingly they are being extradited to Rwanda to face criminal charges, or being tried in countries like Belgium or The Netherlands for crimes committed during the genocide. On the other hand, the Rwandan army and government (in which the secret services play a powerfully pervasive role) are repeatedly accused of hounding their enemies, including through assassinations and false charges. Even more seriously for the government's reputation, UN reports and NGO documents have provided extensive evidence that war crimes have been committed by Rwandan military forces, both during the civil war and after the genocide, both inside and outside Rwanda.

---

[12] Talk by Frederick Golooba-Mutebi, 'In pursuit of safe motherhood: A Rwanda case study', at the conference 'Rwanda From Below', organised by the IOB, Institute of Development Management Antwerp University, 29–30 June 2012.

The Rwandan state has proven remarkably resilient to criticism. Most of its critics are accused of denying genocide, or of promoting Hutu grievances and extremist causes. Having inherited the formidable structure of the Rwandan state, the present regime controls most of its structures from the top national level to local units of ten households. Ordinary Rwandans are in constant touch with local state officials, elected or appointed, paid or voluntary. More and more of these public officials are women, in an impressive experiment in gender equality. Adherence to national laws and local regulations involve detailed requirements for housing standards such as crop varieties, the drying of clothes, the wearing of shoes and even personal hygiene (Ingelaere 2007). A host of complex, overlapping regulatory mechanisms mean that most Rwandans are keen to remain on the right side of the authorities. They must obtain official permission to move from one local authority to another. The typical 'urban drift' and growth of slums typical of post-conflict situations elsewhere is not as visible in Rwanda. The question remains: does relative peace, high economic growth and the orderly co-existence of people previously polarised by war and genocide justify the very high degree of social control and political authoritarianism so often noted in today's Rwanda?[13]

Conclusion: Never Again?

In terms of many indicators, the domestic context inside Rwanda is favourable compared with that of many of its neighbours. And it is hard to disagree that one 'major distinguishing feature of politics under the RPF from politics under its predecessors is the government's demonstrable willingness, its numerous weaknesses notwithstanding, to transcend the politics of ethnic and regional exclusion in all spheres of public life' (Golooba-Mutebi 2008: 35), a form of 'developmental patrimonialism' as identified by David Booth, Goolooba-Mutebi and other researchers of the Africa Power and Politics Program of the Overseas Development Institute (ODI). Close control by the state authorities may be the price Rwandans pay for social peace and economic growth of the country. Mostly, however, post-genocide rhetoric of 'never again' is used to limit 'public opinion' freedoms. The aim of preventing genocidal ideas from spreading is of course a legitimate one. For some of Rwanda's rural poor, the best way to

---

[13] This is a question being posed by the ODI's Africa Power and Politics Program (APPP), see for example a working paper by Booth and Golooba-Mutebi, 2011.

ensure that they support 'never again' in practice, may be to simply focus on fighting poverty.

The militarisation of elites throughout the African Great Lakes region has been hastened by events since 1990–94. Enrichment strategies of political and military elites have been linked with violent attacks against terrorised civilians, and warfare between rival militias and armies, a pattern reinforced in DRC since 1996. The whole African Great Lakes need modes of economic enrichment that do not depend on the use of forced labour and violent military force, especially in DRC. Some believe that Rwanda's domestic economic development offers a peaceful alternative. Others question this, since the counterpart of peace and stability in Rwanda may be the 'underbelly' of war, civilian economic exploitation and terror in Eastern DRC. As a hub, however, Rwanda has growing attractions for investors and tourists living far beyond the Great Lakes region.

As a result of the Rwanda genocide, efforts to prevent genocide were renewed, especially in the US, where Genocide Watch was created by Gregory Stanton, a George Mason University professor. The aim of Genocide Watch is to 'predict, prevent, stop, and punish genocide and other forms of mass murder... to raise awareness and influence public policy concerning potential and actual genocide... [and] to build an international movement to prevent and stop genocide'.[14] The eight stages of genocide have been identified by this organisation, and are based on examples such as Rwanda and the Holocaust. Labelling, polarisation and administrative systems are all viewed as preludes to systematic genocides, and yet these processes are also part of most 'normal' states. Rwanda's genocide has served to highlight the need for long-term monitoring of potentially genocidal situations on the basis of knowledge of 'triggers' and structural factors that make genocide more likely to be conceived of, acted on, ignored and denied.

For today's Rwandan government and leadership, the road ahead is challenging. For poor Rwandans it is daunting. To facilitate the peaceful resolution of conflict in the future, it may be that the post-genocide Rwandan leadership could consider one model from the region, namely the Leadership Code of former Tanzanian President Julius Nyerere, which proposed that if public officials faced critical comments from the general public, they should welcome these and listen to their content, rather than

---

[14] Genocide Watch, Mission statement, viewed 10 June 2012, from http://www.genocide watch.org/aboutus.html.

view critics as a threat. Critics, from this perspective, can help inform public officials about how service provision for citizens might be improved. A spirit of openness may place too high an expectation on government officials in any country. Yet there are promising signs that many middle and lower-ranking civil servants and public officials are working for positive change and improvement in services inside Rwanda today. The hope is that senior leaders might also listen to critics more openly in future, and enable the entire population to finally feel secure that genocide will never recur. If these hopes are fulfilled, a 'new' Rwanda may emerge.

Further Reading

Bangwanubusa, T., 2009, *Understanding the polarization of responses to genocidal violence in Rwanda*, PhD thesis, Peace and Development Research, University of Gothenberg.

Barnett, M., 2002, *Eyewitness to a genocide: The United Nations and Rwanda*, Cornell University Press, Ithaca and London.

Callamard, A., 1999, 'French policy in Rwanda', in H. Adelman & A. Suhrke (eds), *The Rwanda crisis from Uganda to Zaire: The path of a genocide*, pp. 157–84, Transaction Publishers, New Brunswick, NJ.

Clark, P., 2010, *The Gacaca Courts, post-genocide justice and reconciliation in Rwanda: Justice without lawyers*, Cambridge University Press, Cambridge.

Eltringham, N., 2004, *Accounting for horror: Post-genocide debates in Rwanda*, Pluto Press, London and Sterling, VA.

Eriksson, J., *et al.* 1996, 'Response to conflict and genocide: Lessons from the Rwanda experience, Synthesis report of the joint evaluation of emergency assistance to Rwanda', viewed 13 June 2012, from http://www.oecd.org/derec/50189495.pdf.

Golooba-Mutebi, F., 2008, 'Collapse, war and reconstruction in Rwanda: An analytical narrative on state-making', Crisis Paper Working Series No. 2, DESTIN, LSE: London.

Gourevitch, P., 1999, *We wish to inform you that tomorrow we will be killed with our families: Stories from Rwanda*, Picador, London.

Government of Rwanda, 1995, 'Genocide, impunity and accountability: Dialogue for a national and international response', Recommendations of the conference, Kigali, November 1–5, Office of the President (Kigali).

Guichaoua, A., 2005, *Rwanda 1994. Les politiques du génocide à Butare*, Karthala, Paris.

Hintjens, H., 2001, 'When identity becomes a knife: Reflecting on the genocide in Rwanda', *Ethnicities* 1(1), 25–55.

Ingelaere, B., 2007, *Living the transition: A bottom-up perspective on Rwanda's political transition*, IOB Discussion Paper 2007/2, IOB, Antwerp.

Mamdani, M., 2001, *When victims become killers: Colonialism, nativism and
the genocide in Rwanda*, Princeton University Press, Princeton.

Otunnu, O., 2000, 'An historical analysis of the invasion by the Rwandan
Patriotic Army (RPA)', in H. Adelman & A. Suhrke (eds), *The Rwanda
crisis from Uganda to Zaire: The path of a genocide*, pp. 31–59, Transaction Publishers, New Brunswick, NJ.

Prunier, G., 1995, *The Rwanda crisis 1959–1994: History of a genocide*, Hurst
& Company and Columbia University Press, London and New York.

Straus, S., 2006, *The order of genocide: Race, power and war in Rwanda*,
Cornell University Press, Ithaca and London.

Taylor, C., 1999, *Sacrifice as terror: The Rwandan genocide of 1994*, Berg,
Oxford.

Uvin, P., 1998, *Aiding violence: The development enterprise in Rwanda*,
Kumarian Press, Bloomfield, CT.

References

Bale, J., 2002, *Imagined Olympians: Body culture and colonial representations in Rwanda*,
    University of Minnesota Press, Minneapolis.

Bangwanubusa, T., 2009, *Understanding the polarization of responses to genocidal violence
    in Rwanda*, Ph.D. thesis, Peace and Development Research, University of Gothenberg.

Barnett, M., 2002, *Eyewitness to a genocide: The United Nations and Rwanda*, Cornell Uni-
    versity Press, Ithaca and London.

Booth, D. & Golooba-Mutebi, F., 2011, *Developmental patrimonialism? The case of Rwanda*,
    Working Paper No. 16 (APPP), ODI, London, viewed 20 August 2012, from http://www
    .institutions-africa.org/filestream/20110321-appp-working-paper-16-developmental-
    patrimonialism-the-case-of-rwanda-by-david-booth-and-frederick-golooba-mutebi-
    march-2011.

Callamard, A., 1999, 'French policy in Rwanda', in H. Adelman & A. Suhrke (eds), *The
    Rwanda crisis from Uganda to Zaire: The path of a genocide*, Transaction Publishers, New
    Brunswick, NJ.

Clark, P., 2010, *The Gacaca Courts, post-genocide justice and reconciliation in Rwanda: Jus-
    tice without lawyers*, Cambridge University Press, Cambridge.

Eltringham, N., 2004, *Accounting for horror: Post-genocide debates in Rwanda*, Pluto Press,
    London and Sterling, VA.

Eriksson, J., *et al.* 1996, 'Response to conflict and genocide: Lessons from the Rwanda expe-
    rience, Synthesis report of the joint evaluation of emergency assistance to Rwanda',
    viewed 13 June 2012, from http://www.oecd.org/derec/50189495.pdf.

Golooba-Mutebi, F., 2008, 'Collapse, war and reconstruction in Rwanda: An analytical nar-
    rative on state-making', Crisis Paper Working Series No. 2, DESTIN, LSE: London.

Gourevitch, P., 1999, *We wish to inform you that tomorrow we will be killed with our families: Stories from Rwanda*, Picador, London.

Government of Rwanda, 1995, 'Genocide, impunity and accountability: Dialogue for a national and international response', Recommendations of the conference, Kigali, November 1–5, Office of the President (Kigali).

Guichaoua, A., 2005, *Rwanda 1994. Les politiques du génocide à Butare*, Karthala, Paris.

Hintjens, H., 2001, 'When identity becomes a knife: Reflecting on the genocide in Rwanda', *Ethnicities* 1(1), 25–55.

Ingelaere, B., 2007, *Living the transition: A bottom-up perspective on Rwanda's political transition*, IOB Discussion Paper 2007/2, IOB, Antwerp.

Mamdani, M., 2001, *When victims become killers: Colonialism, nativism and the genocide in Rwanda*, Princeton University Press, Princeton.

Midlarsky, M., 2005, *The killing trap: Genocide in the twentieth century*, Cambridge University Press, Cambridge.

Melvern, L., 2004, *Conspiracy to murder: The Rwandan genocide*, Verso, London & New York.

Montagu, A.M.F., 1953, *Man's most dangerous myth: The fallacy of race*, Harpers, New York.

Mosse, G.L., 1978, *Toward the final solution: A history of European racism*, J.M. Dent & Sons, London, Melbourne and Toronto.

Otunnu, O., 2000, 'An historical analysis of the invasion by the Rwandan Patriotic Army (RPA)', in H. Adelman & A. Suhrke (eds), *The Rwanda crisis from Uganda to Zaire: The path of a genocide*, pp. 31–59, Transaction Publishers, New Brunswick, NJ.

Prunier, G., 1995, *The Rwanda crisis 1959–1994: History of a genocide*, Hurst & Company and Columbia University Press, London and New York.

Straus, S., 2006, *The order of genocide: Race, power and war in Rwanda*, Cornell University Press, Ithaca and London.

Taylor, C., 1999, *Sacrifice as terror: The Rwandan genocide of 1994*, Berg, Oxford.

Uvin, P., 1998, *Aiding violence: The development enterprise in Rwanda*, Kumarian Press, Bloomfield, CT.

Vansina, J., 2004, *Antecedents to modern Rwanda: The Nyiginya kingdom*, James Currey & Fountain Publishers, Oxford/Kampala.

Verwimp, P., 2006, 'Machetes and firearms: The organization of massacres in Rwanda', *Journal of peace research* 43(1), 5–22.

Waller, D., 1993, *Rwanda: Which way now?*, Oxfam Professional, Oxford.

CHAPTER FOURTEEN

THE LIBYAN CIVIL WAR AND THE RISE OF THE 'RESPONSIBILITY TO PROTECT'

Sara Kendall

Introduction

The 'Libyan civil war' refers to the conflict that began with an internal uprising against the regime of Libyan president Mu'ammar al-Qadhafi in mid-February of 2011 and is said to have ended with the death of Qadhafi and the termination of North Atlantic Treaty Organisation (NATO) operation 'Unified Protector' in late October of 2011. The uprising is frequently described as forming part of a broader 'Arab Spring'; mass popular protests that began in neighbouring Tunisia and spread throughout the Middle East and North African region (Joffé 2011). However, ongoing conflict between different groups within Libya reveals that the end of external military intervention did not necessarily translate into the establishment of peace, and this case study raises a number of timely questions about the relationship between conflict and peacebuilding. Of the case studies considered in this text, the Libyan case is the most recent and, as a consequence, it has the least settled historical record at the time of writing. As a contemporary and evolving set of events, the history of the conflict in Libya is still being written, with continuing hostilities, political developments, and the increased involvement of international institutions such as the International Criminal Court.

The Libyan civil war emerged out of the population's frustration with decades of authoritarian rule, led to international intervention backed by the United Nations Security Council (UNSC), and culminated in the extra-judicial killing of former Libyan president Qadhafi. Other members of the former regime have been indicted by the ICC through a UNSC mandate that, for the first time, linked the emerging doctrine known as the 'responsibility to protect' to practices of international criminal justice (Stahn 2012). The removal of the Qadhafi regime from control over a major oil-exporting power in a strategically important region has been regarded as a constructive development for many Western states, but the continuing instability reveals deeper tensions within Libya that are compounded by regional grievances and a historically underdeveloped state structure.

This chapter places the history of the modern Libyan state in a broader context and describes the rise of Mu'ammar al-Qadhafi to power before moving to a description of the 2011 civil war and its aftermath. Knowledge of Libya's history of invasions and colonisation and its status as a major oil exporter is key to understanding the development of the Qadhafi regime, with its limited state structure, regional tensions, and fraught relationship with the West. These elements continue to contribute to the ongoing instability of the Libyan state following the mass uprisings that overturned the regime in 2011.

1. *Libya before Qadhafi*

The causes of and justifications for the conflict in Libya are rooted within a more recent history of extended autocratic rule and a longer history of imperial rule and colonisation.[1] The territory of what we now refer to as the modern state of Libya had been inhabited by Berber tribes that frequently came under foreign control. Parts of the territory had been under the influence of the ancient Greeks, including the Greek colony of Cyrene, and in the fourth century the Roman emperor established the provinces of Libya Superior and Libya Inferior. In the seventh century the Arab Muslim expansion into the North African region covered what is now Libyan territory, encountering varying degrees of Berber resistance. The period of Islamic rule stretched from the seventh century until much of the territory came under Ottoman influence nearly a millennium later. Ottoman Turks occupied Libya's contemporary capital, Tripoli, in the mid-sixteenth century, after which it was ruled as a province of the Ottoman Empire. As Ottoman imperial power was waning during the nineteenth century, a religious revival led by the Sanusiyah religious order—the family of the future Libyan king Idris—took hold throughout the region, and Arab resistance to the Turkish occupation strengthened.[2] Italian colonial governance would displace external rule by the Ottomans, reflecting the

---

[1] For an account of these dynamics during the colonial period and their effects, see: Ahmida 2008.

[2] See: Simons 2003.

decline of the Ottoman Empire and the expansion of European powers at the turn of the twentieth century.[3]

An influx of Italian settlers and the establishment of an Italian colony in neighbouring Tunisia predated Italian efforts to colonise Libya. In 1911 Italy declared war on Turkey as a precursor to its invasion of Libya, and in 1912 the Ottoman sultan ceded Libya to the Italians.[4] Many Libyans were unwilling to abide by a treaty that they had not participated in, and the conflict between Italians and Libyans continued, with the Libyans supported by remaining Turkish forces. After violent efforts to suppress the Libyan population, Italy became involved in World War I on the side of Britain fighting against Germany and the Ottoman Turks. Facing waning influence in their colony, the Italians acknowledged Sayyid Muhammed al-Idris of the Sanusis as the hereditary emir of Libya in 1917. Libyan nationalists made limited gains in the following years as the Italians devolved some power to the three Libyan provinces, but renewed Italian interest in Libya under Mussolini led to further violent incursions in the 1920s and 1930s. The Italian conquest forcibly displaced many Libyan communities and led to the establishment of concentration camps, and Libyans were killed in large numbers during this particularly bloody period of Italian intervention (Simons 2003). By 1934 Italy had unified Tripolitania and Cyrenaica, two of the three provinces, and by 1938 Mussolini declared that Libya formed part of the Italian Kingdom.

The modern history of independent Libya is thought to begin in 1951 with the establishment of the Sanusi monarchy, but the transition from colonial rule to independence took several years and involved transitional assistance from the United Nations (UN).[5] Italy formally relinquished its sovereignty over Libya in February 1947. The issue of Libyan independence was taken up by the UN General Assembly in 1948, and the following year the Assembly passed a resolution creating an 'independent and sovereign state' of Libya. The UN oversaw the transition from colony to sovereign state; as one commentator has argued, the UN was 'the midwife of independent Libya' (Simons 2003: xi). Later that month Libya's National Assembly—composed of members drawn from the three provinces of Tripolitania, Cyrenaica and Fezzan—declared that Libya would be established as a federal state. In December 1950 the National Assembly

---

[3] For an account of the Italian colonisation, see: Ahmida 2009.
[4] For an account of this period in Libyan history, see generally Vandewalle 2012.
[5] See generally Pelt 1970.

created the United Kingdom of Libya, and Idris al-Sanusi was offered the throne. In October 1951 the National Assembly promulgated the Libyan constitution, and in December that year the United Kingdom of Libya proclaimed its independence. The kingdom was to be headed by King Idris, who enjoyed Western support and was closely aligned with the United States (US) and United Kingdom, with whom the country traded rights to military bases in exchange for financial and military assistance. One commentator notes that the Libyan Kingdom's patrimonial political system 'started Libya on the road of political exclusion of its citizens, and of a profound de-politicisation that continues to characterise it today' (Vandewalle 2012: 5). Indeed, political parties were banned in the aftermath of Libya's first general election in February of 1952, and state building was generally neglected through the years of the Sanusi monarchy (1951–1969).

2. *Libya under Qadhafi*

High-quality petroleum was discovered in Libya in 1959, which radically shifted the state's strategic position in the global economy and transformed it into an independently wealthy nation. Libya's petroleum law, which had originally been passed in 1955, was amended in the early 1960s to increase the Libyan government's share of the oil revenues, and the state began exporting petroleum from its Mediterranean ports. Libya joined the Organisation of Petroleum Exporting Countries (OPEC) in 1963 and established its own national oil company in 1965. The oil industry in Libya was fully nationalised in 1970 after the overthrow of the Libyan monarchy and Qadhafi's rise to power, leading to even greater revenues for those in charge of the government.[6]

As the state grew increasingly wealthy from the revenues of oil exports, discontent spread as the benefits reached little of the Libyan population. Rather than serving to unify the Libyan state, the Sanusi monarchy had been associated with the Cyrenaican region in Libya and with Western influence. The pan-Arab views of neighbouring Egyptian president Gamal Abdel Nasser were growing in influence, characterised by anti-imperialism and a socialist reform agenda, and these views shaped a growing nationalist revolutionary movement in Libya. On 1 September 1969, a military

---

[6] See Vandewalle 1998.

coup carried out by a group of junior military officers overthrew the Sanusi monarchy while King Idris was out of the country.[7] Mu'ammar al-Qadhafi, a military lieutenant active in the movement, was named chairman of the Revolutionary Command Council, the ruling body of the newly proclaimed Libyan Arab Republic. Qadhafi proclaimed himself Colonel and was known by that title throughout his long rule.

In the years that followed, the Revolutionary Command Council under Qadhafi engaged in extensive reforms of the state, demanding increased revenue from foreign oil companies, revising the legal system in conformity with Islamic law, and creating 'popular committees' to govern various sectors of Libyan society. In sharp contrast to the Sanusi monarchy and its close links with foreign powers, under Qadhafi, the foreign-owned hospitals and banks were nationalised, British and US troops were pressured to withdraw, and Italian-owned property was confiscated.[8] Based in part on the pan-Arab philosophies espoused by Nasser, Qadhafi developed his own concepts of governance that appeared explicitly in 'The Green Book,' his ideological primer first issued in 1975. Qadhafi envisioned a Libyan society in which the people would directly manage politics and the economy, and he advanced a concept of statelessness—denoted by the new Arabic term 'jamahiriya', or 'state of the masses'—that was meant to promote solidarity and equality among tribes, though in practice this led to the concentration of power among a small Libyan elite. The concept of jamahiriya became institutionalised in 1977 with the establishment of the Socialist Peoples' Libyan Arab Jamahiriya, a direct democracy governed through local popular councils. Although Qadhafi officially stepped down from power, he continued to maintain considerable. *de facto* power over the Libyan state.

The rising price of oil on the global market in the 1970s led to massive revenues from oil exports, and the Libyan state under Qadhafi began to explore its geopolitical strength in the global arena. In 1973 Libya embargoed oil exports to the US as a consequence of US support of Israel, and the following year it nationalised US oil companies operating within Libyan territory. There were signs of internal dissatisfaction with the regime, however, with student demonstrations against the Libyan state in Benghazi in 1975 and an attempted coup against Qadhafi by two Revolutionary Command Council members. The Libyan state's extensive security

---

[7] For a collection of accounts of this period, see Vandewalle 2008.
[8] Vandewalle (2012) gives a helpful timeline of these events.

apparatus and ability to quash domestic dissent allowed Qadhafi to continue to govern against the will of segments of the Libyan population despite theoretical commitments to direct democracy.

Under Qadhafi's influence, Libya became increasingly distanced from the Western powers during the late Cold War period. With its revenues from exporting petroleum it was able to back militant organisations throughout the world, from Northern Ireland to the Philippines. For their part, Western powers—and particularly the US—generally supported right-wing dictators and militants opposed to the Soviet Union. Meanwhile, Qadhafi allegedly supported the training of pan-African revolutionaries at Libyan camps as his attention shifted from a pan-Arab to a pan-African vision.[9] Libyan state agents were also associated with alleged acts of state-sponsored violence carried out against Western targets, including the killing of a British police officer during a protest against the deaths of Libyan dissidents in London, as well as the bombing of a Berlin nightclub. The US carried out retaliatory air strikes on targets in Tripoli and Benghazi in response to the nightclub bombing, which resulted in civilian deaths and condemnation by the UN General Assembly. Perhaps the most notorious incident during this period was the 1988 bombing of a Pan Am flight, which exploded over Lockerbie, Scotland en route from London to New York. The UNSC condemned the bombing and called on all states to assist in apprehending and prosecuting those responsible, and it passed resolutions strengthening economic sanctions against the Libyan state.

The Lockerbie bombing led to an extended period of negotiations between Libya and Western powers. In 1991 the US and the United Kingdom charged two Libyans with responsibility for the bombing, and the UNSC passed a resolution requiring Libya to cooperate with the investigation. Struggles over the trial continued, as Libya claimed that it would only permit a trial to take place in a neutral country under Scottish law. In 1998 the US and the United Kingdom agreed to a trial in the Netherlands, which opened in 2000 and concluded in 2001 with one conviction of a Libyan intelligence officer and one acquittal.[10] The Libyan state accepted

---

[9] Extensive testimony of these training camps and Qadhafi's pan-African philosophy were documented during the trial of former Liberian president Charles Taylor before the Special Court for Sierra Leone. Qadhafi was alleged to have supported the training of Taylor and other revolutionary leaders, including Sierra Leonean Revolutionary United Front leader Foday Sankoh and current president of Burkina Faso Blaise Compaoré.

[10] See generally Weller 1992. The sole convicted individual, a former Libyan intelligence officer, was released from his incarceration in Scotland and returned to Libya in 2009 due to ill health, a decision that generated considerable international criticism.

'civil responsibility' without admitting guilt in paying reparations to victims to help facilitate the lifting of UN sanctions against Libya in 2003.

Around the turn of the new millennium, the Libyan state began to
recast its relationship with the West. Falling petroleum prices and a high
rate of unemployment within Libya may have contributed to fostering
what one commentator describes as 'a remarkable set of adjustments and
compromises' that marked an 'emerging pragmatism' (Vandewalle 2012: 7).
Qadhafi announced in 2003 that Libya would not pursue the developments
of weapons of mass destruction, and after agreeing to a compensation
framework for victims of the Lockerbie bombing, the UNSC subsequently
voted to lift sanctions against Libya. At the diplomatic level, relations
were warming between Libya and the European Union, the United Kingdom, and the US, with state visits and the re-establishment of embassies.
Measures were also taken to liberalise the Libyan economy as the state
drifted away from some of its previous economic practices, though Libya's
strong security apparatuses remained intact against the backdrop of weak
governmental institutions and little to no civil society. The events of the
2011 civil war in Libya unfolded in a time of renewed global engagement
coupled with ongoing domestic repression, with the compounded frustra-
tions of over forty years of life under the sway of Qadhafi.

3. The 'Arab Spring' and the Libyan Uprising

The term 'Arab Spring' is commonly used to refer to protests that began
in Tunisia, with the self-immolation of vendor Mohamed Bouazizi in protest against his treatment by local officials in late 2010, and spread across
North Africa and the Middle East in the months that followed. In Libya,
the uprisings began in the eastern part of the country following the arrest
of a human rights lawyer, Fathi Terbil, on 15 February 2011. Terbil had
been representing relatives of more than one thousand prisoners who
had allegedly been massacred by security forces in an infamous Tripoli
prison in 1996. After a protest demanding Terbil's release, a 'day of rage'
was announced for 17 February, which resulted in mass protests in many
of the eastern parts of Libya that had been historically opposed to the
Qadhafi regime.

Originating in Benghazi, Libya's second largest city, the protests spread
throughout the country in the following days, resulting in tens of thousands of demonstrations against the Qadhafi regime's harsh rule, failure to
address economic inequalities, and restrictions on political freedoms. The

eastern city of Benghazi had been the traditional stronghold of the Sanusi dynasty, and demonstrators were seen carrying the flag of the former Kingdom of Libya and images of King Idris. The protests were followed by a brutal response from state security forces, with Qadhafi showing no signs of entering into negotiations with protesters. Top Libyan diplomats resigned, including the deputy Libyan representative to the UN, who claimed that Qadhafi was using mercenaries to attack demonstrators and suggested that Qadhafi's prompting of his supporters to counter-attack may trigger genocide. Within five days the protestors had taken control of Benghazi. On 25 February 2011 the UN Human Rights Council created an International Commission of Inquiry on Libya to investigate the increasing violence against Libyan civilians.[11] The following day, the UNSC issued a unanimous resolution, Resolution 1970, calling for an immediate end to the violence, levelling sanctions against Qadhafi and his close advisors, and referring the situation to the International Criminal Court (ICC) to investigate 'widespread and systematic attacks' against the Libyan population.

Following the Security Council resolution, the Libyan opposition announced the formation of the National Transitional Council (NTC) in Benghazi. Qadhafi declared his intent to hunt down the opposition, a threat that drew increased international attention. On 17 March 2011 the Security Council passed a second resolution, Resolution 1973, which authorised member states to 'take all necessary measures...to protect civilians and civilian populated areas' in Libya under the authority of Chapter VII of the UN Charter. Regional organisations such as the African Union and the League of Arab States took opposing positions about whether a no-fly zone authorised by the resolution should be instituted, with the African Union calling for a negotiated settlement rather than direct military engagement. Despite differing views over the use of force within the international community, US and European forces began air strikes against Qadhafi forces on 19 March. Five days later, NATO assumed authority over the military campaign that had been mandated by Resolution 1973.

---

[11] The UN Human Rights Council appointed Canadian Philippe Kirsch, former President of the ICC, Egyptian M. Cherif Bassiouni, an established international criminal law scholar; and Jordanian Asma Khader, a human rights advocate and former Minister of State and Minister of Culture in Jordan. The Commission's mandate was, among other things, 'to investigate all alleged violations of international human rights law in Libya'; this mandate was later broadened to include violations of international law more generally.

In contrast to the previous unanimity of the Security Council's response to Libyan state violence with Resolution 1970, different approaches began to emerge concerning Resolution 1973. The air strikes were opposed by China, India and Russia, all of whom had abstained from Resolution 1973. Instead they demanded a cease-fire and claimed that allied forces had exceeded the United Nations' mandate by putting Libyan civilians at risk. The African Union called for a cease-fire and the suspension of NATO air strikes in the following month. The UN Secretary General's special envoy to Libya attempted to negotiate terms for a cease-fire between the Transitional National Council and the Libyan government, but the parties disagreed on the terms, with the Libyan government requiring an end to NATO bombings before a cease-fire would be implemented. Libyan state forces and Qadhafi sympathisers made significant gains on 19 March 2011 when Qadhafi announced that the army would begin an assault on Benghazi, but the troops were forced back by a combination of local resistance and an intervention by French forces acting under NATO. In retrospect this failed assault on Benghazi by pro-Qadhafi forces marked a turning point in the conflict, as the opposition continued to gain strength with the support of the NATO operation 'Unified Protector'.

Within a relatively short period of time, it became clear that key Western powers were considering the possibility of regime change and were moving to recognise the National Transitional Council as a legitimate interlocutor. In mid-April, the presidents of the US, the United Kingdom and France had stated publicly that 'it is impossible to imagine a future for Libya with Qadhafi in power'.[12] Meanwhile, in their negotiations with the UN special envoy, the National Transitional Council maintained that a cease-fire would not be successful unless Qadhafi was removed from power. South African president Jacob Zuma met with Qadhafi in late May and relayed his unwillingness to step down, noting that the Libyan leader would support a political solution rather than abdicating power. However, momentum among international partners continued to build around the need for Qadhafi to relinquish power and the possibility of a political solution appeared to be waning.

At the end of May 2011, the UN-backed International Commission of Inquiry released the first of two reports on the alleged violations of

---

[12] The joint article 'Libya: A pathway to peace', co-authored by British Prime Minister David Cameron, French President Nicholas Sarkozy, and US President Barack Obama, appeared on 15 April 2011 in *Le Figaro*, *The Times*, and *The Washington Post*. The text is available on the British Foreign and Commonwealth Office website.

international human rights law in Libya.[13] The report was based on interviews with victims, witnesses, Libyan government representatives and
civil society organisations, and it concluded that further investigation was
necessary to fulfill the Commission's mandate given the difficult investigative circumstances it faced in a situation of ongoing conflict. The UN
Human Rights Council extended the Commission's mandate to the following year.

In the months that followed, opposition forces gained ground and were
approaching Tripoli by August 2011. By the end of the month there were
clashes between rebels and regime loyalists in Tripoli, and by 22 August
the pro-Qadhafi forces had ceded control of the city with relatively little
resistance. As opposition forces gained access to his compound in Tripoli,
Qadhafi's whereabouts became increasingly unclear, suggesting that his
authority was waning. Qadhafi maintained a low profile in his hometown
of Sirte while diplomatic relations continued to strengthen between the
NTC and members of the international community. An international conference in Paris in early September announced support measures for the
Libyan opposition, and later that month the UN General Assembly voted
in favour of the National Transitional Council assuming the Libyan seat at
the UN. After just over nine months of fighting to maintain control of the
country he had ruled for more than forty years, Mu'ammar a-Qadhafi was
captured and killed near his hometown of Sirte on 20 October 2011, probably by Misrata-based opposition forces who captured him after debilitat-
ing NATO airstrikes were carried out against his fleeing convoy. NATO
denied knowing that Qadhafi was in the convoy, and numerous actors
called for an investigation into the capturing and killing of the Libyan
leader. With liberation declared by the NTC chair following Qadhafi's
death and the formal end of NATO operation 'Unified Protector' on 31
October, Libya's civil war appeared to be over, though hostilities remain
ongoing as of the time of writing.

4. *UN Commission of Inquiry findings: Crimes of the Libyan Conflict*

In their final report issued in March 2012, the International Commission
of Inquiry on Libya found that Qadhafi government forces committed
international crimes, including crimes against humanity and war crimes,

---

[13] See Human Rights Council 2011.

during the Libyan civil war.[14] The Commission determined that the regime had used excessive force against demonstrators during the early days of the uprising in February 2011, leading to injuries and deaths that suggested a centralised state policy of violent repression. In addition to these breaches of international human rights law, the Commission also found that Qadhafi forces engaged in war crimes such as unlawful killings, torture, and sexual violence. The final report claims that these crimes were carried out as part of a 'widespread and systematic attack' against a civilian population, suggesting that these crimes may also be categorised as crimes against humanity.

The report also finds that war crimes and breaches of international human rights law were committed by anti-Qadhafi forces (referred to as *thuwar*), who were found to have executed and tortured perceived Qadhafi loyalists. The Commission was unable to determine whether Qadhafi's death constituted an unlawful killing due to the lack of a first-hand account and inconsistent accounts from secondary sources, and it called for additional investigation. Meanwhile, the Commission documented several NATO air strikes that led to civilian deaths and damages to civilian infrastructure without an identifiable military target. Although the Commission found that NATO did not deliberately target Libyan civilians, it claimed that it was unable to draw conclusions on the basis of the information provided by NATO and recommended further investigation.

The Commission's investigation operated during an overlapping time period with the ICC's investigation into the Libyan situation, and two of the Commissioners have previous connections to the ICC. As an independent fact-finding body, the conclusions of the Commission of Inquiry do not carry the same legal weight as the findings of a court or tribunal. The crimes of the Libyan civil war remain to be litigated, either by the ICC or by a domestic legal institution, as the following section explains.

5. *Legal Responses: The 'Responsibility to Protect' and the International Criminal Court*

UNSC Resolution 1970 was only the second time that the Security Council had used its power to refer a situation to the ICC. It had acted previously in the situation of Darfur, Sudan, though without unanimous support (the

---

[14] See Human Rights Council 2012.

US and China had abstained). This referral represented the first time that all five permanent Security Council members had acted affirmatively to refer a matter to the ICC after the failure of the Libyan state 'to protect its population', reflecting the gravity of the violence in Libya and the general consensus at the time that coordinated action was necessary at the international level. The referral enabled the ICC's Prosecutor to open an investigation into the grave crimes committed in Libya during the period of the conflict, and on 27 June 2011 the Court issued an arrest warrant for Qadhafi, his son Saif al-Islam, and the Libyan head of intelligence Abdullah al-Senussi for alleged crimes against humanity committed through the state security forces.

Security Council Resolution 1970 marked the first time that the emerging norm known as the 'responsibility to protect' was tied to the referral of a situation to the ICC. The phrase came to prominence after a 2001 report sponsored by a Canadian-funded commission articulated a shift from the language of 'humanitarian intervention' to the notion of the 'responsibility to protect', a concept that gained currency in UN policy discourse in the years that followed. The norm asserts that states are obliged to protect their citizens from mass atrocity crimes, and in the event that a state fails to protect its population, the international community has the responsibility to intervene. Under the 'responsibility to protect' norm, the use of military force is only to be considered as a last resort after peaceful measures and coercive measures such as economic sanctions have failed: 'Military intervention can only be justified when every non-military option for the prevention or peaceful resolution of the crisis has been explored, with reasonable grounds for believing lesser measures would not have succeeded' (International Commission on Intervention and State Sovereignty 2001: xii).

Resolution 1970 referring the ICC case explicitly used 'responsibility to protect' language and was supported by all five permanent members of the Security Council. This resolution did not actually authorise the use of military force through reference to protection, however, but instead demanded an immediate end to the violence, levelled sanctions against the Qadhafi regime, and referred the Libya situation to the ICC. Resolution 1973 went farther, and it marked the first time that the Security Council approved the use of force in support of the 'responsibility to protect'. The resolution permitted member states 'to take all necessary measures ... to protect civilians and civilian populated areas under threat of attack in the Libyan Arab Jamahiriya', and with China and Russia abstaining, it did not receive full support of the permanent members of the Security

Council. The subsequent military action carried out under the authority of these resolutions was thus not as widely supported among Security Council members as the ICC referral in Resolution 1970. Within the Middle East and North African region the ICC referral was originally supported, though support may have waned following NATO's military intervention. Following the first air strikes by US and European forces, the Arab League, the African Union, China, Russia and Germany expressed concern about the use of force. As reports surfaced of civilian casualties, China, India and Russia demanded a cease-fire, and NATO members Germany and Turkey claimed that military strikes exceeded the mandate of Resolution 1973. NATO members were divided over the interpretation of the UN mandate, though NATO eventually assumed leadership over the military campaign.

This first invocation of the 'responsibility to protect' norm revealed competing visions of how it ought to be interpreted in practice. The referral of the situation to the ICC and the establishment of an investigative commission appeared to be widely supported, but many states expressed discomfort with authorising military action on this normative basis. As the Libyan conflict marks the inaugural use of the 'responsibility to protect' in UNSC resolutions, it will be important to watch when and how this norm is invoked beyond Libya as part of the 'peace and security' mandate of the UNSC.

Meanwhile, the Security Council referral of the Libyan situation to the ICC under Resolution 1970 has generated its own questions about the appropriate venue for adjudicating the crimes of the Libyan civil war. The Libyan state has contested the jurisdiction of the ICC in claiming that it is capable of carrying out domestic trials. Under the principle known as 'complementarity', the ICC was designed to serve as a court of last resort in the event that a state is unwilling or unable to carry out trials in its own national jurisdiction. The transitional government has indicated that it intends to set up a domestic mechanism to try former members of the Qadhafi regime who engaged in mass crimes. The admissibility challenge by Libya, still pending at the time of writing, has been beset by issues of state cooperation as members of ICC staff—including defense counsel for Saif al-Islam—were detained in Zintan, Libya for several weeks by a militia group and accused of spying. ICC staff members theoretically enjoy diplomatic immunity while on ICC business, and the detention raises cooperation issues with the international court and may jeopardise the state's claim to be able to offer fair trials within the Libyan court system. The outcome of this admissibility challenge—which, if successful, will result in trials carried out in Libyan courts—serves not only as a marker of stability within Libya, but also as a test of how the evolving notion of complementarity will be interpreted by the ICC.[15]

Conclusion: Democratic Transitions, Ongoing Hostilities

In July 2012, Libya held its first democratic elections since 1965, which were widely regarded as free and fair. A two hundred member General National Congress was elected to replace the National Transition Council, and the Congress was tasked with electing a Prime Minister and organising parliamentary elections for 2013. Although the Prime Minister was subsequently elected in September 2012, this development was overshadowed by the killing of the US ambassador to Libya and three other staff members on 11 September 2012 in an attack on the US consulate in Benghazi.

The attack on the US consulate was one of the more reported examples of ongoing hostilities within the Libyan state. Despite formal appearances of a political transition, the state struggles to project authority over Libyan territory in a period characterised by fragmentation and devolved military power. Post-Qadhafi Libya is full of numerous armed groups, some of whom fall under the command of the defense ministry and others who may have ties to militant organisations abroad. Some of this fragmentation can be attributed to the philosophy of 'statelessness' or *jamahiriya* espoused by the Qadhafi regime,[16] but it is also a product of a longer history of regional tensions and fragmented strategies under imperial and colonial rule. Libya's position as a major petroleum exporter has generated a great degree of Western attention, and its transitional government continues to receive considerable support from global powers. However, as some critics of liberal peace-building practices have pointed out, Western donors who are interested in providing technocratic advice to states still involved in or emerging from armed conflict may bring certain presumptions about state-building and rule of law promotion that do not mesh with circumstances on the ground (Richmond 2010).

---

[15] For updates on legal developments in the Libyan situation, see the ICC website: www.icc-cpi.int.

[16] According to the Commission of Inquiry, *Jamahiriya* was a term 'created and used exclusively in Libya to describe the "State of the masses" and to reflect the aim of the regime: a country liberated not only from colonial or neo-colonial rule but also from partisan and bureaucratic obstacles'. See also Vandewalle 2012.

The history of the outcome of the civil war and of post-Qadhafi Libya remains to be written, but one dimension is already evident: the formal end of the Libyan civil war marked by the withdrawal of NATO troops in late October 2011 does not tell the full story of the conflict. Qadhafi's death and the regime change it brought is but one facet of a complex set of relations in this materially rich and politically unsettled region of the world, where external interventions have structured almost two thousand years of its history.

Further Reading

Ahmida, A.A., 2008, *Forgotten voices: Power and agency in colonial and postcolonial Libya*, Routledge, New York.

Alaaldin, R., 2012, 'Libya: Defining its future', *After the Arab Spring: Power shift in the Middle East?*, IDEAS reports No. 11, London School of Economics, London.

Anderson, L., 1986, *The state and social transformation in Tunisia and Libya, 1830–1980*, Princeton University Press, Princeton.

Baldinetti, A., 2009, *The origins of the Libyan nation: Colonial legacy, exile and the emergence of a new nation-state*, Routledge, New York.

Bellamy, A. & Williams, P., 2011, 'The new politics of protection? Côte d'Ivoire, Libya and the responsibility to protect', *International Affairs* 87(4), 825–50.

Brahimi, A., 2011, 'Libya's Revolution', *The Journal of North African Studies* 16(4), 605–24.

Hoffman, J. & Nollkaemper, A. (eds), 2012, *The responsibility to protect: From principle to practice*, Pallas Publications/Amsterdam University Press, Amsterdam.

Human Rights Watch, 2012, 'Unacknowledged deaths: Civilian casualties in NATO's air campaign in Libya', Washington DC.

O'Brien, E. & Gowen, R., 2012, *The international role in Libya's transition: August 2011–March 2012*, New York University Center on International Cooperation, New York.

Pelt, A., 1970, *Libyan independence and the United Nations: A case of planned decolonization*, Yale University Press, New Haven.

United Nations General Assembly, 2009, *Implementing the responsibility to protect: Report of the Secretary General*, UNGA Doc. A/63/677, viewed 2 October 2012, from http://www.unhcr.org/refworld/docid/4989924d2.html.

Vandewalle, D., 1998, *Libya since independence: Oil and state-building*, Cornell University Press, Ithaca.

———. (ed.), 2008, *Libya since 1969: Qadhafi's revolution revisited*, Palgrave Macmillan, New York.

Weller, M., 1992, 'The Lockerbie case: A premature end to the "New World Order"?', *African Journal of International and Comparative Law* 4(2), 302–24.

Wright, J., 2010, *A history of Libya*, Hurst & Company, London.

References

Ahmida, A.A., 2009, *The making of modern Libya: State formation, colonization, and resistance*, The State University of New York Press, Albany.

Human Rights Council, 2011, 'Report of the International Commission of Inquiry to investigate all alleged violations of international human rights law in the Libyan Arab Jamahiriya', A/HRC/17/44, 31 May 2011.

———, 2012, 'Full report of the International Commission of Inquiry to investigate all alleged violations of international law in the Libyan Arab Jamahiriya', A/HRC/19/68, 8 March 2012.

International Commission on Intervention and State Sovereignty, 2001, 'The responsibility to protect', International Development Research Centre, Ottawa.

Joffé, G., 2011, 'The Arab Spring in North Africa: Origins and prospects', *The Journal of North African Studies* 16(4), 507–32.

Pelt, A., 1970, *Libyan independence and the United Nations: A case of planned decolonization*, Yale University Press, New Haven.

Richmond, O., 2010, 'The rule of law in liberal peacebuilding', in C. Sriram, O. Martin-Ortega & J. Herman (eds), *Peacebuilding and rule of law in Africa: Just peace?*, pp. 44–59, Routledge, New York.

Simons, G., 2003, *Libya and the West: From independence to Lockerbie*, Centre for Libyan Studies, Oxford.

Stahn, C., 2012, 'Libya, the International Criminal Court, and complementarity: A test for shared responsibility', *Journal of International Criminal Justice* 10(2), 325–49.

Vandewalle, D., 1998, *Libya since independence: Oil and state-building*, Cornell University Press, Ithaca.

———, 2012, *A history of modern Libya*, 2nd edn., Cambridge University Press, New York.

Weller, M., 1992, 'The Lockerbie case: A premature end to the "New World Order"?', *African journal of international and comparative law* 4(2), 302–24.

Wright, J. 2010. *A history of Libya*, Hurst & Company, London.

INDEX

www.ingramcontent.com/pod-product-compliance
Lightning Source LLC
Chambersburg PA
CBHW070359270326
41926CB00014B/2613